The RCIA:
Transforming the
Church

A Resource for
Pastoral Implementation

Thomas H. Morris

PAULIST PRESS
New York ■ Mahwah

Library of Congress Cataloging-in-Publication Data

Morris, Thomas H., 1956–
    The RCIA : transforming the Church : a resource for pastoral implementation / Thomas H. Morris.
    p. cm.
    Bibliography: p.
    ISBN 0-8091-3047-5 : $9.95 (est.)
    1. Catholic Church. Ordo initiationis Christianae adultorum. 2. Initiation—Religious aspects—Catholic Church. 3. Catholic Church—Doctrines. I. Title.
BX2045.I553M67   1989
265' . 13—dc19
                                                                        88-35258
                                                                        CIP

Published by Paulist Press
997 Macarthur Boulevard
Mahwah, NJ 07430

Printed and bound in the
United States of America

Contents

Part Two: Implementing the Rite

Part Three: Specific Pastoral Issues

Dedicated to
my family
and to all manner of families
being created today
that seek to live authentically
the Gospel of Jesus Christ

Abbreviations*

EACW = *Environment and Art in Catholic Worship*, United States Catholic Conference, 1978.

EN = *Evangelii Nuntiandi*, Pope Paul VI, 1976.

LG = *Lumen Gentium* (*Dogmatic Constitution on the Church*), Vatican II (21 November 1964), *Documents of Vatican Council II.*

MCW = *Music in Catholic Worship*, United States Catholic Conference, 1972.

NCD = National Catechetical Directory, *Sharing the Light of Faith*, United States Catholic Conference, 1979.

RCIA = *Rite of Christian Initiation of Adults* (approved ritual edition for dioceses of the United States), United States Catholic Conference, 1988.

SC = *Sacrosanctum Concilium* (*Constitution on the Sacred Liturgy*), Vatican II (4 December 1963), *Documents of Vatican Council II.*

* All quotations from these official texts are in their original translations, which may at times be non-inclusive.

Introduction

My earliest recollections of "adults entering the church" are rather typical of Catholics prior to the restoration of the Rite of Christian Initiation of Adults (RCIA) in 1972. These adults went for private instruction with the parish priest for a few weeks, sometimes a few months. After sufficient knowledge of the faith was demonstrated, they could choose a sponsor or godparent, and then baptism or acceptance into the Catholic Church was celebrated. Usually the celebration was a private matter, attended by family and friends. An important part of the celebration was the first reception of holy communion. The party followed, and then it was the responsibility of the new Catholics (usually with the help of the priest and some family members) to better acquaint themselves with the ins and outs of Catholic life. Except in those rare parishes that were already caught up in the liturgical renewal, this was the manner of "becoming a Catholic" for most adults.

Years later, after completing my theology degree and having had experience in religious education, I moved into full-time parish ministry as the director of religious education. What I found in the parish I served, and in many parishes around us, was a process very similar to the one I remembered from a while ago — convert classes. Since we were in the post-RCIA era, there were new names associated with the program. People now gathered as a class rather than individually, and there were more public celebrations (only in the sense that they occurred during the regular schedule of services). Yet despite all of that, the orientation of the program was the comfortable and familiar instruction of material by the clergy, followed by public ceremonies at the scheduled dates.

Since those first days in the parish, a lot of experience, study, reflection, and grappling with the RCIA has happened in my life. Through the direction of some fine pastoral people, I slowly learned how to translate my theological study of the Rite of Christian Initiation of Adults into a pastoral implementation of the rite. That translation was given flesh by a number of men and women who trusted me to join

1

them on their journey of faith in the catechumenate. Eventually, I became involved in helping other pastoral ministers learn the art of this translation in order to pastorally implement the RCIA. I have had the good fortune of working as a team member with the North American Forum on the Catechumenate, as well as giving presentations and workshops on the RCIA. Additionally, I teach a graduate theology course on the pastoral implementation of the RCIA at DeSales School of Theology in Washington, D.C. In that course, I am able to wrestle with my experience of the RCIA with people in ministry formation.

It is from those experiences of study, pastoral work, workshops, and teaching (and the necessary dialogue that happens in each of those settings) that I bring to you these reflections on the pastoral implementation of the Rite of Christian Initiation of Adults. These reflections are not meant to offer a complete sacramental theology of the RCIA, though there will be some theology offered. There are already fine texts available to help set a firm foundation for someone coming fresh to the RCIA. Nor are these reflections meant to be an explicit recipe of "how to do" the RCIA, offering a syllabus of what is to be covered, and a time line as to when to cover everything. As you will discover, I strongly discourage such a model, and any resources available today that suggest so neat a package for implementation should also be discouraged. Rather, these reflections are one more attempt to enflesh the translation of the rite into pastoral life. You will find some theory, guidelines, explanatory models, and direction to help you embrace the RCIA and allow it to live with the particular people in your particular pastoral setting.

This resource is divided into three sections. In part one, we discuss some foundational issues for implementing the RCIA, such as the history of the rite, ministries, and forming an RCIA team. Part two deals specifically with the periods and steps of the rite, highlighting certain dimensions that could influence how a parish implements the rite. Part three deals with some pastoral issues that arise when implementing the rite, such as annulments, presiding at prayer, and spiritual direction.

The purpose of this resource is pastoral. It shies away from being simply practical. *Practical* is too cut and dry, too matter of fact, too sterile. *Pastoral*, on the other hand, is creative, empowering, dynamic. The implementation of the RCIA in any setting that has become practical usually suffers from minimalism (catechetically, liturgically, ministerially). Such programs are often convert classes disguised in new clothes. This resource is meant to help move from such practical programs toward a rich and empowering process in the life of the parish community.

The best place to begin any reflection on the Rite of Christian Initiation of Adults is with the rite itself. Nothing else can replace it. This resource will be most helpful and effective if you have taken the necessary time to read and reread the rite, becoming familiar with the process of conversion that the rite highlights. Throughout this resource, reference will be made to the RCIA, using the 1988 edition approved in November 1986 by the National Conference of Catholic Bishops for use in the dioceses of the United States (commonly called "the white book").

I want to thank the many people who have influenced and shaped this resource, especially the people with whom I have shared catechumenate ministry over the years: team members, catechumens and candidates, and sponsors. In particular, I want to express my deep gratitude for the support and encouragement given to me throughout this project by Brad McMinn. His friendship and care have sustained me when it was easier not to work on this resource. Additionally, I am inspired by the commitment and dedication of the pastoral staff at St. Rose of Lima parish in Gaithersburg, Maryland. Their vision of mission for service has both enriched and challenged me. I also wish to thank the staff and team members of the North American Forum on the Catechumenate. Their commitment and support for the implementation of the RCIA throughout the United States and Canada has been felt by a large number of people. I am especially grateful to Jim Dunning, President of Forum, for the insights and suggestions he offered to me after reviewing this text. Lastly, I want to thank David Haas for sharing with me his energy and enthusiasm for the implementation of the RCIA.

We have seen the developments of many worthwhile programs to aid in the renewal of the parish community. But programs end, and new programs need to be created to carry the momentum. Not so with the RCIA. The RCIA is not a program, but an on-going and developing process of initiation and renewal in the parish community. If the RCIA is implemented as a program, eventually it becomes one more thing we do. If we allow the RCIA to stand on its own in the parish community, I think we will discover a wealth of wisdom and insight in helping both individuals and the community recognize and respond to the compassionate presence of God. I offer these reflections to you as my contribution to this exciting process.

Thomas H. Morris
Easter Sunday, 1988

Part One

Foundational Issues

1

The Rite of Christian Initiation
of Adults: The Context

EVANGELIZATION

"The preaching of the gospel to the men of our times, full as they are of hope, but harassed by fear and anxiety, must undoubtedly be regarded as a duty which will redound to the benefit not only of the Christian community, but of the whole human race" (*Evangelii Nuntiandi*, n. 1). Pope Paul VI's exhortation in *Evangelization in the Modern World* is a call to all the baptized to continue to live faithfully the mission of Jesus, the Christ. This mission is the proclamation of the reign of God, which is the in-breaking of "liberation from everything that oppresses men, but which is above all liberation from sin and the Evil One" (EN, n. 9). Such liberation, this salvation from our God, is at the heart of preaching the gospel.

Evangelization — from the Greek *euangelion* — means to "proclaim good news, to bear glad tidings." It is neither proselytizing nor moralizing. Rather, it is the witness of those men and women who have been grasped by the "good word" proclaimed in the Christ event, the paschal mystery: human liberation and salvation in and through Jesus, the Christ. An essential dimension of evangelization is witness.

Evangelization is necessary for Christian initiation. Men and women hear the gospel proclaimed, by word and deed, and come to a particular Christian community as a result of this initial stirring in faith. The process whereby adults both hear and respond to this gospel in the Catholic community is called the Rite of Christian Initiation of Adults.

WHAT IS THE RCIA?

The Rite of Christian Initiation of Adults (RCIA) was the last of the sacramental rites revised after Vatican Council II. Its promulgation in 1972 marked a significant shift in the practice of welcoming new adult members into the Catholic community. It is safe to say that most parishes up to this time (and even after the provisional English text was made available in 1974) followed a similar format: convert classes or instruction given by the parish priest to the individual. The RCIA dramatically shifted the focus: men and women, responding to an often inexplicable call, are formed at the hands of the local community around the word of God, discerning and welcoming God's invitation to embrace life in the Catholic Christian community, and thus serving the mission of Jesus in the world today.

The RCIA is a restoration of the ancient practice of initiation into the church: a process of discerning and ritualizing stages of conversion, leading to sacramental initiation through the sacraments of baptism, confirmation, and eucharist celebrated at the Easter vigil, thus empowering men and women for lives of service, charity, and justice as witnesses to the reign of God. It is the parish community, through its witness, worship, service and catechesis, that offers the invitation and support necessary for men and women to be initiated into the church.

Initiation into the Christian community is not concerned about programs which come and go, but rather in reorganizing the very structure from which our programs develop. That is why the RCIA is not a program but a sacramental process. Though the RCIA is explicitly celebrated during a period of from one to three years, it reflects a sacramental attitude that is at the heart of all Christian living: conversion. From this experience of conversion (and conversion means a "turning" of the whole person, not just the intellect), one is empowered by the Spirit to proclaim the gift received: liberation and redemption in and through the person of Jesus, the Christ.

The RCIA is one rite. However, it is divided into various periods that respect the individual's journey of faith. These periods of initiation formation are marked by community celebrations that serve as transitions or steps throughout the rite. The periods of the RCIA and their accompanying transition celebrations are: the Period of Evangelization or Precatechumenate, the rite of acceptance into the Order of Catechumens, the Period of the Catechumenate, the rite of election, the Period of Illumination or Purification, the Celebration of the Sacraments of Initiation, and the Period of Postbaptismal Catechesis or Mystagogy.

These various periods are a process of *formation* to the gospel. The RCIA helps facilitate the experience of God for those seeking full initiation into the community. This formation to the gospel becomes the seed for renewal in the parish community not only because there are new members in the community, but because the actual formation team for the RCIA is the parish community. The catechumens challenge the parish by asking hard questions: Why are you Catholic? What do you believe? Why do you believe? Why would I be happier if I joined your community? How is God alive here? The parish needs to ask and answer these questions of itself over and over again. As the parish members witness to their sense of being ambassadors for God, they deepen their appreciation and use of God's gifts in the community. An active RCIA keeps the winds of renewal always current in the parish.

If one reads the RCIA — the introduction, guidelines, and ritual texts — one discovers a profoundly intricate weaving of various threads: catechesis centered on the lectionary, witness in the liturgical assembly based on one's conversion story, acclamations that flow from the experience of the catechumens, music that integrates the conversion experiences with the community's worship, presiders familiar with the stories of the catechumens, and a parish community willing to commit itself to people with whom it has grown. The threads of catechesis, ministries, parish witness, liturgical music, and sponsorship all weave together to create this event we call initiation. Without the particular threads, we risk empty rituals and disconnected catechesis. Initiation can become an opportunity to help people discern God's call to be formed to the cross of Jesus Christ in the midst of this particular Catholic community. The catechesis must be celebrated ritually; the rituals must be grounded in sound catechesis. The two are intertwined: There can be no separation without ripping the fabric.

HISTORICAL PERSPECTIVE

The Rite of Christian Initiation of Adults is a result of the mandate from Vatican Council II for the restoration of the catechumenate process. Echoed in various places in the council documents, such as the Constitution on the Sacred Liturgy (*Sacrosanctum concilium*), n. 64f, the Decree on the Pastoral Office of Bishops in the Church (*Christus Dominus*), n. 14, and the Dogmatic Constitution on the Church (*Lumen Gentium*), n. 14, the thrust of the restoration of the catechumenate is clearly expressed in the Decree on the Church's Missionary Activity:

Those who, through the Church, have accepted from God a belief in Christ should be admitted to the catechumenate by liturgical rites. The catechumenate is not a mere expounding of doctrines and precepts, but a training period for the whole Christian life. It is an apprenticeship of appropriate length, during which disciples are joined to Christ their Teacher (*Ad gentes divinitus*, n. 14).

As a direct result of the mandate that "the catechumenate for adults, comprising several distinct steps, is to be restored and brought into use at the discretion of the local ordinary" (SC, n. 64), the Congregation for Divine Worship prepared the Rite of Christian Initiation of Adults, approved by Pope Paul VI in 1972. A provisional translation of the text — not a provisional *ritual* — was approved for use in the United States in 1974. In 1986, the United States Catholic Conference approved the ritual edition of the RCIA for use in the United States that included additional combined rites (for both the unbaptized and the baptized) and national statutes for implementing the RCIA (published in 1988).

The restoration of the RCIA recovers a long history of initiation theology and praxis within the Christian community. Although there is no explicit model of initiation in the Christian scriptures (such as the periods and stages of the RCIA), there are some biblical themes that are central for initiation and that suggest a model for initiation in the first century: the proclamation of the kerygma (i.e. the saving events of God in Christ), the call to repentance and conversion, the response of faith, the immersion in water (or the water bath) as the central symbol for baptism, and the presence of the Spirit. Except in the case of households coming to baptism, the baptism into the death and resurrection of Jesus was for adults.

During the second century, as a theology of baptism became more developed, private catechetical schools emerged for the instruction of adults, such as the one founded by Justin Martyr. However, since there was often a lack of time for these adults to reflect on the implications of accepting the Christian faith, we see a high level of apostasy and heresy later emerging from some members of the community. Because of this, communities began to establish basic criteria for access to baptism: sorrow for sins, faith in the church, and conversion or transformation of life. The period of formation began to be extended.

The writings of Hippolytus (ca. 215) — which tend to reflect the larger tradition of the time — give us a more complex picture of the process of initiation. By this point there were stages of initiation: a period of inquiry with a preliminary examination to determine if the individual was capable of hearing the word, an extended catechumenate (three years), another examination to determine readiness to be chosen for baptism, the period of election as a time of retreat, baptism through water immersion at the vigil of Easter, and, finally, a period of reflection on the mysteries celebrated (mystagogy).

Throughout this period, as reflected in the writings of people like Clement and Origen, the process of initiation into the saving death of the Lord was a prolonged process of conversion and repentance, marked ritually within the community. The expectation was one of lifetime fidelity and commitment to the demands of the gospel.

A dramatic shift occurred in the Christian community in 313 A.D. — a shift that would affect the initiation practice of the community. With the Peace of Constantine, Christianity moved from being an underground church to being the preferred church of the state. It became politically advantageous to enter the Christian faith, and so there were mass conversions and baptisms that began to break down the process of the catechumenate, resulting in a decline of people strongly committed to the radical message of the gospel. By the ninth century, there were hardly any signs of the catechumenate, though as late as the twelfth century, something like the catechumenate was still going on in Rome.

Eventually there was the breakdown of the initiation sacrament into three separate sacraments in the church in the west. Previously, the sacramental initiation was celebrated in the presence of the bishop. As the community grew, the presbyters were appointed to preside at the water rite, leaving the second anointing to the bishop. The separation in time between the water bath and the second anointing became larger and larger. As a corollary to this, the practice of infant baptism as soon as possible increased due to Augustine's teaching on original sin.

With the disintegration of the catechumenate process, we see the rise of regulations and legislation surrounding sacramental initiation, culminating with the Council of Trent (1545–1563). Prior to Trent, Peter Lombard had already established a listing of the sacraments — which reflected the theology and practice of the times — that separated the initiation sacraments into separate sacraments. Lombard's list of seven sacraments was approved by Trent.

Theologically, the practice of initiation became frozen at Trent. Pastorally, however, from the sixteenth century forward, the growth of missionary activity resulted in large numbers of baptisms. Eventually, the missionaries became concerned about the preparation for baptism and started to develop models of initiation that began to bear a resemblance to the initiation practice of the early Christian community. Renewed interest in the process of sacramental initiation became heightened with the liturgical movement of the twentieth century, coupled with the recovery of ancient texts such as the *Didache* and Hippolytus' *Apostolic Tradition*. These influences, alongside the great strides in the catechetical movement, contributed to the mandate to restore the catechumenate process at Vatican Council II.

THEOLOGY OF THE RCIA

The basic theology of the RCIA can be found in the introduction to the rite. In order to help give an overall picture of the dynamics of the rite, we will briefly explore some theological principles that are operative in the rite. These principles will be developed in various ways throughout the resource.

(1) The RCIA is intended to facilitate the experience of conversion and the response of faith (RCIA, n. 1). At the heart of this experience is the proclamation of the kerygma, the saving death and resurrection of Jesus Christ. Embracing the gift of salvation is embracing the demands of the reign of God.

(2) The RCIA respects the individual experience of conversion, offering a process that accommodates and adapts to one's journey in faith in the midst of the community (RCIA, n. 1, 2, 4, 5).

(3) The RCIA creates a dynamic for adults to share faith together. Hence, it is meant for groups of adults while respecting the individual's experience of God (RCIA, n. 1, 3, 5). The rite does make provisions for the initiation of children of catechetical age (RCIA, n. 3).

(4) The RCIA is celebrated in the midst of the community and is a challenge to the community to deepen its own conversion (RCIA, n. 4).

(5) The RCIA emphasizes the close relationship between liturgy and catechesis. Growth in faith is ritualized in various ways throughout the RCIA (RCIA, n. 6). The proper time to celebrate the rituals of the RCIA will be influenced by both the individual's conversion and the liturgical calendar (RCIA, n. 18–30).

(6) The RCIA recognizes that growth in faith that leads one to commitment happens gradually and in discernible periods (RCIA, n. 7).

(7) The RCIA bears a markedly paschal character. The proper time for celebrating the sacraments of initiation is the Easter vigil (RCIA, n. 8, 23).

(8) The RCIA affirms the responsibility for ministry and service of all the baptized. Furthermore, both explicitly and implicitly, the rite calls for a variety of ministries for full implementation (RCIA, n. 9-16).

(9) The RCIA recognizes the importance of incorporating the particular needs and demands of the community and the candidates. The ritual celebrations need to authentically express the conversion experience of the candidates. Therefore, the rite encourages the appropriate adaptation of the RCIA at all levels (RCIA, n. 32-35).

(10) The RCIA provides a new context and model for sacramental catechesis: evangelization, conversion, the response of faith, and mission. All of this is formative and dynamic, responding to the initiative of God. The further exploration of the various periods and steps of the RCIA will underscore this understanding of sacramental catechesis.

Ultimately, the theology of the RCIA is about conversion.

CONVERSION AND THE DEVELOPMENT OF FAITH

The RCIA is not a program, but a sacramental formation process that prepares individuals and communities for a particular way of life. Conversion is at the heart of that way of life. The RCIA facilitates the conversion experience.

Conversion is a turning around, an about-face. In a variety of ways, the individual encounters a transformation of values that empowers that individual to turn from what is inauthentic to embrace the truly authentic. In religious terms, conversion is the surrender of oneself to the all-loving God, who calls us to fullness of life. It is God asking us to give what we thought we could not give.

Authentic conversion is transformative. Not only does it result in a radical change in the individual, but it informs and affects every dimension of the individual's life. Furthermore, there is a qualitative change in the individual's manner of life that rings true.

One experiences an empowerment to move beyond self to a new sense of self, the process of self-transcendence. While one can be open to this experience, and can facilitate the possibility of self-transcendence, one cannot "do" it. As a dimension (and result) of conversion, self-transcendence is a dynamic openness to full and authentic human living. Ironically, it is in the very process of not seeking self-transcendence that one enters into this transformative process. One finds self only in losing self. Losing self — embracing the path of conversion — is not about self-destruction. Rather, it is about entering into life in intelligent, rational, and responsible ways, thus allowing values for their own sake to be the driving force of life. The shift is from individual satisfaction to the values that promote the vision of the reign of God. One is able to recognize a new identity: self in relationship with God.

The Hebrew scriptures express the notion of conversion within the context of the covenant relationship. Over and over again, God is inviting God's people to simply allow God to be their God, to accept God's gift of life and relationship. The Creator God desires to give life — without this life, one lives in isolation and bondage. Acceptance of the covenant with God is what can deliver them from their bondage and isolation precisely because acceptance of the covenant is allowing God to be God — thus imparting the gift of life and relationship. The response to the covenant is a penitential heart (i.e. a heart that is open to hear God's saving word and available to receive the very life of God). Conversion is turning around from sin (i.e. the way of those not in true relationship with life) to a personal and loving relationship with God as expressed in the covenant.

The Christian scriptures develop this notion of conversion further with the radical acceptance of Jesus as the one who brings life. *Metanoia*, the Greek word most frequently used to convey the message of conversion, is a change of direction — from a way of life that fosters death to Jesus, who brings the fullness of life. This is all experienced within the context of the proclamation of the reign of God and the demands the reign of God makes for transformed living.

Conversion, then, is the change that happens when we allow God to love us enough that we are reformed, refashioned into men and women who value each other and our relationships in self-sacrificing love. The conversion manifests itself in different ways (e.g. intellectually, morally, affectively), but it is always a radical shift from one way of being to another. There is a breakthrough . . . a new vision.

The transformation effected by conversion comes at a price. The old dies so the new can live. Therefore, the conversion process can be likened to a grieving process. The literature on death and dying suggests a series of steps toward acceptance of death: denial, anger, bargaining, depression, acceptance. The significant point here is not that one becomes resigned to death, but that one accepts death. This acceptance can only happen when one realizes that the experience of dying is itself meaningful and the person willingly embraces the experience.

The encounter with God's unconditional love that results in conversion is similar: an encounter with God's love (usually mediated through others), the grappling to understand and accept, the struggle to discern the true and the real, the on-going conversation and questioning for the true and the real, the emergence of an awareness that sees things as they are and the willingness to embrace them, the immediate change that results because of this embracing, and the subsequent changes that occur on every level of life because of the transformation.

The catechumenate process is helping people awaken to the stirrings of God to a renewed life, a turning to a more authentic embrace of life. The process is named conversion. The language that helps articulate the invitations of God is the language of symbol.

SYMBOL

It is difficult to talk about certain experiences. Words seem to fail us when we try to express our love and affection for someone. They seem even more inadequate when we try to explain the depth of our love for our beloved to a third party. The reason for this is that these experiences — love, pain, fear, hope, and others — are packed with meaning. Nothing we say or do can exhaust the meaning of the experience; there is always something more. These experiences, however, are common to all of us and we have found a manner of speaking about them that respects the depth of the message while still conveying the basic meaning and message we want others to know. The language we use is the language of symbol.

Symbols are the language we use to speak of the richness of reality. Symbolic discourse is the most common form of communication we have with each other. Daily we express our fears, sentiments, hopes, and dreams to each other through symbolic gestures: a kiss of welcome, a supportive hand on one's shoulder, an embrace for the sorrowing, slamming the door in someone's face, or a smile — whether it be a warm, inviting one or a cold, cynical one. All of these symbols communicate a message to the other.

Symbols are not the same as signs, though some signs can also be symbols. A ring can be a sign of marriage. It can also be the symbol of the love and commitment behind that marriage. Symbols point to the inexplicable and help create the very presence of that which they point to. In the world of symbols, there is a wealth of meanings that are evoked and actualized in the encounter with the symbol. Because of this wealth of meanings, symbols evoke a response from various dimensions of a person, not just the intellect.

Symbols, therefore, affect the whole person. One moves from fact (what is seen or encountered) to meaning (the interpretation of the symbol). This experience of symbol will be influenced by one's previous history with the symbol (or the meanings evoked by the symbol), as well as the culture's experience of the symbol. For example, the experience of the symbol of bread broken and shared will necessarily include the individual's previous experience (or personal history) of shared food or bread, such as the memory of grandmother baking bread on Sunday afternoon and the sense of care and security that such a memory elicits. Additionally, the individual will be opened and exposed to the culture's experience of the same symbol, such as bread feeding the poor, or as a staple of life. Not only is the individual affected by his or her own personal interpretation and experience of the symbol, but the symbol also carries the wealth of meaning that a culture (and the history of that culture) has both experienced with and invested in that symbol — broken bread as symbol can be sharing in the life of each other, fostering care and support, and embracing the needs of the poor.

Thus symbols help communicate the inexplicable, the profoundly evasive, the simplest of truths. Bread ripped, oil smeared, wine poured — all speak of a world being transformed and our participation in that very transformation. There is a radical new presence in this transformation: God-present-with-us. As little as we can explicitly name and point out the experience of love in concrete and final terms, how much less can we name fully the real presence of God in our midst. Symbols are religious language.

And since symbols evoke a response from the whole person, from every level of our person, then symbols have the power to not only transform the world, but to transform our lives. When we are awakened to the power of symbols in our lives, the possibility occurs for new life, for transformation, for conversion. The language of conversion is the language of symbols.

Faith in God is both experienced and expressed through symbols. The sacramental life of our community is rooted in the power of symbols to evoke and heighten our presence to God's mystery. Eventually we formulate this experience — because it is too great for us to encounter fully — into statements of faith and belief. Our creeds and doctrines are symbolic summaries of a rich and profound history of the experience of God as salvation through Jesus.

Since faith is articulated and experienced through symbols, the RCIA becomes an important experience of naming and experiencing the symbols of our community. As one becomes immersed in the power of the symbols of our faith, one is opened to the possibility of transformation, of conversion. Then there is a qualitative change in one's life. One becomes a disciple.

MYSTAGOGY: THE END IS THE BEGINNING

The focus of the Rite of Christian Initiation of Adults is not membership. Membership is the result of programs. It is clear from the rite that its focus is somewhere else: "The rite of Christian initiation presented here is designed for adults who, after hearing the mystery of Christ proclaimed, consciously and freely seek the living God and enter the way of faith and conversion as the Holy Spirit opens their hearts" (RCIA, n. 1). The RCIA is concerned about relationship with God, a relationship that both frees one and empowers one for service. The RCIA is concerned about discipleship.

Christian discipleship is the response to the call to follow Jesus, learning to live the vision of Jesus that proclaims the reign of God. Discipleship is about a way of life, a qualitative difference in our actions and attitudes. It is embracing the paschal event wholeheartedly.

The RCIA is formation for discipleship. Therefore, the movement of the RCIA is toward the period of mystagogy or post-baptismal catechesis (RCIA, n. 244–251).

Mystagogy, the fourth period in the ritual initiation process, is appropriately a reflection on the experiences of the mysteries, specifically the paschal event. The Greek root for mystagogy is *myo*, meaning to close one's eyes and shut one's ears; it is the experience that leaves one awe-inspired, and therefore cannot be spoken of adequately. Mystagogy is the struggle to articulate from within the symbols of the mysteries, and at best is a cipher, pointing to the inexplicable. To speak of mystery is to speak of the religious dimension of experience, an experience of God. The entire initiation process is to help facilitate individual and communal conversion, to facilitate the possibility of being in love with God. Mystagogy is a period to integrate effectively this religious dimension of experience for it to be authentically fulfilling and empowering. Mystagogy thrusts one into the power of the initiation experience: missioned to serve the reign of God.

What does this mean, to be missioned to serve the reign of God? The answer to that question will necessarily inform our initiation praxis. If service to the mission of the reign of God is a private affair, with private graces, then initiation will also be very private, culminating in the celebration of the Easter sacraments. But if our vision of the mission of the reign of God is more than a private affair, then our initiation practice will view the Easter sacraments not as the goal of the initiation process but as empowerment for service. The goal of the initiation process becomes immersion in the ministry of Jesus, the Christ.

Mystagogy, then, is not the end of initiation, but really the beginning. The demands of mystagogy, therefore, are informed by our understanding of discipleship. Briefly, we will explore two basic movements in discipleship: call and response (vocation), and mission and service.

Call and Response. Vocation is the way of life one chooses in response to the call from God. This call from God is both personal and public. In its personal dimension, God calls us to a full and authentic humanity. God invites us, through the exercise of our human freedom, to move beyond ourselves in intelligent, reasonable, responsible, and loving ways to be obedient to the will of God. The will of God, fundamentally, is the well-being of all people. Therefore, God calls us in the ordinary of our lives to embrace a way of life (vocation) that allows God's Spirit to be made manifest in the world: the Spirit of compassion, of justice, of love. Christian vocation is the personal way one responds to God's call, whether that is in the diverse ways of lay life or in canonical religious life and the priesthood. The universal call of God affirms the egalitarian nature of vocation: no one vocation is better. Rather, the quality of a vocation is witnessed to by the manner and style of life of the individual in response to God.

The call from God, however, is not a private grace. There is the public dimension of vocation: witness and service to the world community. The public side of vocation can be associated with the mission of the church.

Mission and Service. Mission is to be sent. When one allows oneself to be opened further by the power of the Spirit, when one experiences liberating grace, then one is empowered to move beyond oneself in service of the world. The mission of the church, and therefore of all who are initiated into the community, is to continue the very mission of Jesus the Christ: to proclaim, in word and deed, the reconciling and compassionate presence of God, who desires to liberate and embrace all held in bondage. The Christian proclamation is that God is at our side. Once we have experienced this redemptive love (the initial move-ment of vocation), we are thrust forward to make concrete and explicit this love through self-sacrificing love. The focus of our actions becomes the needs of our neighbor. Charity is love enfleshed in service. Thus, all members of the church, laity and clergy, have the responsibility to live the mission of Jesus in their concrete, daily existence.

This mission is lived not only in the realm we might define as "reli-gious." Rather, we recognize that both the church and the world are the very places of the liberating redemption of God. The incarnation affirms that God manifests God's love in and through the created world. The world, and all creation, is fundamentally good and poten-tially celebrative of God's love. Yet we also recognize that within hu-man structures, such as institutions, there lies the possibility of the dehumanizing forces of sin. Whenever we choose to create institutions that dehumanize and oppress others, or whenever we choose to support such existing institutions, then we choose a way of life named sin. The church's mission is to proclaim another order or manner of living: freedom from all forms of oppression for all people so that human dignity may be affirmed and human authenticity may be embraced. The death and resurrection of Jesus serves as God's *no* to senseless hu-man suffering and God's *yes* to men and women that God is on our side. A constitutive dimension of Christian life, as affirmed by the 1971 Synod of Bishops' *Justice in the World*, is the work of liberation and jus-tice that is rooted in the experience of God's salvific love. The public side of vocation is a commitment to serve the world community through acts of justice and mercy. Such a commitment is at the heart of the baptismal commitment of every Christian.

The period of mystagogy in the RCIA is a time to help the neophyte embrace this vision of mission because he or she has encoun-tered the empowering presence of God in the Easter sacraments (as well as in other ways). Mystagogy becomes a transition time. It helps prepare the neophytes, and through them the entire community, to embrace the demands of the gospel to evangelize the world community and to witness to redemptive love through lives of self-sacrificing love. Such witness is concrete and historical, and is situated in the ordinary of one's life. The distinctive call of the laity is to bring the radical message of Jesus to the workplace, the home, and the social world, not in a manner akin to proselytization, but by a qualitative difference.

The vision of mission for the reign of God, which becomes the integrating focus of mystagogy (although it has been operative throughout the initiation process), sets the agenda for initiation minis-try. Initiation ministry is about Christian living, which is active living, active witnessing to the powerful presence of God in the world that forms us together as a community of brothers and sisters. The vocation and mission of the initiated is to be faithful followers of Jesus, to be disciples. "Thus every layman, by virtue of the very gifts bestowed upon him, is at the same time a witness and a living instrument of the mission of the Church herself, 'according to the measure of Christ's bestowal' (Eph 4:7)" (*Lumen Gentium*, n. 33).

2

Getting Started
in a Pastoral Setting

MODELS FOR IMPLEMENTATION

What does the RCIA "look like" in a parish? How is it implemented? At least three basic formats or models — with nuances and variations that respect local need — have emerged as people begin the pastoral task of implementing the RCIA. Each model builds on insights gleaned from the previous model.

In the first model, the primary work and concerns about initiation belong to the catechist — often a priest. The format is lectures or presentations with information about the Catholic Church. The various periods and stages of the rite are not followed. Or if they are, they are followed only in name. The image is that of a classroom presentation.

This is an inadequate model. In fact, it runs contrary to the spirit and vision of the rite. This model clearly gives the message that faith is predominantly — if not exclusively — information. Receive this information, show good will and true desire and we will baptize you. The church passing on its faith is symbolized by the one person giving information. While this may be comfortable and familiar to many of us, this is not sacramental catechesis.

As people spend time reflecting and studying the RCIA, they often move from this model. Aware of the stages and periods of the RCIA, they begin to construct a model that respects the distinctions of the stages and periods, as well as recognizing the differences in focus and catechetical methodology. This model — model two — is a very popular and common model, especially for parishes beginning to implement the rite.

Model two recognizes the need for a period of inquiry or the precatechumenate that is informal and focused on story telling. Perhaps the gatherings are at the parish center or in parishioners' homes. After recruiting, advertising, and interviewing people, the precatechumenate sessions begin in September. After about eight gatherings — and the necessary discernment for readiness — the candidates celebrate the rite of acceptance into the order of catechumens on the First Sunday of Advent. The catechesis proper to the period of the catechumenate — usually a series of presentations and reflections on basic Catholic issues that may also include dismissal catechesis based on the lectionary — continues throughout the catechumenate period until the approaching Lenten season. Throughout this time, the catechumens and candidates have been journeying with the support of a sponsor, as well as celebrating various blessings and anointings. After discerning readiness to celebrate the Easter sacraments, the catechumens and candidates celebrate the rite of election, enter the period of purification during Lent, and celebrate the initiation sacraments at the Easter vigil. The whole initiation process reaches its peak at this moment of celebration. The neophytes continue to meet with the team, usually during the week, and often with less regularity. This continues until Pentecost. During the summer months, the team regroups, does some training modules together, and begins the process of recruiting and interviewing prospective candidates for the approaching September's precatechumenate gatherings. (See Illustration 1.)

Model two is the way many of us begin to implement the rite. And as a beginning, it has some merits. There is the recognition of the various periods. The structure such a calendar provides helps keep the process well organized and functioning. But the longer people try to implement the rite using model two, and the more time and energy teams exert in getting to know the dynamics and vision of the rite, the more inadequate they find their experience with model two. Basically, model two does not reflect the dynamic sense of the RCIA. In fact, there are some real problems with this model with its very strong overtones of an academic calendar:

(1) The Spirit is not bound to the academic calendar. Men and women come seeking more information about the community at the time appropriate for them. Sometimes it is because of a crisis, other times because of an upcoming marriage, or because of someone at work who inspired them, or a nagging need to belong, or ... the list is endless. What is common to all of these experiences is that they happen when they happen, and not on September 1. We do a disservice to people to send them away and ask them to come back in September, giving them a book to read while they wait.

(2) Each person in the RCIA process has a unique story of conversion. Some people will need an extended period of inquiry, while

Illustration One.

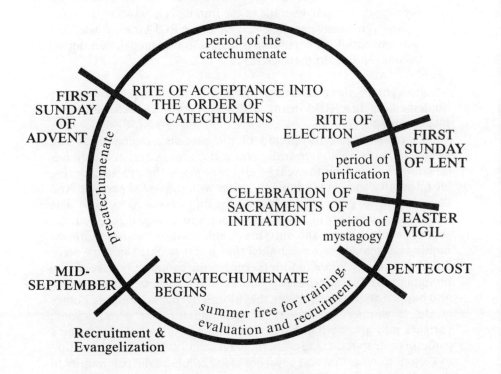

period of the
catechumenate

RITE OF ACCEPTANCE INTO
THE ORDER OF
CATECHUMENS

FIRST
SUNDAY
OF
ADVENT

precatechumenate

RITE OF
ELECTION

FIRST
SUNDAY
OF LENT

period of
purification

CELEBRATION OF
SACRAMENTS OF
INITIATION

period of
mystagogy

EASTER
VIGIL

PENTECOST

MID-
SEPTEMBER

PRECATECHUMENATE
BEGINS

summer free for training,
evaluation and recruitment

Recruitment &
Evangelization

23

others will have had a great deal of exposure to the community already. And the length of the catechumenate itself will vary for
each person. Model two forces people to conform to our time
schedule for conversion, thus refusing to respect the uniqueness of
each person's experience of God.

(3) The RCIA is directed toward mystagogy: reflection on the mysteries that empower us for mission. The celebration of the Easter
sacraments, while a very special and sacred moment in the journey, is not the end of the process. The RCIA is designed to bring
one to mission. The entire process needs to be focused on
mystagogy — the style of life of the initiated (servants of the reign
of God). For many parishes, the goal of the RCIA is the Easter sacraments, with little care for mystagogy. In that model, sacraments
become ends unto themselves.

In light of these concerns, there are many parishes that are
implementing the RCIA using a different kind of "scheduling" —
model three.

In model three, the period of the precatechumenate has two
unique qualities about it regarding time: It is always available, and it is
on-going. Throughout the year — all year long — the precatechumenate or inquiry team is available to gather with interested persons. And
they continue to gather for as long as the inquirers need to do so. The
shape and personality of the inquiry group will change throughout the
year as people move in and out. One possible option can be to form an
inquiry household (or households) that meets weekly (let's say every
Tuesday evening). When inquirers come to the community, they can be
brought to the Tuesday evening gathering. While these gatherings can
also happen at the parish center, the informality of parishioners' homes
creates a warmer atmosphere of welcome for new people. Some
parishes may also wish to have more than one household for inquiry
gatherings, or to rotate the gatherings seasonally. The important thing
to keep in mind is that whenever someone comes to the community to
discover more about the community, the parish staff (and hopefully,
the parish itself) knows where and when the inquirers are gathering
that particular week.

When the individual discerns a desire and readiness to enter the
community, the rite of acceptance into the order of catechumens is
celebrated. If the parish has provided gatherings throughout the year
for inquiry, then it is safe to assume that not everyone will discern
readiness to enter the church at the same time, much less for the First
Sunday of Advent. Yet at the same time, the parish does not want to be

celebrating this rite so regularly that its importance and significance loses its impact on the community. A possible option would be to plan three or four Sundays during the year when the rite of acceptance into the order of catechumens would be celebrated. Such a model respects the individual's journey in faith (various times of celebrating the rite helps people to more honestly discern their readiness), while helping to establish a liturgical rhythm in the community. The times of celebrating the rite can also vary to provide greater participation by the parish community. Depending on the readiness of the candidates, the parish may or may not celebrate the rite at all the scheduled times.

During the period of the catechumenate, the catechumens meet regularly to grow in their awareness of God's invitations to them of conversion and community. The shape and structure of these gatherings, which we will discuss later, will vary with each community. But it seems reasonable that the catechumens will meet weekly for an appropriate period of formation — usually a year or more. A possible option would be for the catechumens to gather weekly at the community's worship and be sent with a blessing after the homily for their catechetical gathering (known as dismissal cathechesis). In some parishes the catechetical gathering — prayer, reflection on the scriptures of the day, looking at the Catholic faith — may not be reasonably done on Sunday morning. Later we will discuss the value of dismissal catechesis. For now, let it suffice that in those parishes where a full catechetical gathering cannot happen on Sunday, the parish at least provide dismissal from the liturgy with a period of prayer and reflection on the Sunday scriptures. The catechumens can gather again during the week for further exploration into the scriptures and the issues of Catholic faith. The problem with this model is that catechesis can be reduced to a classroom model. The preferred option is a full catechetical gathering on Sunday morning.

The period of purification is celebrated during the Lenten season. Care should be given during the weeks beforehand to help discern with the catechumens and sponsors the individual's readiness to celebrate the Easter sacraments. The rite of election is celebrated on the First Sunday of Lent, preferably at the cathedral with the other catechumens of the diocese. The parish community can celebrate a rite of sending of its catechumens and candidates to the cathedral liturgy, which may include the enrollment of the catechumens into the Book of the Elect. The Easter sacraments — baptism, confirmation, and eucharist — are celebrated during the Easter vigil. Because of the centrality and importance of the paschal event in connection with sacramental initiation, the initiation sacraments should be celebrated at other times than the

Easter vigil only in extraordinary circumstances. The decision to move the celebration of the initiation sacraments to another time of the year should not be made lightly.

The period of mystagogy continues through the Easter season. The neophytes (newly initiated) continue to gather with the community at Sunday worship, but now there is no dismissal because the neophytes are full members of the community. However, the catechumens — those who have not discerned readiness for the Easter sacraments — continue to gather for Sunday dismissal and catechesis. Weekly, either after the Sunday eucharist or during the week, the neophytes gather to continue to reflect on the scriptures and to explore the meaning of the mysteries they have celebrated (the Easter sacraments), as well as to discover more fully their call to mission. After Pentecost it is recommended that the neophytes continue to gather monthly for another year — as a means of support to each other, and to provide on-going formation and reflection in the faith.

Model three respects the vision and demands of the rite while providing a pastorally sensitive and workable model for pastoral implementation of the RCIA. (See Illustration 2.) Parishes will nuance and adapt the insights of this model in ways that work best in their particular situation. Some people will find the development of this model difficult at first — especially if they are just beginning the implementation of the RCIA. This model is one possibility of how a parish can implement the rite. This does not mean we necessarily begin here — but rather are moving toward this vision. We may need to begin with some adaptation of model two. But what is crucial is that we recognize what we are doing: striving to develop a richer pastoral expression of the rite that is faithful to the spirit and norms established in the rite itself. Model three provides a jumping board for such an implementation.

Throughout the remainder of this resource, the process of initiation suggested in model three will be operative. Adapt and adopt.

WHOM IS THE RCIA FOR?

The Rite of Christian Initiation of Adults is a restoration of the catechumenate process for the full sacramental initiation of unbaptized adults into the Catholic Church. While there are many adults who are not baptized, the experience of many pastoral ministers has been that a number of people who come to our communities are already baptized in another Christian community, or are baptized but uncat-

Illustration Two.

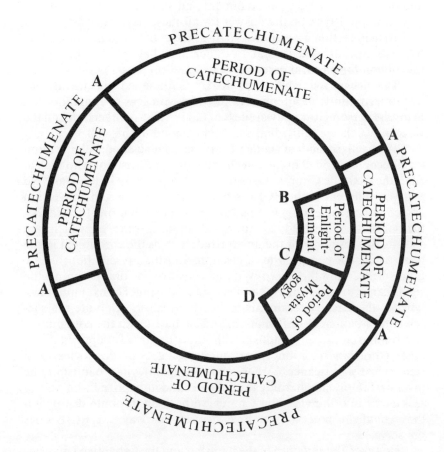

Precatechumenate: Available all year long.
A: Rite of Acceptance (scheduled at various times during the year)
B: Rite of Election (Lent I)
C: Celebration of Easter sacraments (Easter vigil)
D: Mystagogy ends at Pentecost, but full service for the reign of God continues
Catechumenate: Continuous from one to three years

echized Catholics, or are Catholics who have been alienated from the community and wish to return. Does the RCIA effectively serve these and other adults seeking nourishment and support from the community? Can the RCIA be the answer for all these pastoral needs?

To help facilitate a response to these concerns, each pastoral situation will be addressed separately, indicating what seems to be a possible option for pastoral care.

The unbaptized adult: The RCIA is designed specifically for unbaptized adults. It attempts to provide a process of initiation that helps the person grow in awareness of God's call to conversion and the ways in which the individual can best respond to this call.

The baptized adult in another Christian denomination: A large number of people enrolled in the catechumenate are Christians who wish to enter the Catholic Church. Does the RCIA serve these individuals? No and yes. Inherent to the RCIA is the marking of stages of conversion and commitment leading to a baptismal covenant. During the process, the journey is marked by liturgical rituals, some of which are specifically designed for the unbaptized, such as the enrollment in the book of the elect in the rite of election, and the presentations of the Lord's Prayer and the Creed. Without sensitive pastoral planning, the significance of these rituals can become confusing. For example, election for the Easter sacraments is clearly a call to celebrate the sacraments of baptism, confirmation, and eucharist with the community. Celebrating election for baptism with someone already baptized in another Christian tradition raises questions of both theological and ecumenical significance. (Are we claiming the previous baptism to be invalid?) Simply shepherding the baptized and unbaptized who wish to seek entry into the Catholic Church without appropriate distinction throughout the process is a disservice. In this way, the RCIA does not serve.

However, the situation of the baptized and the unbaptized may not necessarily be very different. Of course, a lot of this will depend on the baptized Christian's involvement in his or her community of faith. The process of sacramental catechesis that underscores the RCIA — evangelization, catechesis, conversion, ritual celebration, integration — seems to be appropriate and workable with adults who are baptized in other Christian denominations provided that the necessary distinctions are made throughout the process, especially during the ritual celebrations. We will specify these distinctions when we address the various periods of the RCIA.

In the most ideal situation, the catechesis necessary for the unbaptized and the baptized would be done differently and even separately — not so much as a mark of distinction but to recognize the difference in religious background. However, in many ways, the questions and concerns of both groups are very similar at this point in the process. Therefore, most parishes will merge the formation process of both the unbaptized and the baptized who wish to affiliate with the Catholic Church.

One more note. The length of formation for the baptized Christian entering the Catholic Church will differ for each one, depending on religious background and previous exposure to the Catholic community. The RCIA provides a ritual for the celebration of reception of baptized Christians into the full communion of the church. This celebration, while appropriate for celebration during the Easter season, need not be celebrated only at that time. The 1988 ritual edition for use in the United States, approved by the NCCB in 1986, includes combined rites in the RCIA for the baptized and unbaptized, thus responding to the pastoral praxis in this country, as well as separate rites for the baptized.

The baptized Catholic adult who is uncatechized: Some adults have been baptized in the Catholic Church — and that's where it ended. For various reasons, the adult was never raised in the Catholic tradition, and never celebrated eucharist and/or confirmation. Because of their very limited exposure to the Catholic tradition, it is appropriate that the same pastoral concern and questions raised in the previous section on the baptized Christian in another religious denomination apply here. In fact, it will often be the case that the individual from another Christian denomination has more religious backgound than the uncatechized Catholic.

There are some adult Catholics, though, who experienced initial catechesis as a child, often through grade school. Some of these adults have celebrated both eucharist and confirmation. Others have not. Sometimes these adults return to the church prior to marriage, hoping to celebrate confirmation. Whatever the reason or the circumstances, the principles of the RCIA are helpful with these adults. However, although the principles apply, usually the formation process will need to take place separately from the uncatechized adults. The questions and concerns of adult Catholics seeking to complete their Christian initiation are going to be very different than those of the new members of the community. There will be memories and stories of the church they knew — however different or similar they are to the church now — that will need to be dealt with and responded to pastorally. Also, depending on their background and level of involvement in the community, the period of formation will differ. Initially a parish may be limited in resources and be forced to include these adults in the RCIA process. Hopefully, as the RCIA takes firmer root in the parish, these adults can become part of a separate group of Catholics seeking to complete their Christian initiation guided by the theology of the RCIA.

The baptized Catholic adult who has been alienated from the community and seeks to return: Similarly to the catechized Catholic who has not completed Christian initiation, the alienated Catholic has specific concerns and questions that need to be addressed. More often than not, these are not the concerns of the catechumens. A pastoral process needs to be established within the community for the pastoral care of alienated Catholics similar to a new order of penitents, as has been suggested by some sacramental theologians. In responding to these persons' needs, though, we need to bear in mind that the alienation is not always caused by the individual. We as a Catholic community have not always been faithful to Jesus' call to compassion and charity. As we restore the order of penitents in the church, we will need to begin to explore the role of not only the forgiving church but the forgiven church.

The baptized Catholic adult who is looking for some updating and spiritual support: Deep within all adults is a hunger and desire to grow in faith, to deepen our relationship with God, ourselves, our neighbors, creation and the cosmos. Parish programs for adult formation are needed to supplement and enrich the community's worship and service. The RCIA is not the place for this. While the RCIA gives helpful insights and direction for adult faith formation, the RCIA is specifically designed for sacramental initiation. Adults seeking to deepen their Catholic way of life need to be directed to scripture study groups and other adult formation programs. The renewal of the church through the RCIA and other means, as well as the heightened awareness of our need for God, will exhibit a renewed interest and demand for good and effective adult formation programs in our parishes.

The initiation of children and adolescents: The question of the initiation of children and adolescents will be addressed in the final section of this book. Suffice it to say for now that, unless the RCIA is family based (i.e. households serving as teams for inquiring households), the children and adolescents are probably best served in a similar process with their peers.

The RCIA is a powerful and effective process for sacramental initiation. However, we need to be careful and not turn it into the panacea for all adults coming to the church. The needs and concerns of each individual will help establish the appropriateness of enrolling the person in the RCIA. Unfortunately, some parishes place all adults in the RCIA without differentiation. The excuses for this vary — they all need the same thing, we don't have enough staff, there are not enough people in the group, and so on. We need to carefully evaluate who is enrolled in the RCIA and why they are enrolled.

As previously mentioned, the 1988 ritual edition of the RCIA approved by the United States bishops for use in the dioceses of the United States includes a series of combined rites for the unbaptized and the baptized completing initiation. The distinction is necessary for theological and pastoral reasons and should be maintained throughout the celebration of the RCIA. However, since the formation process is so similar for both groups, and to avoid the cumbersome repetition of "catechumens and candidates for full communion," the terminology appropriate for the unbaptized (during precatechumenate — candidates; during the catechumenate — catechumens; during the period of purification — the elect; during mystagogy — the neophytes) will be used for the remainder of this resource except where it will be necessary to indicate distinctions between the unbaptized and candidates for full communion.

INFORMATION VERSUS FORMATION

Some of the most frequent questions asked about the RCIA concern themselves with doctrine: "What do we teach?" "When is it appropriate to bring in church teaching?" "Do we only do scripture sharing?" "Is reflection on the Sunday readings enough?" "How will they know what it means to be Catholic?" A too frequent criticism of lectionary-based catechesis is that it is soft on doctrine. Translated, this can mean, "The scriptures are important *but* people need to know Catholic doctrine in order to be Catholic." These are valid concerns. Catholic teaching is an important dimension of Catholic faith. Often, however, a misunderstanding of catechesis, and sacramental catechesis in particular, can lead one to an inordinate concern over doctrine.

The model of catechesis that has influenced a great many (if not all) adults in the church today is best reflected in the Baltimore Catechism model. Information is given — through readings, lectures, or even question-answer memorization — and the ability to return this information often equaled faith. "Does he know the faith?" was often understood as intellectual assent. Information and teaching is an important dimension of catechesis, but only one dimension. Information alone does not help make a person's "faith become living, conscious, and active, through the light of instruction" (National Catechetical Directory, n. 32).

The National Catechetical Directory, *Sharing the Light of Faith*, defines the task of catechesis as fostering mature faith (NCD, n. 33). "It [catechesis] is a form of the ministry of the word, which proclaims and teaches. It leads to and flows from the ministry of worship, which sanctifies through prayer and sacrament. It supports the ministry of service, which is linked to efforts to achieve social justice and has traditionally been expressed in spiritual and corporal works of mercy" (NCD, n. 32). The NCD establishes the four dimensions of effective catechesis to be word (didache), worship (leiturgia), community (koinonia), and service (diakonia) (NCD, n. 39).

The vision of the NCD and the RCIA is one of *formation* catechesis. People come to an awareness of salvation in God through the scriptures and instruction (word), through the prayer and sacramental life of the church (worship), through the shared life of the believers (community), and through the active participation of justice and action for the gospel (service). "Catechesis is a lifelong process for the individual and a constant and concerted pastoral activity of the Christian community" (NCD, n. 32).

Furthermore, in terms of sacramental catechesis, the NCD highlights the importance of liturgy as educative and formative. Effective sacramental catechesis needs to "promote an active, conscious, genuine participation in the liturgy of the church, not merely by explaining the meaning of the ceremonies, but also by forming the minds of the faithful for prayer, for thanksgiving, for repentance, for praying with confidence, for a community spirit, and for understanding correctly the meaning of the creeds" (NCD, n. 36).

The information component of catechesis is subsumed into the larger vision of catechesis: formation for mature faith. The question needs to be asked again and again of our catechetical activity: Is it balanced with the four components of catechesis (word, worship, community, service)?

In addition to the concerns already raised regarding an information-only approach, the concept of giving information needs to be briefly explored. This seemingly popular model of "giving information" is not an effective image. It suggests that someone has something (facts) that the other person does not have, and gives it away, as if the giver is filling up the receiver with all the facts the receiver can hold. This passive model, which can be somewhat arrogant at times, does not guarantee that the receiver will actually integrate and internalize the facts — the receiver need simply receive (demonstrated by the receiver's ability to repeat back the facts). It would seem that such a model does not foster faith, a response to our relationship with God.

Education, in its best sense, is quite the opposite of this information-giving image. Education, from the Latin root *educere*, means to train, to help one come to awareness, to insight. Education (or teaching) of the faith is the ministry of helping people name — by using the symbols of the community, such as our creed and doctrines — their experience of God as salvation. Our creed and doctrines are the church's expression of its experiences of God as salvation that are brought together and formulated in statement for the community's corporate profession of faith (i.e. their profession of belief in this experience of God). Therefore, only giving the information without helping people *begin* to name the experiences that root these expressions of faith seems backward. A more natural sequence suggests that we first help people name experiences of God's salvific presence, and then share with them the community's formulas for articulating this salvation in our midst — our Creed. Then the Creed becomes both a response and an invitation. As response, it enlarges the individual's personal experience with the richness of the tradition. And as invitation, it recognizes that none of us can exhaust or fully comprehend the meaning of God's salvation, thus calling all of us forward to new experiences of mystery.

If we move from the model of information-giving to formation in faith, where can we turn for effective catechesis in the RCIA? And how do we honor the insights of faith formation and still bring the best of Catholic teaching to inquirers and catechumens? The source of all our catechesis needs to be the formative documents of the community: our scriptures. Catholic faith and teaching are both rooted in and emerge from the scriptures. Later in the catechumenate section, we will deal more specifically with lectionary-based catechesis. Here we will explore briefly how the teachings of Catholic faith can emerge naturally from a catechesis rooted in the scriptures, especially the community's cycle of Sunday readings.

People unfamiliar with lectionary-based catechesis understandably are confused about the role and place of the teaching of Catholic doctrine. The concept itself — catechesis based on the Sunday scripture readings — seems to be more focused on scripture study and not on the on-going articulation of this faith as expressed in church teaching. However, this is not the case. First of all, church teaching has a significant role to play in catechesis, providing it is balanced with the other dimensions of catechesis outlined previously. Second, lectionary-based catechesis respects the natural flow of the community's articulation of revelation as recorded in the scriptures — thus allowing the issues of Catholic life to emerge from the community's proclamation. Third, it ties the liturgical life of the community together with catechesis. Fourth, the best of Catholic teaching is rooted in the scriptures and therefore will emerge during the catechetical gatherings over the course of the catechumenate period. When we discuss how to prepare the catechetical gatherings during the catechumenate, we will explore in more detail where and when we insert the issues of Catholic teaching.

The other confusion about lectionary-based catechesis — and this is usually from those who practice a First Sunday in Advent to a First Sunday in Lent catechumenate — is whether or not the essentials of Catholic teaching will be covered sufficiently if they come from the lectionary and not from a syllabus. The National Catechetical Directory is helpful here.

The NCD lists in chapter five the principal elements of the Christian message for catechesis — the essentials referred to above. Since it is normative that people enrolled in the catechumenate process are engaged in an extended period of formation, one is able to see how these issues of Catholic teaching will naturally emerge from the lectionary. Candidates for full communion — who may not be enrolled in the catechumenate process for as prolonged a period — can supplement the formal catechetical gathering with materials provided by the RCIA team. A tool, such as the *Catholic Faith Inventory* developed by Kenneth Boyack, Robert Duggan, and Paul Huesing (Paulist, 1985) can serve as a useful facilitating instrument.

A brief description of the essentials of Catholic teaching as explained in NCD Chapter 5 will help us to remove the mystique over what Catholic doctrine needs to be covered:

Mystery of the One God (NCD, n. 83–84): Personal presence of God in the history of salvation; the Trinity; revelation in Jesus Christ; covenant relationships with God; worship of God in liturgy, communal prayer, and personal prayer; God's will; the desire for God.

Creation (NCD, n. 85–86): Creative work of God; relationship of creation and salvation; the human person as climax of God's creation; the on-going presence of God in and through creation.

Jesus Christ (NCD, n. 87–91): Salvation and reconciliation in Jesus Christ; continuing mission of Jesus; Jesus, truly divine and truly human; proclamation of the reign of God; life, death and resurrection of Jesus; the meaning and destiny of life most fully revealed in Jesus Christ.

The Holy Spirit (NCD, n. 92): Presence of the Holy Spirit in the world and in the church; ministry.

The Church (NCD, n. 93–96): Origins and foundations; the new people of God; servant; prophetic and priestly roles; hierarchical structure; role of pope and bishops; infallibility and inerrancy; on-going renewal of the church; community of people; universal call to holiness; vocation; unity in the church; ecumenical respect; mission of the church to bring the message of salvation; call to serve the world community.

The Sacraments (NCD, n. 97): Christ, the sacrament of God; the church, the sacrament of Christ; sacraments as actions of Christ; purpose of sacraments for sanctifying humanity, building up the body of Christ, and giving worship to God.

The Life of Grace (NCD, n. 98–100): Sin; original sin; personal sin; effects of sin; grace as God's generous and free gift of self, a sharing in God's life; Christ's offer of grace is universal and everlasting; sacraments as sources of grace; on-going conversion; role of penance in conversion; discipleship; fulfillment in Christ; beatitudes as way of life; living the reign of God.

The Moral Life (NCD, n. 101–105): Call to holiness; concrete expression of love; fidelity to moral norms and values; genuine human freedom; value of the truly good; true morality as accepting humanity restored in Christ; natural moral law; judgments of conscience; moral decision-making; informed conscience; discernment; guidance of the church in moral questions; specifics of moral life in light of the ten commandments, sermon on the mount, and the last supper discourse; duties toward God, others, and self.

Mary and the Saints (NCD, n. 106–107): Mary, model of faith and charity; Mary, mother of God and mother of the church; the immaculate conception; the assumption; the communion of saints.

Death, Judgment and Eternity (NCD, n. 108–110): Christian understanding of death; personal and final judgment; hope; final union with God; the return of Christ is glory.

Hopefully, one can recognize, based on good experiences of preaching, that all of these essentials are raised continually throughout the year at the Sunday liturgy. An effective catechesis that flows from the lectionary, and is informed by the preaching on the texts, will be able to address these issues throughout the liturgical year.

The goal of catechesis in the RCIA is to facilitate conversion. Concretely, this does include a basic awareness and understanding of Catholic life and teaching. The key emphasis here, though, is *basic*. We are about providing an environment for the response of faith to grow to a new level of commitment. Included in this commitment is a lifelong process of growing in awareness of Catholic Christian doctrine.

Catechesis during the RCIA is intimately woven with the community's liturgical life. They interpenetrate and support each other. Initiation into the Catholic community calls for a shift in our thinking from an information model that primarily is concerned with knowledge of the faith to a formational model that seeks to integrate this knowledge with the heart and the will.

GETTING STARTED

Parishes start to implement the RCIA when people come seeking more information about the Catholic way of life. However, it is the rare parish situation that can immediately begin to implement the full rite. Normally, there will be stages of growth and development. Given all this, what are the essentials? Where does a parish begin?

There is nothing in the RCIA that is not essential. However, with limited resources and limited staff, a parish can begin slowly. In this case, less is more. Following are some suggestions for getting started.

- Form a catechumenate team. If you do not have people inquiring already into the life of the community, then you have the leisure of setting up an RCIA team without the added pressure of immediate catechesis for inquirers. Without delay, a wise coordinator will begin to seek out people who will be able to serve on the team in a variety of capacities, as will be discussed in chapter three.
- Recruit and train sponsors. An extremely important link in this chain is the sponsor. Often sponsors feel inadequate or incapable of serving in the ministry unless they are given some basic formation and insight into how the process works. Even if there are no candidates, begin to solicit sponsors now.
- Choose inquiry households. Be prepared to have a place (and a ready team) for inquirers. If you are able to begin with gatherings in parishioners' homes, it will make it easier to expand the precatechumenate in a full-year process.
- Begin to prepare for dismissal catechesis. Even if there are no catechumens, spend time with the catechetical team on a regular basis unpacking the Sunday texts and highlighting the issues of Catholic life and teaching. Use this time for catechist formation.

- Do some serious long-range planning. This does not mean making a schedule. It means tentatively planning a few rites of acceptance, deciding the best time for the rite of sending, and marking in the scrutinies, and also determining when is the best time to celebrate the dismissal rite.
- Begin to talk about it in the parish. Let parishioners know about the process of sacramental initiation. Highlight the importance of conversion and the development in faith for the parish community. Encourage preaching and teaching on the reign of God. Facilitate in whatever way possible the growth of the parish community so that it will be a community of the baptized that is willing to embrace and form men and women seeking our way of life.

3

Ministries in the RCIA

INTRODUCTION

The challenge of official ministries in the church has been to hold in tension two important dimensions of ministry: remaining rooted in the ministry of Jesus while at the same time adapting and developing to meet the needs of a particular people in a particular time and place. The RCIA offers a vision of ministry that attempts to do that. On one hand we have the traditional expressions of ministry, especially the ministry of baptism: bishop, presbyter, godparent. The RCIA expands this vision of ministry — explicitly and implicitly — to include the ministry of the baptized community, the formative role of the sponsor, and the office of catechist. These ministries are explicitly called for in the introduction to the rite. However, because of the ministry of the baptized community that is articulated in the rite, it can be argued that the rite implicitly calls for other roles of active service in the RCIA, such as hospitality and the catechumenate team.

The term ministry, the recognition of ministries, and the proper function of ministries is often a point of confusion and debate. Even in the early Christian community, we see evidence of differences in the understanding and functioning of ministries. In the Jerusalem community, we see ministries revolving around the role and function of the Twelve (i.e. those who walked with Jesus) and the elders of the community. Rooted in the experience of the synagogue, this model of ministry eventually expands — because the needs of the Hellenistic community were not being met — to include the seven (the deacons). At the same time, the church in Antioch, under the guidance of Paul, struggled under a different model of ministry as articulated in 1 Corinthians 12:27f. The controlling image was the body of Christ, with the variety and diversity of gifts — apostles, preachers, teachers, and the other expressions of service. There were two different understandings and perceptions of the function and order of ministries — ones that would cause some heated arguments between the two communities.

Eventually, the responsibility of ministry becomes associated with the offices of the episcopacy, presbyterate and diaconate. For most of us, this was our understanding of ministry until Vatican Council II. With the council, new questions about ministry gave rise to new studies on the role and function of ministries. Of special interest was the call of the baptized to service and how this service is expressed.

EXPLICIT AND IMPLICIT MINISTRIES IN THE RCIA

Within this context, the RCIA promotes an important vision of ministry for initiation. While acknowledging the role of service of the more traditional ministries — bishop, priest, deacon — the RCIA clearly states that the responsibility of initiation rests in the hands of the baptized community. It is important to note that this is stated in various ways throughout the RCIA. However, it is specifically stated in the Introduction under the title "Ministries and Offices": ". . . the people of God, as represented by the local Church, should understand and show by their concern that the initiation of adults is the responsibility of all the baptized" (RCIA, n. 9).

As indicated earlier, the RCIA suggests both explicit and implicit ministries, offices, and opportunities of service for the full implementation of the RCIA.

MINISTRY OF THE PARISH COMMUNITY (RCIA, N. 9)

The primary minister of initiation in the RCIA is the parish community. The quality of their lives, the concern and interest they show, the manner of worship, the commitment to social action, all of this is the where and how of the RCIA. People come to a particular community to become part of that community. It is the community's responsibility not only to welcome them, but to show the interested persons what makes the community distinctive, what makes it a Catholic Christian community. Ultimately, the community needs to ask: Why do we initiate? Into what do we initiate?

All of this suggests a level of awareness in the community. Shaped by authentic worship and good pastoral leadership, the community grows in its awareness of its own baptismal commitment: to serve the mission of the reign of God, to be leaven in the world. It is because of this living witness to the ministry of Jesus that the community is eager to welcome new members into its midst, to help in this service to the world community. The community is enlivened by its experience of the presence of the Risen One healing, reconciling, empowering them to lives of charity, justice, and compassion. It is in this spending of oneself that the community discovers salvation in its midst.

Therefore, the involvement of the community in the initiation process is both primary and key. It is into this particular community that one receives welcome. Therefore, the community needs to know and meet the candidates and catechumens. The names of those who seek full initiation in the community should be familiar to all and should be a regular part of the community's prayer. Welcome needs to be extended, not only at parish gatherings, but also into the homes of members of the parish. The community actively participates in the ritual celebrations of initiation, extending its support in prayer and witnessing.

MINISTRY OF SPONSORS (RCIA, N. 10)

Sponsors are members of the local community who are chosen to accompany the candidates and catechumens through the initial periods of conversion. Sometimes the sponsor is a friend of the candidate — perhaps the person the candidate first went to talk to about the Catholic Church. Often the sponsor is someone from the parish who has volunteered to serve as this important and special companion. The sponsor needs to be a fully initiated member of the church, as well as an active member of the parish community. In addition to being a direct support to the candidate or catechumen, the sponsor will also assist in the discernment process for the candidate, as well as in giving testimony at the rite of acceptance into the order of catechumens.

The responsibility of the sponsor for a particular catechumen ends at the rite of election, when the responsibility for the catechumen is assumed by the godparent. The sponsor of someone expressing a desire to celebrate full communion in the Catholic Church continues with the candidate throughout the process.

MINISTRY OF GODPARENTS (RCIA, N. 11)

The godparent is the individual who accompanies the catechumen through the final periods of the RCIA and continues as a companion with the individual throughout life. The godparent must be a fully initiated member of the Catholic Church; a person fully initiated in another Christian denomination may serve as a godparent as long as there is also a fully initiated Catholic as a godparent. The godparent, who is chosen by the catechumen, formally begins his or her role at the rite of election. Election is the formal pronouncement of the catechumen's readiness for full sacramental initiation. Thus, the on-going companion who will witness and affirm this commitment formally begins the journey with the catechumen. Realistically, the godparent has probably been part of the catechumen's journey already.

The godparent is chosen because of his or her witness to the Christian life, character, and level of friendship with the catechumen. Because the role of godparent is more than a ceremonial function — indeed it is a commitment of lifelong friendship in the Lord — the choice and formation of godparents needs to be given the same level of consideration as with sponsors. The popular practice of requesting people to serve as godparents for our children based on purely social or obligatory reasons has contributed to the functioning of godparents as purely ceremonial witnesses. Hopefully the on-going relationship stressed in the RCIA will inform the practice on the level of infant baptism. The same is true of sponsors for confirmation.

Godparents give testimony at the rite of election, witness the celebration of the Easter sacraments, and remain part of the catechumen's life as they together struggle and grow in faith. Sometimes a catechumen may ask his or her sponsor to serve as godparent. While this may be appropriate, the sponsor needs to recognize the on-going nature of this responsibility. Candidates for full communion do not choose godparents for full sacramental initiation. They retain the relationship established with their godparents at baptism. However, it might be good to include their godparents in this process of initiation to help establish the connection with their own baptism as well as to express ecumenical sensitivity.

MINISTRY OF THE BISHOP (RCIA N. 12)

The bishop, as shepherd of the diocese, presides over the entire process of initiation. It is his responsibility not only to regulate the RCIA in his diocese, but to promote the formation of candidates and catechumens. In the early church, it was the bishop who welcomed the new members into the community. The bishop continues this role of guidance and support indirectly and directly. Indirectly, through the competent leadership he appoints in parishes and diocesan offices that function to serve the RCIA (such as the diocesan RCIA Office, Office of Worship, and Office for Religious Education) and which provide adequate care and formation for catechumenate teams as well as for those enrolled in the RCIA. Directly, the bishop presides at the rite of election celebrated at the cathedral or at regional gatherings, as well as

bringing the neophytes (newly initiated) together during the Easter
season to celebrate the eucharist together.

The parish pastoral ministry team (pastor, associate pastors,
deacons, pastoral ministers) is responsible for providing for the care of
the candidates and catechumens. The RCIA needs to hold priority for
the staff or else it will not hold priority for the parish community.
Specifically, this means the necessary investment in resources, time,
talent, supervision, and direction to the various people involved in the
process. The staff can regularly participate in the process as members
of the RCIA team. Their regular presence to the catechumens and candidates not only offers support, but helps to establish personal
relationships with them. The decisions that need to be made during the
RCIA are the responsibility of the parish pastoral ministry staff, or the
person(s) they designate (such as the RCIA coordinator). Specifically,
they are responsible for the approval of the choice of godparents, the
appropriate adaptation of the rites, and the discernment throughout
the process. It is advisable that at least once during the year (and preferably a number of times) the staff meet informally with each of the
catechumens. This gives the catechumens a chance to become better
acquainted with the pastoral leadership of the parish, as well as opening an avenue to discuss personal issues, if needed.

In addition to sponsors, catechists have the greatest contact with
the catechumens. They meet with them regularly to share faith, pray the
scriptures, and share in the Catholic tradition. The catechists are to
take an active part in the preparation and celebration of the rites. Their
catechesis needs to be adapted to the liturgical year. As we will discuss
in chapter six, the ministry of catechesis is an echoing of the gospel.
One dimension of this is information. However, catechesis is more than
information; it is formative. Thus, the skilled catechist will be sensitive to growth in faith, conversion, and appropriate expressions of
prayer.

Each period of the RCIA has a different focus. It would be appropriate to have different catechetical teams to serve during each of the

periods: a precatechumenate team to help facilitate the early stirrings of faith and initial conversion; a catechumenate team to help pass on the essentials of the Catholic tradition within the context of the liturgical year, thus facilitating God's call to conversion; a team to serve during the period of purification and illumination that can facilitate the Lenten retreat for the elect (with an on-going RCIA, there will probably be catechumens and elect at the same time and therefore the need for different catechetical teams); the postbaptismal (mystagogy) catechesis team responsible for reflection on the mysteries (sacraments), as well as integration into the community through lives of service and charity.

Additionally, there are "informal" catechists — the men and women of the parish who often come to one or more catechetical gatherings to share their own experiences of marriage, prayer, or ministry.

ADDITIONAL ROLES OF SERVICE

The RCIA clearly holds the vision that the primary responsibility of initiation rests in the hands of the community of the baptized. To facilitate this process, other roles of service have developed in parishes, flowing from the general ministry of the baptized. Some of these roles of service are:

The RCIA Coordinator. As one implements the RCIA, it becomes clearer that the full implementation of the rite requires the coordination of a variety of ministries. It would be foolish for one person (or pastoral staff) to attempt to implement the RCIA alone — as well as being contrary to the vision of the rite. One designated person can serve as coordinator — to do just that, coordinate. It would be this person's responsibility to see that all the ministries are well serviced and resourced, as well as for providing the overall choreography to the rite. In places that function at a high level of implementation, this role of service not only is essential, but will require a large commitment of time and dedication. This responsibility may initially fall into the hands of the DRE or one of the pastoral associates. However, it eventually may evolve either into a full-time staff position, or within the care of a person responsible for sacramental catechesis in the parish. If anywhere in the rite one deems it necessary to have someone skilled and trained in theology and ministry, it would be in this role of service.

Hospitality. An initiating community is a community of welcome and hospitality. Throughout the RCIA, there are hospitality needs: celebrations, welcoming into parish functions, Sunday morning coffee and doughnuts. Parishioners can become involved in the RCIA through the coordination and extension of hospitality.

Communications. The parish community, in order to welcome and serve, needs to know what is going on. Throughout the year, they need to hear about the various periods of formation, their role in the process, the people who are joining the community. The sponsors, godparents, and other team members need to stay informed as well. A group of people whose primary role is on-going communication to the RCIA team and parish community will deepen the level of involvement and ownership by all.

Prayer Partners. In addition to the explicit sponsorship of candidates and catechumens, various members of the parish can be involved in the RCIA by serving as prayer partners. This would include parishioners or groups of parishioners actively remembering in prayer one of the catechumens throughout the process. This would be a wonderful way of involving the homebound in the RCIA and of recognizing their baptismal spirituality as well.

Liturgical Ministers. In addition to the pastoral team, the RCIA demands the active involvement of liturgical ministers — especially musicians — for full and rich celebrations of the rites. This requires a shift from liturgical planning to liturgical preparation that incorporates the experience of growth in faith and variety of conversions experienced by the catechumens. Along with the pastoral staff and RCIA team, the liturgical ministers adopt and adapt liturgical rites of the RCIA so that they may authentically express the experience of the catechumens within this particular community. This would require a "listening in" to the movement of the Spirit in the catechumenate and in the parish community.

Spiritual Directors. Sometimes a catechumen will desire to seek additional companionship in the process of naming and owning his or her conversion. The parish needs to make available men and women gifted in the art of spiritual direction or accompaniment. In chapter thirteen, we will discuss in more detail the role and function of spiritual direction in the RCIA.

Outreach. One sign of the interiorization of conversion is the outward expression in service. Catechumens will experience the call and desire to give away the gift they are receiving in the RCIA through concrete expressions of charity and service. Sometimes it is helpful to provide someone who can assist them in discerning how they can best serve the larger community, as well as which explicit avenues of service are available to them (such as soup kitchens, shelters for the homeless, visiting the sick, assisting in child care, or other expressions of charity).

The initiating community will continue to discover additional expressions of ministry flowing from the RCIA experience. Implementing the rite seems to have a ripple effect — we risk bringing a variety of people together to help with the formation process, the RCIA moves closer to the center of the parish's worship, more people will want to become involved, the variety of ministries that can develop become more extensive, the parish community becomes more involved and deepens the level of renewal that can happen in the community, the parish community expresses this renewal in forms of charity and justice resulting in more people wanting to affiliate with this community . . . and the on-going cycle of formation and initiation of both individuals and the community continues.

FORMING AN RCIA TEAM

The process and ministries we utilize to implement the RCIA make an important statement about how we view initiation and the role of the community. If we are committed to a vision of church that calls forth the gifts of all the baptized for service, then we are working toward a collaborative model of ministry. Collaboration requires the differentiation of ministries while respecting the fundamental responsibility of all the baptized. It is from a collaborative model for ministry that the concept of a RCIA team can emerge.

Usually one person is designated to be responsible for the RCIA in a parish — the RCIA coordinator. The coordinator could choose to do most of the implementation alone. The results would be a definite vision of church, ministry, initiation — all of which would probably suggest a very privatized experience of church — and one burnt-out person. Of its very nature, the RCIA is communal and its implementation is communal.

The RCIA coordinator will need to surround himself or herself with two teams of ministers. The first team comprises all the individuals who are sharing gifts in the RCIA process — catechists, hospitality, environment, communications, sponsors, and so on. The second team is a smaller group of individuals who represent the various ministries in the RCIA and work with the coordinator to oversee the general development and implementation of the rite. This second team — commonly called the core team — could be as small as three to

four or as large as twelve to fourteen. Whatever the size, the core team
needs to represent all the various ministries in the RCIA.

Recruiting the Team

How do people become involved in the RCIA? Usually through
word of mouth. The best publicity is the feedback from friends and
neighbors. So begin small and provide wonderful care and support.
The message will quickly get around.

Another way to get team members is to begin to ask around. Who
are the people in the parish who are good care givers, willing to share
faith, friendly, prayerful — basic active members of the community.
The basic active members need not be the "faithful fifty" who are
always called upon to do things. Rather, they are the ordinary Jane and
Joe in the community who need to be asked, who are waiting to be
invited to help serve the parish.

The bulletin can be an effective communicator in the parish.
However, avoid blank ads such as "We need catechists for the RCIA"
or "We need sponsors for the RCIA." This limits your ability to help
discern with the individuals their own gifts for service. A more general
announcement will still attract people, and will give you the opportunity to help place them where they can be of best service.

Some parishes offer an "RCIA gathering." The gathering is an
evening of reflection about baptismal spirituality and the RCIA. Its
purpose is to expose people to the RCIA and its ministries to the needs
in the parish. While the gathering needs to be open to everyone in the
parish — and be advertised as such — certain individuals may be
given a special invitation to attend because they are prospective team
members. The format of the evening can vary, but some basic elements
would include a short overview of RCIA, prayer time, and reflection on
ministry. No one is coerced or forced to make a commitment. Rather,
people are invited to explore their own baptismal spirituality. At the
end of the gathering, an opportunity for joining one of the teams
can be provided.

What are the qualities of people who serve on RCIA teams?
Basically, they need to be men and women from the community who
honestly struggle to live the gospel in the ordinary ways of life. As people of prayer, they have come to trust their experience of God in the
Catholic community and desire to share that experience with others.
Because they are each unique, the team members will bring different
gifts and talents — leadership skills, hospitality, humor, critical sense,

intuition — and different perspectives of living as church — single, progressive, divorced, married, traditional, and so on.

We need to remember that team members are volunteers. People volunteer to help out for a variety of reasons. However, beneath all the reasons are two basic ones — one external and one internal. The external reason usually has to do with contributing to this particular group, and hoping to gain some sense of affiliation, support, and a sense of accomplishment and worthwhileness — that my contribution counts. The internal reason usually has to do with some inner need or desire that the individual hopes to have fulfilled by participating with this group, such as a deepening of my hunger for God, or coming to a new awareness of my relationship with God. Whatever the reasons, the RCIA coordinator will need to help the team members name their needs, and then help them feel some satisfaction and fulfillment of those needs. If they are not being cared for, the volunteers will go somewhere else to have those needs satisfied. Thus, good resourcing and support for your team are essential.

Minimally, this means providing on-going gatherings for the team for support and personal enrichment. Some topics that need to be discussed with the team throughout the year are:

- Overview of RCIA — process, history, theology. Each team member should either have his or her own copy of the rite or easy access to a copy.
- Conversion and Faith Development. The team needs to be sensitive to the dynamics of conversion and faith in their own lives in order to be attentive to them in the catechumens' lives.
- Storytelling and Faith Sharing. The team will need to begin to develop a basic level of naming and telling their experience of God in order to share the faith of the community and help the catechumens enter into this same process of naming God's activity.
- Basic Communication Skills. The team will need to practice basic skills for effective communication: active listening, feedback, appropriate confrontation and challenge, affirmation and support, and so on.
- Basic Catechetical Skills. Those involved in catechesis will need to spend some time exploring methodological options to provide the finest opportunities possible for the catechumens.
- Burnout in Ministry. The RCIA tends to engender enthusiasm and high levels of commitment from team members. However, if the

team does not reflect on realistic expectations and develop skills for stress, the result could be burnout.

- Time to talk about their needs, concerns, and so on. In addition to these training modules (and any other your team needs), the team members need time together to simply talk about their experiences with the RCIA, to inform and be formed together in support and care.

The Core Team

The second team the RCIA coordinator may work with is the core team. This smaller team would be responsible for the general implementation of the RCIA. The members of the core team, who come from the RCIA team mentioned above, meet more regularly to discuss the needs and direction of the RCIA. Depending on the size of the basic team, the core team could be composed of:

- RCIA coordinator.
- Member from the pastoral staff. It is advisable that if the RCIA coordinator is not a part of the pastoral staff, one member of the staff join the core team to represent the needs and concerns of the pastor and staff.
- Liturgy coordinator. This person serves as liaison with the liturgy team and liturgical musicians, bringing them in when necessary as the team prepares for any celebrations.
- Hospitality coordinator. This person represents those who provide formal (receptions) and informal (coffee breaks, greeters) hospitality in the RCIA.
- Catechist coordinator. This person serves the needs of the catechists in the RCIA. If the catechetical team is differentiated into four subgroups — one for each period of the RCIA — it might prove to be helpful to include one representative from each group.
- Sponsor and godparent coordinator. This person keeps in touch with the sponsors and godparents, communicating any of their needs to the team.
- Communications coordinator. This person is responsible for keeping the parish community aware of the RCIA and the various rites when celebrated.

The core team will vary depending on the needs of each individual parish. What is important is that a team of people involved in the RCIA gather to help discern how they can best be of service to both the parish community and the catechumens in this process of initiation.

SPONSOR AND GODPARENT FORMATION

Perhaps one of the most important ministries in the RCIA —
second only to the role of the local community — is the support and
care given by sponsors and godparents. Catechumens and sponsors
meet regularly to discuss the basic concerns, hopes, and fears that
develop as the catechumen listens to God's call in his or her life.

Sponsorship is an important service, and therefore the team needs
to be cautious about who sponsors. Idealistically, everyone in the community is called to be a sponsor. However, given the limits that surround us, we want to provide the best possible experience for the
catechumen as he or she journeys in faith with this community. A
sponsor sensitive to the needs of the catechumen will be of great assistance in this journey.

Sponsors need to be informed up front that their ministry will
involve a large commitment of time: regular gatherings with the catechumen, witnessing for the community, and catechetical sessions.

The formation of sponsors (and godparents, whenever possible) is
similar to the formation of the RCIA team, with stronger emphasis on
faith-sharing skills, shared prayer, reflection on the scriptures, discernment, conversion theories, and communication skills. Sponsors need to
be sensitive to the fact that choosing to affiliate with a community is
both a joyful and a painful process. There is a death to an old way of
life, and the catechumen will often experience something akin to
grieving.

Regular gatherings for sponsors will help them talk about what's
going on in the RCIA, as well as keep them informed of any developments. The following guide for sponsors helps outline some of the responsibilities and expectations of sponsors. These would also be
helpful for godparents, with appropriate adjustments.

GUIDE FOR SPONSORS

The following offers a summary of the role of sponsor. It can be
adapted to include the responsibilities of the godparent.

■ The role of sponsor is one of spiritual friend, of support and care.
You represent the parish community in a special way. You also provide the one-on-one support the person needs during this period of
growth and development. Your role is a privilege and a responsibility
in the parish.

■ Catechumens and sponsors need to meet on a regular basis. The definition of regular basis differs, of course, depending on individual needs. However, the following can serve as a guideline: that catechumen and sponsor meet to talk about the catechumen's faith development and concerns *at least* once every week. The gatherings are meant to be informal sharings — to be supportive and to help clarify some issues for the catechumen. If a particular week passes and you can't be available (or vice versa), then call the catechumen to at least touch base. On-going communication is essential here.

■ What do you do when you meet? Share faith together. You become the resource person for the catechumen, for all those questions he or she has, for those concerns he or she may feel uncomfortable bringing up in the inquiry/catechumenate gatherings. But more importantly, you serve as a support and a friend. Here are some conversation starters: How has your week been? What happened at last Sunday's session? Did you understand what was talked about? You'll find the catechumen has a lot of questions. Feel free to share with him or her your experience of being Catholic, and of being part of this parish.

■ Another vital role of the sponsor is to help the catechumen feel welcome in the parish community. Here are some suggestions as to how you can do this:
— Alert the catechumen to upcoming parish events (lectures, socials) and suggest that perhaps you go together.
— If you are involved in a parish organization, invite the catechumen to one of your meetings.
— Introduce the catechumen to some of your parish friends. While you do not want to overwhelm, you do want to welcome them into the parish family. And the only way they will feel welcome is if you introduce them to parishioners.

■ Be creative, be innovative, be daring. Some sponsors have invited catechumens over for dinner on occasion. Others have met at the local diner for a cup of coffee and a chance to chat. What is important is that you find quality time to welcome this person, to make him or her feel important and special to this parish through you.

■ Questions will be raised, concerns will come up, and you may feel inadequate in handling them. That's fine. Let the catechumen know, "I don't know..." and then find out. Call up one of the team or check it out in the Catholic Encyclopedia or any other resource text. This can become a good learning experience for both of you. The catechumen will learn that the Catholic experience is one that is always new and growing. And you will have the chance to clarify some important questions and concerns you may have had with the community.

■ During the inquiry period, opportunities for the candidates to meet will be made available weekly. Stay informed of the day and place of these gatherings. Hopefully, you will be able to join with the inquiry team and the candidates each week. This will be a good opportunity to get to know your candidate, as well as to set up a time for you to meet privately.

■ If the candidate you are sponsoring chooses to become a member of the Catholic community, he or she will celebrate the rite of acceptance into the order of catechumens. The catechumenate team will meet with you to discuss the importance of this transition for the candidate. During those last days prior to the celebration, your discussions with the candidate will need to focus on why he or she is joining the community, and what he or she will need from both the community and from God. Your witness at the rite of acceptance will be valuable.

■ During the period of the catechumenate, the catechumens will be gathering weekly to pray, reflect on the word of God, and explore the issues of Catholic faith — and how all of this impacts on their daily lives. The catechumenate team will let you know when the catechumens will be gathering. The presence and participation of the sponsors in these catechetical gatherings are important. These gatherings can also serve as a starting point for your weekly gathering with the catechumen.

■ When your catechumen is ready to celebrate the Easter sacraments, he or she will celebrate the rite of election on the First Sunday of Lent. Your witness to the growth and development of the catechumen at this celebration will be valuable. If you are sponsoring a candidate for full communion in the Catholic Church, he or she will celebrate a similar rite of recognition.

■ During the final days of preparation, the catechumen (or elect) will be spending more time with his or her godparent who will continue to be a companion with the catechumen during the years ahead. You are encouraged to continue your relationship with the catechumen. However your responsibility as a sponsor comes to an end at this time. Of course, you are welcome to join with the catechumens and their godparents and families at the Easter vigil. If you are sponsoring a candidate for full communion, however, you will continue in your role as sponsor with him or her throughout the remainder of this formation process.

■ Throughout the year there will be a number of gatherings which will be of service to you as a sponsor. The catechumenate team will provide you with the dates for these gatherings. These will be times of prayer, and discussion of the concerns and issues of the catechumenate process, as well as of providing support and direction for all the sponsors.

Part Two

Implementing the Rite

4

Period of Evangelization and Precatechumenate

INTRODUCTION

The period of precatechumenate is when the individual begins to respond to some stirrings within to seek out this particular community of Catholic Christians. The reasons vary and are as many as there are individuals. This is a period of searching, asking questions, and the initial stirrings of faith.

During the precatechumenate, individuals are introduced to the stories of the Catholic community: scripture stories, stories about the Catholic Church, personal stories of faith, and the stories of the parish. Gathering regularly in the home of someone from the community, or at the parish center, these inquirers raise the questions and concerns they have about following Jesus in the Catholic community. The goal of this period of formation is to help the inquirers come to an initial awareness of God's saving presence in their lives, and to help them discern their initial readiness to embrace the way of life of Jesus Christ. In addition to the support and direction from the catechumenate team, sponsors chosen from the community begin a special ministry of accompaniment with the inquirers to help them in discerning their readiness to embrace the gospel way of life more fully. While the inquirers usually meet as a group, the period of the precatechumenate lasts as long as each individual inquirer needs — this is a period of no fixed duration — thus respecting the individual's journey in faith.

There are no liturgical celebrations during the precatechumenate period. The guidelines provide for an optional reception of inquirers, but are clear that this is not a ritual celebration (RCIA, n. 39). Rather, if desired, it can be a gathering of the community to meet and support the inquirers. Throughout the precatechumenate period, there may also be opportunities for short prayer experiences (RCIA, n. 40).

THE PRECATECHUMENATE

The period of the precatechumenate is a time of evangelization, of beginning to name the good word that in Jesus there is freedom and life. There are various dimensions of evangelization that are operative during the period of the precatechumenate.

1. *Development of relationships and experiences of trust.* The precatechumenate is a time for people to begin to feel at home — with the community, with specific individuals in the community, and with themselves. It is only in an environment of genuine care and concern that people begin to entrust themselves and others with their questions, their concerns, their story.

People come seeking entrance into the church for various reasons. Whatever the reasons why they come, the reason they stay is due to the quality of the relationships that are established.

Since the precatechumenate is a period of welcoming and at-homeness, the logical place for these gatherings is in parishioners' homes. Households throughout the parish can be used for gatherings at which questions about Catholic life can be answered. As the RCIA develops in a parish, there may be a number of households that have gatherings on different evenings to accommodate the various needs and demands of the inquirers.

The motivation for developing relationships of trust and centers of welcome is to create a space where the individual inquirer can experience a basic respect for his or her life journey. The focus is on the inquirer, not on membership. When our focus shifts, and it can in subtle ways, we are bordering on manipulation. It is then that we create false environments that are not authentic.

2. *Questions and storytelling.* The precatechumenate is about questions and about stories. Usually, inquirers come with more questions than stories, until they realize they have permission to tell their story. Then the stories come.

Stories are our basic mode of communication with each other. When we want to share something of ourself, when we want to understand someone, when we want to include others, we begin to tell and listen to stories. Storytelling is a language of self-disclosure.

Real storytelling happens best when there is a caring and trusting environment, when people don't have to fear being judged or evaluated because of their story. Then they can tell stories — simple ones, significant ones, transformative ones, funny ones. When people begin to tell stories about their lives, they also begin to discover questions about their lives.

Most of the questions that inquirers come with are either profound life-questions (e.g. why is there suffering?) or questions of interest (e.g. why do Catholics light candles in front of statues of saints? Isn't that idolatry?). During the experience of storytelling, new types of questions often emerge: personal questions (what do I really want?), questions of truth (how do I really discover who I am?), questions of value (what is really important in my life?), questions of responsibility (what am I choosing to do with my life?). Storytelling becomes one way of facilitating people asking better questions about themselves and others and their relationships.

In dialogue with the stories the inquirers bring, the period of the precatechumenate is also filled with the stories of the community: the stories told by team members and sponsors, the stories of the parish community, the stories of Jesus and his followers, other stories from the Hebrew and Christian scriptures, the stories of men and women in the Catholic community who led inspiring lives (saints) . . . and more stories. When we begin to tell stories, others begin to tell stories. When we begin to move to another level of storytelling that raises questions of meaning, others join us in the search.

3. *Naming the experiences.* The precatechumenate, though, is more than a rap group or a discussion club. We raise stories, we ask and answer questions so that we can begin to name them, so we can begin to look at all of them from a new perspective, from a new vantage. The precatechumenate is the beginning of helping inquirers experience that in their life stories — the ordinary and extraordinary, the painful and the joyful, the calm and the stormy — are those places where we can come to meet and know God. It is the beginning of recognizing the stirrings of God within our human lives and relationships.

4. *Initial faith in Christ and initial conversion.* And not only do we begin to name God in our experience, but we begin to name a call from God within our experience. Inquirers are provided with the opportunity to explore their life within a new frame of reference: the story of Jesus. And from this, they may feel drawn, compelled, invited. Questions may be answered, but usually a deeper longing begins to become more apparent. "I came here because I wanted to become Catholic to marry my fiancée. But something has happened. I can't explain it. There is something more in all of this. I want to find out what it means for *me*."

The precatechumenate helps the inquirers establish and name a relationship with God. And not just any relationship with any God, but a loving relationship with the God revealed most fully in Jesus and proclaimed within the Catholic Christian community.

Some inquirers will be ready to tell stories. Others will have good questions. Others will have an established love relationship with God. All of them, in different ways, will need to come to a point where they can say, "Being in the Catholic community does make a difference in my life." Not that they can articulate the difference at this time. Rather, it's an inkling, a stirring, a dim light. But it is nonetheless a conviction.

And being in the Catholic community means being in relationship with God as revealed in Jesus. Again, the meaning of this may be very simple. But it is real. And it is worth committing oneself to. It is worth saying yes to the gospel of Jesus proclaimed in the Catholic community.

The period of precatechumenate — a period of evangelization — is about facilitating the possibility of this initial conversion. It is helping people name their current reality (the story of their lives), their possibility (God's desire for them), and the movement to allow all of this to emerge (responsibility).

THEOLOGY OF REVELATION

All of this is rooted in a dynamic theology of revelation, which is affirmed in the Dogmatic Constitution on Divine Revelation (*Dei Verbum*) from Vatican Council II and rearticulated in the National Catechetical Directory.

Revelation is not extrinsic, that is, something outside of us. A static notion of revelation holds that it is "information," truth locked away that we need to uncover. When we hit on the right combination, we will have all the truths revealed.

Rather, revelation is God's self-communication with us. It is God's desire to stand in union with us, to share life with us, to offer the gift of loving presence. Through this process of revelation (i.e. communication, being invited into God's very self), one comes to a heightened and more intense awareness of God's presence and love. The Christian tradition holds that the fullness of God's revelation — the on-going and fresh gift of God's self to the community — is most complete in Jesus, the Christ, and that it is in and through Jesus that we come to know God: the God who creates us, redeems us, sustains us, and chooses to become intimately involved with us. The incarnation affirms, therefore, that a primary place of God's revelation is in relationship with creation, especially humanity. Revelation, then, is dynamic and on-going. God is continually in relationship with us.

The Catholic community also holds the scriptures and the tradition as sources of God's revelation, thus offering a complement and fullness to the revelation of God in Jesus and in creation.

If we look to the early Christian community, we can see this dynamic sense of revelation in operation. The followers of Jesus experienced in Jesus new possibilities, a new way of life. After his death and resurrection, they began to name this experience of freedom and reconciliation with themselves, others, creation, the cosmos and with God as salvation. Initially, the earliest communities preached the reign of God as proclaimed in Jesus. They preached *what* Jesus preached. Eventually, though, as they reflected on their experience, guided by the power of the Spirit, the community came to affirm that it was precisely in Jesus that they experienced this reign of God. The preaching and belief shifted from what Jesus preached to *preaching Jesus*. Jesus became the preached good. Eventually, this reflection and struggle to name God in their midst (the symbols of the community) became formulated into creedal formulas and eventually into doctrine. But the first level was the experience of God, followed by appropriate reflection and internalization, followed by articulation, followed by formulation. Doctrine, in its best sense, is the articulation of the community of faith. It is the church expressing its experience of God reconciling and saving us in and through Jesus the Christ. Doctrine, as an expression of revelation, is dynamic. It flows from the faith of the community.

This is not to say that doctrine is the product of consensus, opinion, or whim. Rather, doctrine is the formulation of a community's symbol system that authentically empowers the community to a deeper and more integrated response to God's call. Doctrine is an expression of faith. The important point here, however, is that doctrine flows from the religious experience of God in our midst.

In light of this, the catechumenate experience is to help individuals begin to name God's manifestation in their lives and to correlate their experience with the living tradition of the Catholic community. This correlation is a dynamic process of questioning, challenging, searching, resolving. During the precatechumenate, we are beginning to equip the journeyer with the basic skills to learn to seek God in their lives. During the catechumenate period — and throughout the Christian life — the task will be to remain faithful to the dialogue for true self-knowledge and a sense of mission.

Such a dynamic sense of revelation, therefore, suggests that there are not two types of experience — secular and religious. Rather, it suggests that from *within* human experience we can come to meet and know the living God.

HUMAN EXPERIENCE

Are all human experiences revelatory? Do all human experiences — precisely because they are human experience — serve as vehicles for the manifestation of God? Basically, all truly human experiences have the potential of being the bearers of God's manifestation in the world, of God's epiphany. Some distinctions need to be made to help clarify this.

Experience is a rather fuzzy word for many. It is invoked to include everything that happens for an individual — from the intense excitement of a basketball game to the passive resignation of being shuffled about in a crowded subway car. "What an experience that was!" In our discussion of experience, however, we need to be more focused. To speak of human experience presumes some level of conscious interaction by the individual or group with an object (i.e. a person or an event). The person or persons are aware and in dialogue with the object. For example, a father and mother are sitting in the auditorium watching their daughter in her first dance recital. Most probably they are not aware of themselves sitting in the auditorium seats, or of many of the people around them, or even of the temperature in the room unless any of these is a distraction (uncomfortable chair or a cold room). They are focused on their daughter and her dancing. Being in the chair is not a human experience because there is no active and conscious encounter with the chair — it's probably taken for granted. The human experience is the encounter with their daughter, her dancing, each other as they sit there, and the feelings that are emerging throughout the performance (that is, the feelings they acknowledge). In another section of the auditorium, another parent is watching his daughter dance also. However, he is preoccupied with a crisis at the office that may result in the loss of his job. While the dance goes on, he feels restless and squirms in his seat, repeating over and over again in his mind possible scenarios at the office. He feels tired, and the darn seat is so uncomfortable! Suddenly there is a burst of applause and the dance is over. He was looking at the dance but not seeing the dance. For this man, his daughter's dance recital was not a human experience in that he was not consciously present or aware of the dance. His human experience focused on his job, his feeling tired and restless, and the uncomfortable chair. In order for an experience to be a human experience, it requires some level of conscious interaction between a subject (the individual or group) and the object (the dance, the chair, the daughter, the restlessness, and so on).

There are two basic dimensions of human experience. The first dimension is the level of the ordinary, the level of the sensory. One has a visible, sensible encounter with the world. The chair is uncomfortable, the dance is lively, the woman is cold, the iron is hot, the tree stands tall. This first dimension of human experience encounters things and people *as they are.*

The second dimension of human experience is the depth dimension, the level of interpretation and meaning. One shifts to move behind the sensory to possible meanings of the interaction. The fidgeting in the seat may mean the person is preoccupied, the tree standing tall may inspire values of truth and beauty, the touch of the beloved may inspire love and affection. The depth dimension of human experience breaks one open to a new level of awareness; it is a disclosure situation. Because of it, one enlarges his or her basic world vision or horizon. New levels of meaning emerge that are interpreted from a variety of perspectives. One particular interpretation or perspective is the religious dimension.

The religious dimension of the secondary level of human experience is the particular way of viewing these depth experiences that opens one up to seeing within these moments the mystery we call God. There is the recognition of an invitation to a new relationship with the holy. That experience of God is then allowed to come to stand within the community's tradition for verification.

When we move from the sensory to this secondary level of human experience — when we name beauty, truth, hope, love — we discover that the depth and immensity of the experience far exceed any words or phrases we can use. Depth experiences bring us to the limits of human language. And so we use rich and multifaceted symbols to express, however inadequately, the depth experience. Our earlier discussion on symbols highlights the appeal to the whole person and the inability to exhaust the meaning of symbolic discourse.

Thus, there are not two types of experiences: secular and religious. Rather, there is the religious dimension of human experience. Technically, it is inaccurate to talk of religious experience unless it is nuanced to mean the religious dimension of human experience.

Every depth experience, therefore, has the potential of being a religious experience. If one is able to interpret the experience within the framework of a religious tradition, one can come to a new sense of meaning and a mediated encounter with the holy. This mediated encounter — there is never a direct experience of God — affirms the sacramental and incarnational dimension of the experience of God.

This is very different than an understanding of religious experience (or the religious dimension of human depth experience) that is lacquered over life. There is no depth, no meaning. Rather, there is the polishing off of every experience with religious language. This rather facile use of religious language leads one to a private and individualistic expression of religious experience, and hence God. God, in this context, stands outside of human history and human experience.

One of the tasks of evangelization is to help people articulate levels of meaning in their life and then to enter into dialogue with the Christian tradition's expression of these same meaning-makers. Hence the truth of the gospel needs to be proclaimed (and authentically interpreted) in order to provide a credible and meaningful challenge to the contemporary man and woman's interpretation of their depth experience. Then the gospel can serve as invitation.

During the precatechumenate, we are helping the inquirers to begin to develop a heightened sensitivity to the depth dimension of human experience by helping them to create a space wherein they can trust that experience, name that experience, tell that experience, and then dialogue that experience with our Catholic Christian tradition. The period of the precatechumenate takes storytelling very seriously.

THE INITIAL INTERVIEW

As we mentioned earlier, people come to our community for a variety of reasons and due to a variety of influences: a Catholic spouse, fiancée or fiancé, the influence of other Catholic people, a search for community and relationships, a feeling of emptiness, a desire to start a new life, the response to evangelization, a death in the family, a feeling of guilt for past deeds, and so on. More often than not, however, the reasons for staying change radically as the individuals begin to allow the healing hand of God to emerge for them within this community.

Each person's needs and concerns will be different. And each will come with a very different background. Hence, the process of formation, while respecting the basic steps and periods of the RCIA, will still be structured in such a way as to respect those differences. Someone who has had very little exposure to the Catholic community and is unbaptized will probably enter into a more extensive process than someone from another Christian denomination who is able to name explicit calls from God for deepened conversion.

One way to assess the needs of the inquirer, as well as helping the catechetical teams best serve the inquirers, is through an initial interview. The initial interview or conversation, while affording the team the opportunity to get necessary information about the inquirer, is really an act of hospitality and welcome. Someone comes seeking more information. We respond with a chance to talk with someone from the community, who will also use the opportunity to share some initial insights and perceptions about the parish, the formation process of the RCIA, and the needs of the inquirer.

The initial interview often sets the tone for the inquirer for quite some time. If the individual felt welcomed and cared for during the conversation, he or she will be more willing to invest time seeking this community. If the interview or conversation is rather distant or sterile, new questions will emerge for the inquirer, mainly: What could I possibly want from here? Thus, it is important that the initial interview be conducted by someone with basic communication skills. It seems appropriate that unless there is an interviewing team that can be trained for this service, the initial interview be with either the RCIA coordinator, a member of the pastoral staff, or someone designated for this function.

There is some basic information you will need to know early on. However, avoid giving the inquirer a form to fill out. This has all the appearances of an application or registration process. Rather, in an informal conversation, the questions and concerns can be raised with the inquirer. You can explain to the inquirer that you will be taking down some of the information shared so you can better serve him or her. Also, if you plan to share any of the information with other team members, such as the inquiry team, you will need to let the inquirer know as a sign of respect for confidentiality.

Some areas that you may wish to address in the initial interview include:

- Specific concerns: What are the specific questions and concerns the inquirer has at this time?
- Religious background: What is the inquirer's experience or sense of God, religion, prayer?
- Church affiliation: Is the inquirer unbaptized? Baptized? If baptized, what is the Christian denomination of affiliation? Was the baptism in the trinitarian formula (in the name of the Father . . .)? How involved was the inquirer in that community? Why the move to Catholicism?

- Connection with Catholic Church: What has been the inquirer's experience of Catholicism? How did the inquirer find out about the Catholic Church? This parish?
- Marriage background: Is the inquirer single, married, divorced, planning to remarry, and so on? These marital questions will need to be assessed early in case there is need for pastoral care regarding marriage issues.
- Basic information: What is the inquirer's full name, address, phone, work phone, occupation, and so on?
- The RCIA: Explain the process of formation in the parish for the RCIA. It would be important to be clear that there is no pre-set guaranteed time line for initiation.
- New questions: In light of the discussion, are there any new questions or concerns? How can we specifically help right now?

At the end of the conversation, the inquirer can be invited to attend the next precatechumenate gathering. Arrangements can be made to meet the candidate so she or he does not have to come to this new home alone. Sensitivity to the needs of the inquirer in this new environment is important.

FORMING THE PRECATECHUMENATE GROUP

The precatechumenate gatherings work best when they take place in the homes of people from the parish. The team and pastoral staff will need to know the location, day, and time of gatherings. The size and style of the group will change as people move in and out of the precatechumenate. However, it is advisable that the group not get too large or else it will be difficult to foster an environment for sharing and discussion. If there are a large number of inquirers, a parish may choose to have a number of precatechumenate groups meeting at different times to accommodate the needs of the inquirers. The various small groups could come together periodically to touch base with each other. Another format could be to rotate the location of the gatherings every few weeks. Except in the situation when there are only one or two inquirers, it does not seem to be a good idea to separate the inquirers into individual households (one-on-one). The sense of community, however basic and primitive at this point, that is established in the homes helps the inquirers develop a sense of trust and affiliation.

CATECHESIS DURING THE PRECATECHUMENATE

There is no set agenda for the precatechumenate. In light of all that has been said already, suffice it to say that the precatechumenate is about storytelling, naming God's call, and initial conversion. The format for gatherings is very informal. The agenda is determined by the questions and concerns of inquirers. The team may want to have some basic tools ready to encourage the questions and storytelling, but these tools and activities are always secondary to the needs of the inquirers.

Following are some tools that have been used effectively in precatechumenate gatherings.

- *Biography sharing:* Encourage everyone to share something about themselves and their lives. As new people join the group, it helps for everyone to briefly go around again and introduce themselves. Usually, each time the group tells something about themselves, new and unique dimensions emerge.
- *Journaling:* Early on, the inquirers can be given a journal or notebook and encouraged to begin a journaling process that could include reflections gleaned from the gatherings, new questions, their history, their hopes, and so on. Journal keeping is not the same as diary writing. The latter is usually a record of events. Journaling attempts to move to a level of meaning and interpretation of experiences. Basic journaling skills and techniques could be given to the inquirers.
- *Life Map:* In order to help inquirers situate their present search within the larger context of their life, one journaling technique is the life map. The inquirers are asked to think of major transition points in their life (perhaps ten or twelve), beginning with their birth and ending with the present moment. These marker events can be drawn as if they were a road, indicating the highs and lows of the events and the periods between them. These serve as possibilities for discussion. Throughout the RCIA they can be encouraged to fill in the details of this map.
- *Church Tour:* Art, architecture, and sacred space have always served the community in a variety of capacities. One service has been catechetical. The life of both the local community and the larger church can be discussed during a church tour. Spending time with the pictures, statues, windows, carvings, and so on, are all ways of basic instruction. Bring the inquirers to the sacristy, show them

vestments and vessels. Open the reconciliation room. Bring them into the sanctuary and show them the altar. Help them feel at home.

■ *Parish History:* Parishes preserve their history in a variety of ways: photos, anniversary journals, booklets. Spend time discussing the life and growth of the parish, indicating some of the unique features of this particular parish community.

■ *Parishioners:* Invite members of the community to visit with the inquirers. Have a cross-section of people: old, young, involved in organizations, and so on. Ask them to spend a few minutes sharing who they are and why they are part of this parish. Allow the inquirers to ask questions about life in the parish.

■ *Liturgical Year:* There are some beautiful liturgical calendars published that are relatively inexpensive. Have one available to show the inquirers the various seasons and movements in the life of the community as indicated on the liturgical calendar: feasts, Ordinary Time, Advent, Lent. Talking about these seasons and the various colors of the liturgical year is a good way of telling some of the stories of our faith.

■ *Symbol-Making:* Provide opportunities to help inquirers name and discuss basic life symbols as well as personal symbols. Perhaps those who would rather not write in their journal could draw or describe a symbol that captures the day's experience for them. These symbols, followed in sequence, can begin to tell the story of the inquirer during this period of life.

■ *Open-Ended Sentences:* These are usually good for discussion. Provide a sheet with a series of opening phrases of a sentence, and allow the inquirers to have time to respond to them. The sentences could be constructed in response to the issues raised in the previous gathering. Some examples:
— My greatest hope . . .
— I'm here because . . .
— When I think of death . . .
— What I really want . . .
— To love . . .

■ *Photo Stories:* Whenever people show family photos, immediately the stories begin to be told. Encourage people to bring in a few photos — perhaps of different periods of their life. This is also a good opportunity to show photos of people and places in the Catholic tradition.

■ *Storytelling:* Needless to say, this is going on all the time throughout the precatechumenate gatherings. As people begin to tell their stories, the team can also begin to tell the stories of the Catholic community.

■ *Telling the Jesus Story:* Throughout the precatechumenate, it will be important to tell the story of Jesus, stories of the Hebrew and early Christian communities, and the Catholic Christian community again and again. This will be most effective when collaborated with the questions and concerns of the inquirers.

■ *Current Events:* An important part of the journey of faith is to be able to recognize the movement of God in the ordinary of life. Encourage inquirers to bring in news clippings to discuss with the group: What's happening? How am I affected by this? How is God present in this? How can I respond? How do we respond? The team may also want to keep abreast of news that would have a particular interest for the inquirers — things they have talked about, newsworthy events in the Catholic community, items or concerns that call us to prayer.

■ *Catholic Trivia:* Encourage the inquirers during the week to think of questions about Catholic life — any questions, such as: What are the candles in front of statues for? Why are priests celibate? Where do we get the hosts? Who chooses the scripture readings at the Catholic Mass? Then choose one member of the team to serve as the responder. The inquirers (and team!) can toss out the questions one at a time to try and stump the responder.

■ *Scripture:* Inquirers need to see the Bible — to recognize its basic structure, how it is broken down into a variety of books, and so on. This can be done very informally. Include a story or passage from the scriptures at each gathering and let them know where it came from. Some of the inquirers from other Christian denominations will have questions about the so-called Catholic books of the Bible.

■ *Written Questions:* At the end of each gathering, the inquirers can be encouraged to spend a few moments, and each can write at least one specific question he or she has about what was discussed, or Catholic life. The questions can be reviewed by the team during the week and used to help prepare for the next gathering.

■ *Prayer:* Regularly the inquirers need to be invited into experiences of prayer. Variety of prayer forms can be used to accommodate the needs and differences of the inquirers. This is a good time to use simple and spontaneous prayer with them, leading them into an awareness of prayer of petition and thanksgiving.

These are only a few examples of the variety of tools the team can use to help facilitate an initial awareness of God's on-going conversion in the inquirer's life.

HOSPITALITY

Throughout the Judeo-Christian tradition, hospitality has always been a central and key virtue. It is welcoming the guest in the name of God. For the Jew and Christian, all men and women are God's children and are due the respect and dignity of such an ennobled people. In recent times, we have seen the diminishment of this important dimension of community life. The precatechumenate provides a good opportunity for a parish community to begin to grow in its awareness of the responsibility of hospitality.

People will choose to respond to God's call to fuller life in the Catholic Christian life when they encounter members of the community who welcome them and willingly share with them the good word of God's presence in the community. Hospitality becomes the first word of welcome for the inquirer.

Various parish organizations can help with hospitality throughout the catechumenate process. With some coordination, a different parish group or organization can provide refreshments for the various gatherings. Child care during sessions could be provided. Transportation can be made available. Invitations to various parish functions, as well as to parishioners' homes, can be extended. The possibilities are endless. The effect is powerful.

Focusing catechesis on the needs and questions of the inquirers is another expression of hospitality. The message becomes clear: We are here to care and support you, to welcome you, to answer your questions (rather than this is what we want from you).

SPONSORS

As the inquirers continue to gather in the precatechumenate households, the coordinator of sponsors — in dialogue with the team — can begin to discern how best the inquirer can experience sponsorship. Each inquirer will have different needs. Spending time listening informally at gatherings will help to select a sponsor for the inquirer who can be a helpful companion. Sponsors can begin to gather occasionally at precatechumenate gatherings. Or perhaps having a social with all the inquirers and sponsors on a periodic basis will give people a chance to meet and get an initial sense of each other. Try to avoid having sponsor and inquirer meet for the first time when they are matched for the remainder of the process. With a minimum of effort, the sponsors can become known to the inquirers before decisions are made.

The sponsor's role at this period of formation is very informal. As the decision for a deepened commitment to the process approaches, the sponsor begins to take a more active role in the life of the inquirer. By the time the inquirer celebrates the rite of acceptance into the order of catechumens, the inquirer and sponsor should have had ample time to know each other and to have the beginnings of a trusting relationship.

TIME LINE

This period of the RCIA is of unlimited duration. This is the time to look around and see what Catholic life is all about. But it is also the time to stop and listen to what God is asking of the inquirer. Some people will be ready to move to a new level of involvement and commitment. Others will want to gaze and explore for a longer period of time. There is no need to rush, there is no hurry. As long as someone is interested and has basic questions, then the precatechumenate team makes themselves available and offers gracious hospitality. Sometimes a person may discern that this particular parish community — or this particular Christian denomination — is not the right place for them. Our response is one of continued support and blessing, encouraging them that we will continue to pray with and for them that they will find their heart's desire. Others will determine that this is the place they can come to know God more deeply. They will ask to join us, to seek their true hope and joy within our community. To them, we also extend our support and blessing. We welcome them into our family — the family of our parish and of the Catholic community.

5

First Step: Rite of Acceptance into the Order of Catechumens

INTRODUCTION

The rite of acceptance into the order of catechumens is the first of the public rites celebrated in the RCIA. During this important ritual, the inquirers publicly declare their intention to continue their journey toward full initiation in the Catholic Church, and the community accepts them, offering its support and witness during the journey. The RCIA is clear regarding its expectations of those who make this first step: "The prerequisite for making this first step is that the beginnings of the spiritual life and the fundamentals of Christian teaching have taken root in the candidates" (RCIA, n. 42).

The rite, which is celebrated at various times during the year depending on need, consists of various parts: receiving the candidates, the liturgy of the word, and the dismissal of the candidates. It is important to note that for all the ritual celebrations of the RCIA, there is the freedom for appropriate adaptation (RCIA, n. 35). Therefore, the structure of the ritual celebrations may differ at times because of pastoral sensitivity, but the essential dimensions of the rituals outlined in these reflections will be incorporated in the celebration.

DISCERNMENT FOR THE RITE OF ACCEPTANCE AND RITE OF WELCOME

The decision to celebrate the rite of acceptance ultimately rests in the hands of the individual inquirer. While there is the necessary dialogue and discernment with team and sponsors, the decision to choose to commit oneself to the gospel within this Catholic community is made by the inquirer.

The team and sponsors aid in this discernment process by reflecting back to the inquirer his or her growth in consciousness and change in lifestyle because of the initial exposure to the gospel within the Catholic tradition. The rite indicates some of the "indicators" that assist us in this discernment of initial conversion (RCIA, n. 42):

- *Evidence of first faith:* Does the individual have a desire to be in relationship with God? Does he or she want to discover more to life?
- *Initial conversion:* Has the individual begun to recognize that his or her life will change because of God? Has there been any preliminary changes and adjustments in the individual's life, attitudes, or actions because of what he or she has experienced to date?
- *Intent to change one's life:* Does the individual desire to leave behind all that is inauthentic? Does he or she desire to live life fully, whatever the cost?
- *Intent to enter into relationship with God in Christ:* Does the individual desire to follow the way of Christ in the gospel? Is he or she able to willingly embrace the demands of the gospel, at least as much as he or she knows of them now?
- *First stirrings of repentance:* Does the individual recognize that there are areas of his or her life that are wounded and broken? Has he or she begun to accept responsibility for areas of failings in his or her own life?
- *Beginnings of the practice of prayer:* Has the individual begun to pray outside of the gatherings? Does he or she recognize that prayer is an essential dimension of Christian life?
- *Sense of church:* Has the individual had the opportunity to discuss basic issues of the Catholic Church? Does he or she have a basic awareness of the distinctiveness of the Catholic Church?
- *Some experience of the community:* Has the individual expressed an interest in getting to know more about the parish, especially through participation in parish activities? Has he or she had the opportunity to meet and spend time with members of the parish?

DAY OF PRAYER

At the end of the period of the precatechumenate, the inquirers and their sponsors need to spend some time reflecting on the importance of this decision to enter the catechumenate. A period of reflection prior to the celebration of the rite can be a positive experience for the inquirers and their sponsors.

Once the decision has been made to enter the period of the

catechumenate, let the inquirers and sponsors know the date and time of the reflection gathering. The Saturday morning prior to the celebration of the rite is a good time. Following the period of reflection, there can be a review of the ritual with the sponsors.

If it is Saturday morning, you may want to ask members of the hospitality team to prepare a breakfast for those gathered. The gathering, while specifically for those entering the period of the catechumenate, could be open to all members of the RCIA community.

There can be a variety of components to the reflection gathering. Following are a few suggestions of elements that can be included in such a gathering:

- *Periods of Private and Communal Prayer:* The gathering can be so constructed as to include communal prayer experiences (such as an adaptation of the Liturgy of the Hours, or a guided meditation in common) and private prayer time (a significant period of quiet time need to be part of the time together).
- *Proclamation of Scripture:* A text can be chosen that highlights the importance of the rite of acceptance and God's call. The text may also be the gospel that will be proclaimed at the celebration of the rite.
- *Inquirer and Sponsor Time:* The inquirers and sponsors may be invited to pair off and spend time together. Reflection questions based on the text and the rite can be given to them at this time, such as:
  — Do you recognize that you need other people to become a full human person?
  — Do you recognize a need for Jesus Christ in your life?
  — Why do you want to become a member of this parish?
  — How have you experienced God in this parish?
  — How is your life beginning to change?
  — Are you willing to follow the way of life of Jesus?
  — Are you willing to accept the challenge of the cross in your life?
  — How can you welcome the word of God in your life?
  — What is it that you ask of God at this time of your life?
  — What do you ask of us as a church?
  — What do you need to help you in your journey of faith?
- *Shared Reflection:* In addition to the opportunities for sharing with one's sponsor, the inquirers can come together with the rest of the participants for a period of faith sharing. This will help to encourage a sense of community as well as provide support during this transition period.

■ *Preliminary Preparation for Rite:* Before ending the reflection period, the leader of prayer can ask the inquirers if there is anything the community can do to help them prepare for the rite. While not discussing the rite itself, it would be appropriate to discuss the significance of the rite (RCIA, n. 42), including the following:
— This is a ritual of commitment.
— The inquirers minister to the community by their desire to join the community.
— The inquirers need only to trust the direction and guidance of their sponsors during the rite.
— Thank the inquirers for their commitment.
■ *Overview of Rite with Sponsors:* After the inquirers have left, the team reviews the rite with the sponsors. A possible model can be:
— Discuss the experience of the reflection day with the sponsors.
— Review the importance of the rite of acceptance.
— Review the role of sponsor during the catechumenate.
— Review the rite, perhaps using a guide sheet for the sponsors.
— "Walk through" the rite with the sponsors in the worship space.

RITE OF ACCEPTANCE AND RITE OF WELCOME

Prior to the celebration of the rite, the candidates and sponsors will have had ample time to discuss the faith journey of the candidates. It would be important that the sponsors help the candidates articulate for themselves the meaning of this decision, as well as what they need and desire from God and this parish community.

As with the other ritual celebrations, the candidates should not rehearse the rite. Liturgical rituals need to be experienced and then reflected upon and discussed. Too often we practice rituals with those who will celebrate them, and the power of the experience is diminished. Therefore, it is strongly encouraged not to walk through the ritual with the candidates but rather allow the sponsors to guide the candidates in the celebration. It is the responsibility of the team and the sponsors to plan the rite, making certain it meets the needs of the local community. As mentioned, the significance and importance of the rite needs to be discussed beforehand with the candidates. The sponsors may also want to tell the candidates about the opening dialogue so as not to cause undue anxiety for the candidates.

It will be important to keep the distinction clear between the unbaptized and the baptized. Because of the frequency of mixed groups, the suggestions for implementation will presume a mixed group, following the translation published by the United States bishops in 1988. The rite will need to be adjusted accordingly if the group is all unbaptized or all baptized for full communion.

Gathering of the Community: The rite suggests the celebration begin outside the church with the candidates present (RCIA, n. 48, 507). However, it may be a richer symbol if the community gathers first and then goes to greet the candidates. Therefore, the community can gather in prayer in the church while the candidates wait with their sponsors in another place (preferably outside). Wherever they assemble, the presider greets the community and briefly explains to them the importance of this day. The following recommendations for celebration are based on an adaptation of the rite that would have the community gather in the worship space prior to greeting the candidates. While the community is gathered, the sponsors can use this time to pray and converse with the inquirers, offering support and helping to ease any anxiety.

Presentation of the Candidates: The RCIA coordinator is then invited to present the candidates to the community. The coordinator tells the community who the candidates are, letting them know something about the candidates.

Affirmation of the Assembly: The presider then asks the community if they are willing to support and welcome these men and women on their journey of faith. After the assent of the community, the presider invites the entire community to go and greet the candidates.

Procession: An antiphon or hymn is sung. When the community reaches the doors of the church, members of the hospitality committee open the doors and the community comes out singing to greet the candidates. In some circumstances (such as inclement weather), it may not be feasible for the community to move to another space (such as outside the entrance or the foyer of the church) to greet the candidates. In those cases, the candidates can be brought to the door of the church, or a representative of the community can be sent out to get the candidates and bring them into the midst of the assembly. Going outside to meet the candidates, however, makes a stronger statement.

Opening Dialogue (RCIA, n. 50, 509): The presider can invite the sponsors to introduce the candidates to the community. After the sponsor has introduced his or her candidate and told us something about him or her (including if preparing for baptism or full communion), the presider asks the candidate what he or she wants from God and the church. The candidate, who has already reflected on these questions, can respond in his or her own words.

Another possibility: the sponsors for the unbaptized can present their candidates first, followed by the questions from the presider. Then the sponsors of the baptized present their candidates. What is important is that the distinction between the unbaptized and the baptized be maintained throughout the rite.

The rite calls for the first promise of the candidates to live the way of the gospel to follow this dialogue (RCIA, n. 52, 511). Some argue that it would be more appropriate first to move to the celebration of the liturgy of the word, affirming that all ritual action flows from the proclamation of the word, and then follow with the first promise. Others argue that it is the first promise and the subsequent signing of the senses that prepares one to receive the word proclaimed in the assembly. In order to explore another option for celebration, we will move the first promise and signing of the senses to after the proclamation of the word.

Procession (RCIA, n. 60, 521): The presider invites the community to welcome these men and women into our midst and to lead them to the table of the word. An appropriate hymn can be sung while the community returns to the worship place.

Liturgy of the Word: The readings are those assigned for the day. The presider may choose other appropriate readings as suggested in the rite (RCIA, n. 62, 523).

First Acceptance of the Gospel: Following the homily, the candidates for baptism are now called forward. The presider asks them if they are ready to receive the gospel as a way of life (RCIA, n. 52, 511). The form of question may be worded in such a way as to include some of the insights gleaned from the initial dialogue.

Declaration of Intent: The candidates for full communion are now called forward (RCIA, n. 512). In similar fashion, incorporating insights from the opening dialogue, the presider asks them if they sincerely intend to explore and complete their Christian initiation with this Catholic community.

Affirmation by the Sponsors and the Assembly (RCIA, n. 53, 513): The presider then addresses the sponsors and assembly, asking if they will support and care for these candidates on their journey of faith in the Catholic Christian community.

Both the first acceptance of the gospel and the declaration of intent are pivotal moments in the ritual. Here is where the focus for catechesis needs to be. This is the public proclamation of the acceptance of the gospel as a way of life, and the acceptance of the Catholic community as an expression of this way of life. It is only because of this public assent that the remainder of the ritual makes any sense. The affirmation by the sponsors and the assembly is the Church's response to this first public statement of faith. It is only after this public statement that the candidates for baptism are called catechumens.

Signing with the Cross (RCIA, n. 54f, 514f): Now the catechumens and candidates (the rite does them separately, but they can be signed together without blurring the distinction) are led by their sponsors for the signing with the cross. It would be effective if they were placed at various spots throughout the church — down the aisles, across the front of the church — so that the assembly can witness the signings.

The presider invites the catechumens and candidates to receive the sign of their way of life, the way of life they have just given assent to. They are marked with the cross on the forehead, ears, eyes, lips, breast, shoulders, hands, and feet. It would be appropriate for the sponsors to sign the body of the catechumens and candidates using full gestures, touching the body with the palms of their hands as they sign them. An acclamation can be sung as each part of the body is signed.

Following the senses, there is a general signing of the whole person "in the name of the Father, and of the Son, and of the Holy Spirit." At this point, the sponsors may choose to give a cross to the catechumens and candidates. If this option is chosen, the sponsors could be wearing the cross during the ritual and then would remove them at this point and place them on the catechumens and candidates.

Presentation of a Bible (RCIA, n. 64, 525): Following the signing with the cross, the catechumens and candidates are given a book containing the gospels. The RCIA coordinator may be the one to present the book to them.

Some possibilities: Have the book opened to a text that has become important to the catechumen during this period of preliminary formation. Or hand the opened book to the catechumen with a prayer of blessing that incorporates what the catechumen mentioned earlier in the initial dialogue. For example, "Jane, earlier you said that you prayed that God would be your foundation and strength. Receive this word of God. May you find that as you pray this with our community, God will indeed be your foundation and strength."

Another possibility would be to hand the lectionary to each of the catechumens, since this will be the primary text for their formation in the catechumenate. This same lectionary would then be given to the RCIA coordinator at the dismissal.

Some people have raised the concern that the presentation of the Bible or the lectionary clutters up an already full ritual. The candidates have already begun to hear the word of God in the precatechumenate gatherings, and some candidates may have done so prior to coming to this community. Hence, the passing on of the text may be inappropriate. Perhaps during the retreat day or near the end of the precatechumenate period the inquirers can receive the word more formally within the catechumenate group. Then the ritual of acceptance and welcome can flow from the word received. Pastoral sensitivity and discernment will be needed by the team to determine how to effectively celebrate the ritual to best meet the needs of their particular community.

Prayer for the Catechumens and Candidates (RCIA, n. 65, 526): The community, using intercessory prayer, prays for the needs of the catechumens in this period of formation. The intercessory prayers can be adapted to specify the needs of these particular men and women, as well as the needs of this particular parish.

Prayer over the Catechumens and Candidates (RCIA, n. 66, 527): The presider brings the prayer together in a prayer of blessing for the catechumens and candidates. The community can be invited to extend hands in prayer over the catechumens with the presider.

Dismissal (RCIA, n. 67, 528): The catechumens and candidates are then dismissed from the assembly to continue to break open the word of God. The presider can call forth the catechist for this particular day, give the lectionary to the catechist, and then dismiss the catechumens. The rite does make provision for the catechumens and candidates remaining for the remainder of the eucharist, but it does so only when there are serious reasons why they cannot be dismissed (RCIA, n. 67c, 528C).

Welcome: Since the rite of acceptance and the rite of welcome are celebrations of initial affiliation and welcome, there should be some small reception following the community's eucharist. Perhaps the catechumens can be present at the rear of the church to greet and be greeted by members of the community.

CATECHESIS FOLLOWING THE RITE

Following the principle that liturgy is to be experienced and then reflected upon, the major movements and experiences of the rite become the "stuff" of the ensuing catechesis.

There will be many feelings present for the catechumens. Give them an opportunity to talk about the experience, as well as their hopes and desires. You may want to direct some of the reflection with questions such as:

— What was it like to be left outside the church?
— What did it feel like when the community came to greet you?

— Did you feel welcomed by the community throughout the service?

— How significant was your promise to follow the gospel way of life? (Reminder: this is the pivotal moment of the rite — the formal pronouncement of their intention and the reception and affirmation of that intention by the community.)

— What was it like to be signed by the cross, the way of life you committed yourself to?

— How did you feel about being dismissed from the community?

— Was there any longing to stay?

— Why do they stay?

PREPARATION REMINDERS

■ The community needs to be informed beforehand about the celebration. This can be done through pulpit and bulletin announcements.

■ The sponsors need to walk through the entire ritual with the RCIA coordinator and presider.

■ The sponsors will need to focus their gatherings with the candidates to raise the questions and issues reflected in the rite.

■ The hospitality people need to be informed of their responsibilities: greeting the assembly as they enter, facilitating the movement of the assembly to the place where the candidates are gathered, facilitating the movement back to the place of worship, and any reception that may follow the celebration.

■ The environment people will need to make sure that the sanctuary is appropriately decorated and that the space where the candidates are signed is uncluttered.

■ The final ritual text, with adaptations, etc., needs to be placed in a ritual book for the presider.

■ A speaker system needs to be set up for the initial dialogue with the candidates, especially if this is outside the church building.

■ If the candidates will receive a Bible, be sure enough are available. If you plan to have them receive the lectionary, be sure the lectionary is nearby.

■ If the candidates will receive a cross to wear, be sure they are available.

6

Period of the Catechumenate

INTRODUCTION

The period of the catechumenate is a prolonged period of formation in the Christian life. The RCIA notes that maturity in faith during the period of the catechumenate is achieved in four ways (RCIA, n. 75): through catechetical, spiritual, liturgical and apostolic formation. The primary catechetical text for the catechumenate is the lectionary, from which flows the basic issues of Catholic teaching. The catechumens are supported in their life of prayer and growth by their sponsors, the catechumenate team, and the whole of the Christian community. Throughout the catechumenate, the catechumens are both nourished and purified by appropriate liturgical celebrations, including the Sunday liturgy of the word with the community. And the catechumens begin to recognize the enfleshment of their growing faith through lives of apostolic service that flow from their experience of the gospel. The catechumens learn the Christian way of life from the Christian community and the community's participation in its own faith.

Ordinarily the catechumens will gather with their sponsors for the Sunday celebration of the liturgy of the word with the local community. After the homily, they will be "kindly dismissed" (RCIA, n. 75.3) to their catechetical session that is based on the lectionary texts. The sponsors, who represent the local community, serve as companions to the catechumens throughout this period of formation. The period of the catechumenate is of different duration for each catechumen. "The time spent in the catechumenate should be long enough — several years if necessary — for the conversion and faith of the catechumens to become strong" (RCIA, n. 76).

During the period of the catechumenate there are many liturgical celebrations. In addition to the liturgy of the word and dismissal catechesis already noted, the catechumens may participate in other rites: celebrations of the word, minor exorcisms, blessings, an anointing, and the presentation of the Creed and the Lord's Prayer (RCIA, nos. 81–105). All of these liturgical celebrations are meant to strengthen the catechumens in their conversion journey of faith, as well as to witness to God's love for them.

DISMISSAL CATECHESIS

Dismissal catechesis needs to be distinguished from lectionary-based catechesis. Usually the two are the same form of catechesis. Lectionary-based catechesis is catechesis that flows and builds upon the Sunday texts. This can be done with the catechumens whenever they gather. Dismissal refers to a particular model of gathering.

What is dismissal catechesis? Dismissal catechesis refers to the "sending forth" of the catechumens during the Sunday liturgy in order that they may further break open the word of God proclaimed in the assembly. The catechumens gather with the parish community to celebrate the liturgy of the word. As an act of hospitality, the community then sends them from the gathering to a place reserved for them to pray and struggle with God's challenge based on the lectionary text. This is an act of hospitality because the uninitiated are not yet welcomed to gather at the table of the eucharist.

During the period of catechesis, the catechumens reflect together, with the guidance and support of the catechumenate team and sponsors, on the lectionary. The issues of Catholic life and worship flow from the text and not vice versa. Dismissal catechesis (and any lectionary-based catechesis) has only one syllabus: the order and structure of the liturgical year (RCIA, n. 75.1). The primary text of the community, the scriptures, indicates the direction the catechesis will go. Issues emerge naturally rather than artificially through imposition. This at first may seem uncomfortable (will we cover everything?). But as we realize more fully that the aim and goal of the RCIA (and all catechesis) is to facilitate God's invitations of conversion and maturity of faith, we can become more comfortable with the formative character of the process. Doctrinal information is important and, usually, naturally flows from the lectionary. Additional resources could be made available. But the "textbook" is the scriptures, particularly as they are structured in the lectionary.

Dismissal catechesis also serves as a formative dimension for the parish community. As these men and women who seek to share fully the faith-life of this community are dismissed, people can't help but ask the question, "Why are they leaving?" Complementary to this question is another (often unarticulated): "Why am I staying? What is so important about our gathering at the table of the eucharist that, even though they can't participate, they don't stay?" Slowly the community begins to question its own fidelity to the mission and mandate of Jesus the Christ. Slowly (and surely) God's Spirit opens hearts in new ways to share community. The catechumens serve as witnesses of God's unfailing love and continual call to renewal.

And dismissal catechesis offers an invitation to the team: How centered are we, in our many, many programs, on the word of God as a formative dimension to our growth, and the growth of those we serve? Is our catechesis a formative one or are we passing on information? Does the word of God, a two-edged sword, become the challenging focus?

Many people are initially reluctant to dismiss the catechumens from the Sunday gathering. The reasons not to dismiss vary, but they don't compare to the on-going impact that dismissal can have on a parish community. The dismissal is a powerful symbol, demanding more of the parish community than of the catechumens.

CATECHETICAL FORMATION

Catechesis is an echoing of the gospel. It is a ministry of the word that proclaims the good word of God in Jesus. It is a full and robust proclamation that invites the full person to a response in faith, a response embodied in charity and justice. The full person is called and challenged in catechesis.

Catechesis during the period of the catechumenate is concerned with helping the catechumen name the experience of God within his or her own life, and respond to that experience of salvation. Additionally, the catechumen needs to come to know the story of the community named Catholic and how, throughout the centuries, we have come to name the experience of God in our midst. If the period of the precatechumenate was a time for storytelling, the period of the catechumenate develops that story into a dialogue. We don't abandon the storytelling and faith-sharing, but we expand it to include the particular story of our Catholic faith.

Earlier in chapter two, we discussed the tension between information and formation. Catechesis is not about passing information. It is about enlivening faith. How can we incorporate the great symbols of our community — including the rich word symbols of doctrine — to empower and enliven the faith of the catechumens? This exciting challenge is the challenge of catechesis: making the word of God — in

scripture and as articulated in the faith of the community — credible
and meaningful. This is not a watering down of the word of God, but
rather a raising up of that word so that it has a bearing on ordinary life.

There are various catechetical models that one can use during the
period of the catechumenate. Whatever model one adopts, the model
needs to respect and integrate the insights of adult learning. Basically,
that means that the individuals are respected as adults with valid questions and concerns. They are there not to get information but to raise up
their life questions for exploration and reflection. Therefore, the place
to begin is with their questions, their concerns, their experience. Also
adults have the ability to sift and find what is necessary and important
for them. There is no coercion or proselytizing with adults. Instead,
there is a genuine trust that what needs to be received will be received.
Since adult learning is a co-learning experience, the catechist will also
need to have a posture of hospitality to receive whatever gift is given to
the catechist from the adult in terms of insights and experiences. No
one comes to the catechetical gathering finished. Everyone comes as a
learner. The bottom line is respect and trust. Adults are also capable of
making their own choices and living with the consequences of these
choices. Catechesis helps inform the decision-making process; it does
not replace the fundamental freedom of a person to respond to life.
Therefore, we don't manipulate adults with our agenda. Rather, we
offer them the truth as we experience and know it and allow them to
receive it in the manner appropriate for them.

Another issue that needs to be addressed is the when of catechesis.
As mentioned earlier, dismissal catechesis lends itself to a full catechetical session. This would mean that the catechumens continue to
gather after the assembly has completed the celebration of the
eucharist. At that time, the sponsors and spouses can join the catechumens for the continuation of the catechesis. For such a gathering, one
would need to plan to meet for at least another 1½ hours after the community's dismissal. The hospitality people can arrange refreshments, as
well as babysitting.

Sometimes the extended catechesis cannot happen following the
dismissal. Don't dismiss the dismissal! Meet for the allotted time
(usually until the community's dismissal) and then regather later during the week.

In some parts of the country, parishes are working together on the
catechumenate. If this is the case, dismissal can happen at the individual parishes on Sunday with some reflection on the word, followed by
the joint session later in the week.

Catechesis also needs to be wholistic. There needs to be variety in presentation that energizes and challenges the catechumens' minds, hearts and wills. Sometimes there will be cause for guided reflections, other times for journaling. Sometimes a presentation will be necessary, and other times some discussion. Perhaps a short reading will get the point across, or else a case study. Music or video will sometimes help. What is important is the diversity of styles that both respects people's learning preferences and also challenges areas that need growth and development — variety not for the sake of variety, but to touch and gently till the rich soil of human life, with all its variety and complexity.

ONE MODEL FOR CATECHESIS

Following is one model that can be adapted for catechesis during the catechumenate. It attempts to be faithful to the insights of adult learning, to focusing on the Sunday lectionary, and to integrating this with the Catholic tradition. It is only *one* of many possible models. It is also important to note that the various movements in this model are rather artificial. Hopefully, the concerns of each movement are being addressed more wholistically, e.g. the issues of Catholic teaching do not have to wait until later in the gathering if they are more effectively responded to earlier on.

Prayer: Each gathering happens because of the presence of the Spirit. Begin with some quiet time, allowing the catechumens to surrender whatever concerns and preoccupations they may have in order to receive the word in their hearts in a new way. The prayer times during the period of the catechumenate are extremely formative. Therefore, provide exposure to a variety of prayer experiences, especially spontaneous intercessory prayer.

Initial Sense of Text: The catechumens are invited to share whatever reactions, feelings or insights they have from hearing the text proclaimed in the assembly, as well as anything they gleaned from the homily. The catechist will need to be alert in order to integrate these reflections into the material that follows.

Meaning for Life: The catechist could then raise basic life questions that the text addresses. The word, as mentioned earlier, is a meaningful word for life today. As part of the preparation for the session, the catechist will need to grapple with the word to discover how it is illuminating and challenging our life. This is then presented to the catechumens in terms of their everyday life (without using religious language). For example, the question may be raised, "Where do I put my time and energy?" A discussion and reflection period concerning what is important to me can then follow. What is important at this point is not to raise the explicitly religious questions ("Is God important to me?") but the ordinary life questions. It will be from these life experiences that the word will be able to dialogue.

Dialogue with Text: Now the catechist can invite the catechumens to listen to what the word of God has to say about these very same life questions. The text can be read again, preferably by one of the catechumens. Usually the gathering will focus on one issue or theme that flows from the gospel text. Homilists can testify to the difficult task it is to merge the three texts. Catechists need not perform similar tasks. In this situation, less is more. Helping the catechumens focus on one issue, one concern raised by the word is sufficient. This is also the time for some basic interpretation of the text for the catechumens.

Integration: Through reflection, dialogue, quiet time and other methods, the catechist invites the catechumens to be challenged by the word. How does the word make new demands in my life? How does the word question what is important to me? Let there be some dialogue between the catechumens' life questions and the proclaimed word.

Living the Tradition: The catechist then invites the catechumens to take another step. Already we have struggled with some basic life questions, and then have seen how the word of God both challenges and informs those life situations offering new hope and meaning for our life, sometimes at demanding costs for change and renewal. Now we turn to the Catholic tradition to see how we have articulated this same experience in our doctrine and belief system. The issues of Catholic teaching are now discussed and explored as they relate to the issues raised by the scripture text. The teaching flows from the proclamation rather than being imposed upon it.

Integration: Again there is the challenge to integrate the Catholic teaching in a way that informs and challenges the catechumens' lives. Reflection questions and discussion will be helpful here.

Mission: The fruit of catechesis is conversion embodied in lives of service and charity. Our time together is not only to hear and be challenged by the word, but to also allow the power of God to effect changes within us, to bring us to a new sense of ourselves. We participate in this in active ways by the quality of our lives. The catechumens, within this context of participation in God's call to conversion, are invited to consider some concrete steps or changes that need to happen in their lives because of today's word as experienced in their life, the scriptures and the tradition.

Closing Prayer: Allow the closing prayer time to include some way that the catechumens — either verbally, symbolically or in silence — can articulate their resolve and seek the grace and support from God and the community to be faithful in their resolve.

There are many possible adaptations and nuances to this basic model. For example, the catechist could provide a reflection question for the catechumens before the liturgy of the word to help focus. Some examples:

- Thirty-third Sunday in Ordinary Time (B): Mark 13:24–32.

  Recall a period when things seemed almost disastrous, out of control, heading for "the end." Who or what offered a glimmer of hope to you at that time (i.e. whom or what could you rely on in the midst of such conflict)?
- Second Sunday of Advent (B): Mark 1:1–8.

  During this past week, when did I have to "prove myself," assert my identity or competency by bragging?
- First Sunday in Lent (B): Mark 1:12–15.

  During this past week, when did I "busy myself with nothing" (e.g. television, radio, snacking — to fill in the void, to fill in time, to chase away the quiet)?

  It is also appropriate to expect the catechumens to prepare the Sunday texts prior to the community's worship. The catechist can provide some preliminary directions and information about praying the scriptures, if this has not been addressed already. Early on, the catechist will want to be careful to address the questions of literalism and fundamentalism and the role of personal interpretation of the scriptures.

  Some of the highlights of the model for integrating the scriptures and the Catholic tradition outlined above are:
- Attempt to make the experience of God concrete in everyday life. That is why the religious dimension of human experience is raised only after the catechumens have struggled with their ordinary human experience. In this way, they can discover the presence of God in the ordinary.
- The catechist must struggle with the scripture and life questions in order to bring a meaningful and credible word to the catechumens.
- The catechist will need to do some investigating of the Catholic issues raised from the text. The best of Catholic teaching is rooted in the community's experience of God as revealed in Jesus and proclaimed in the scriptures. Doctrine is the formulation of that

corporate experience over time. To some degree, the catechetical task immerses one in the on-going nature of the development of doctrine.

■ At various times, the catechumen will need to struggle with the message received and its impact on his or her life. This is not a passive receptivity, but a struggle to name the movements of conversion.

■ Catechesis is only catechesis when there is a movement to bring about the reign of God. This is made manifest in lives of charity and justice. So, too, this model helps the catechumen seek concrete expressions of God's call to conversion, as well as recognizing the need for God to bring about the change.

AN EXAMPLE: MARK 1:14–20

To help illustrate how this model can effectively be used, the gospel from the Third Sunday in Ordinary Time (Cycle B) will be explored. The preliminary movements (opening prayer, initial sense of text) and closing prayer will not be considered.

Meaning for Life: Reflection on "Where do you place your trust? Whom do you rely on?" After some reflection time, discussion about trust and why we place our trust in the people and institutions we chose as a response to those questions. Further reflection would include some basic qualities of someone we trust.

Dialogue with Text: After reading Mark's account of the call narrative, some discussion about call in the Old Testament could follow — namely, call and repentance are closely entwined, and when God calls, it is for some mission. Perhaps some exploration of basic call stories (including Jonah from the first reading) could be explored.

Shift the focus to discussing today's call narrative — to follow Jesus is a response to a call, which includes repentance as one dimension. Other qualities of the call include abandonment (being able to surrender to trust in Jesus) and mission (making us fishers of others).

How does this text challenge, inform, expand what we place our trust in, as reflected upon earlier?

Integration: What in my life keeps me from dropping my net, from saying yes to God? Where is my trust? How can I begin to place more trust in God? What do I need to say yes, to trust God more?

Living the Catholic Tradition: There are numerous Catholic issues that can be raised from this text: repentance, reign of God, discipleship, vocation. The catechist will need to be prepared to focus this section depending on the response to the first part. A logical development at this point would be in terms of vocation: Who am I called to be by God? How does the Catholic tradition understand the responsibility of being named by God? This could include discussion on the reign of God, justice, fidelity to basic values, repentance.

Integration: How does the reflection on the Catholic tradition inform my previous reflection? How do I say yes to God, place my trust in God within the Catholic context? Some basic elements of Catholic life, such as community and worship, can be highlighted as supports for this decision to say yes to God's call.

Mission: How do I enflesh this? How do I allow this to birth newness in me? How do I live out this new level of awareness and freedom? How do I bring the Catholic teaching into my life?

Throughout the catechumenate process, the issues of Catholic life and teaching will be raised numerous times from various perspectives. Since the goal of the catechumenate is to facilitate conversion, we will need to be careful not to "give them everything" we know about the issue. Rather, we gently feed them with this nourishing word. Throughout the catechumenate we will see growth and development — and not only in the catechumens — which will help the catechist focus on certain topics rather than others. This form of catechesis demands a certain trust, a surrender to God's work in the life of the catechumens. We facilitate God's work, we don't program it.

The temptation at this point would be to go to the lectionary and review the cycle of readings, indicating the issues of Catholic teaching that emerge from the texts. From this, one could draw up a listing or chart (a syllabus?) of Catholic teaching. While this could be helpful in establishing the validity of the argument addressed — the basics of Catholic teaching flow from the proclamation of the word in our worship — it also would be forcing issues that may not respect the needs of the catechumens. This is not to say that there is no sense of planning or direction. But it is to say that both the scripture and tradition are living documents that need to be encountered and interpreted appropriately.

Let us return to the text used above: Mark 1:14–20. The catechesis could have taken a totally different, and equally as valid, direction. The life-meaning section could have also focused on: abandonment, values, changes in life and the conditions that facilitate and restrict such changes, or the search for what is meaningful. The exploration of the texts themselves could have focused on: the reign of God, discipleship, community, the messianic promise, or the call to repentance and the response of faith. The issues of Catholic teaching that also could have been addressed are: the relationship between sin-reconciliation-forgiveness, the early foundations/history of the community, baptismal commitment, discernment, or God's will.

The discerning catechist will be able to listen to the needs and concerns of the catechumens while listening to the demands of the scriptures and our tradition, and then allow the two to dialogue. As in the experience of preaching, the catechist has many possible directions he or she can move with the texts. A resource that lists the issues of Catholic teaching, while helpful for initial planning, can become inhibiting and sterile. It would be a greater service to catechists to provide resources on how to enter into the interpretation of the scripture texts and allow Catholic teaching to emerge.

GUIDELINES FOR INTERPRETING SCRIPTURE

There are many good biblical commentaries that offer guidance and direction for the interpretation of scripture within the Catholic tradition. However, the catechist — as well as sponsors, godparents and other members of the team — will need to discover a process for using the commentaries that respects and integrates their own experience of the scriptures. Following are some guidelines for developing such a process that can be used for personal prayer, catechesis and preaching.

A. PREPARATION: COMING TO THE SCRIPTURES

The scriptures are more than religious texts. For the Christian, they are the revealed word of God. Hence, one approaches the scriptures, whether for study or meditation, in a spirit of prayer and anticipation. Prayerful presence to the scriptures becomes an important and necessary posture in order to allow them to speak to us personally and to our life situation.

It is important to recognize any attitudes one brings to the text: one's understanding of the scriptures in general (e.g. Do I take the scriptures "literally"?) as well as any previous encounters with the particular text. Sometimes we think we have exhausted the meaning of a text because we have heard it so many times. But every text has the power and possibility for new meaning. The first step toward such an encounter is our acknowledgement of any pre-understandings we have concerning the text. For example, in the familiar parable of the prodigal son, many people focus on the story of the son who runs away, returns home, and is forgiven by the generous and kind father. With that focus again and again, the message of forgiveness can become stale for some. Recognizing this may allow new insights to emerge, such as the significance of the elder brother and his claim on justice.

After situating oneself in reference to the text and bringing to awareness one's pre-understanding of the text, one can then become open to the text and ask the simple question: What is new? These guidelines for interpretation are similar to any encounter. If we presume the result already, the encounter is barren. But if we can stand in expectation before the painting, or the piano piece, or our friend, something new can come to us.

B. READ THE TEXT: HEARING THE WORD

Coming to an awareness of one's pre-understanding of a text presumes a preliminary reading of the text. One needs to return to the text and read it again, slowly, expectantly. The text has its own authority, its own life. It has something meaningful to say each time it is encountered. Allow yourself to be *present* to the text. There are a variety of ways of reading the text at this point. Read it out loud. Image the text. Converse with the text. Sing the text. The important aspect to keep alive is that the text is ever new.

C. THE MEANING OF THE TEXT:
ALLOWING THE TEXT TO SPEAK

After reading the text, it is appropriate to ask, "What does this mean to me? How does it make me feel? What images emerge for me? What do I think God is saying in this text? What impact does this have on my life?" Although the personal interpretation of the text may not completely reflect the sense of the text, such an interpretation is nonetheless valuable at this point. We must allow ourselves to be drawn into conversation with the text. It is important to write down those feelings, images, insights, prayers, and reflections that occur as we meet the text. It is also important to recognize that the meaningfulness of the text needs time and scholarship to allow it to emerge. Therefore, one does not stop at the private interpretation of the text.

The text has a history of interpretation already. Scholars have done extensive research and study with the text. Now is the time to become familiar with that material (and not before the personal dramatic reading of the text). These scholars, using the tools of critical literary research such as form criticism and redaction criticism, provide for us a context and background for the text. They help us identify the literary genre of the text (e.g. mythic literature is very different from biographical accounts), as well as discover the meaning of particular words and phrases within the culture and time of the writer. We can learn the particular audience the text was intended for (e.g. Palestinian Christians or Hellenistic Christians), its use in the community (e.g. hymn, letter, moral principle), its theological significance within the larger piece of writing (e.g. why Jesus journeys to Jerusalem when he does), and the historicity of the event (e.g. what really happened). All of this is valuable information for us. Luckily, there are many commentaries available to us that serve a wide range of audiences.

It is important to note, though, that the work of interpretation of a text can not rest solely on one's personal encounter with the text as described above, nor on the official commentaries. Rather, there must be a coming together of the two with the text. When a person has respected the text by taking it seriously, by recognizing the agenda he or she brings with him or her to the text, and by informing oneself of current scholarship, one can then allow the text to emerge with new meaning, with new possibilities, with new insights. There is a new coming together of the text with the individual. Both the person and the text have been changed: the person, by the values that emerge from the experience of the text that inform his or her life, and the text, by the individual's particular experience of interpretation. This process takes time. One cannot force the text. Rather, one allows oneself to mull over the text, befriend the text, take it to one's interior home.

D. APPLICATION OF TEXT:
LIVING THE TRUTH

One of the values of allowing oneself to encounter a text (whether that text be verbal, visual, literary, or personal) is that the individual is changed in some way and must assimilate this newness in concrete, categorical terms. We need to apply the meaning that has emerged to everyday life. The process of *exegesis* allows for the truth of the text to emerge and speak. This process is very different from the experience of someone attempting to impose a meaning on the text (proof-texting) to support the individual's claim — a case of manipulating the text to serve one's purpose rather than serving the truth of the text. Once the truth emerges from the text, there is the invitation to live out this truth. One needs to recognize the current needs and concerns of life, and prayerfully explore how this text speaks to these issues.

The guidelines previously mentioned serve as the preliminary process for preparing the text for the catechetical session or preaching. Those guidelines are for the homilist, catechist or facilitator; they help the minister encounter the text. It is only after the individual has wrestled with the text (and that takes time) that he or she then takes up the responsibility of preparing a particular application of the text. It would be appropriate at this time to determine the best way of presenting the text (e.g. mime, acting out, reading aloud). The audience and the issues important to that audience need to be considered. Those people who have been involved in catechetical ministry for a number of years know the essential value of being attuned to the times we live in. We also need to recognize the value of culture and its contribution to effectively communicate with those with whom we share the scriptures.

What becomes central in the pastoral presentation and application of the text is that it be meaningful for the particular audience. Hence, the experience of the minister in coming to meet the text provides the backdrop but not necessarily the lesson. By this I mean that one doesn't bring to the gathering all the research, insights, and reflections from his or her process of interpreting the text. Rather, with all of that as one's foundation, the catechist approaches the text for its message and meaning for the catechumens he or she is working with. The key here is not forcing a meaning from the text on the catechumens, but rather using good catechetical and group skills to effectively (and accurately) convey the text, presenting it in its best form, and allowing the catechumens to meet the text in their own encounter. The catechist serves as a guide, a curator, and a companion.

The scriptures offer the Christian community a powerful and unique experience of God. Through the power of the word proclaimed, we can come to encounter reconciliation and salvation from our God. However this revelation of God can be distorted, and at best hampered, by private interpretations, poor scholarship or the refusal to authentically encounter and interpret the scripture text. The heralds of this message of goodness bear an important responsibility in the community. Part of that responsibility includes taking the time necessary to grapple with that word for the community today, and then authentically proclaiming that message through preaching, catechesis, and sponsorship. It is this word proclaimed that will continue to shape and form us as the people of God.

SPIRITUAL FORMATION

Throughout the entire initiation process, we are helping the catechumens come to a deepened awareness of God's loving presence that brings life. This presence of God is clearly experienced in the midst of the community. Hence, the period of the catechumenate also concerns itself with the immersion of the catechumen into the very life of the community. As one enters more fully into the life and community of the parish, one begins to examine (and hopefully) embrace the moral values that inform a Catholic Christian way of life. All of this — community, moral values — becomes part of the process of spiritual formation. Spiritual is seen as more wholistic and not isolated to an interior disposition. Rather, it is about living life most fully within the community.

The bottom line of the spiritual formation dimensions of the catechumenate is the fostering and development of relationships that help the catechumens respond to the call of conversion. The response of faith that is demanded can only be nurtured and strengthened by a life of prayer.

Initiation into prayer happens best when people pray. The same is true for any love relationship. We can talk about friendship and the commitment of love, yet it is only in the actual living out of such friendship that one comes to a heightened appreciation and understanding of the concepts. We can talk about prayer and prayer forms during the catechumenate. But the catechumens will best understand and appreciate prayer through the experiences of prayer we offer to them.

Catechumens need to be invited to experience a wide variety of prayer forms: praying from scripture, using the imagination in prayer, *lectio divina* (holy reading) as a form of meditative prayer, the prayer of intercession, centering prayer, discursive prayer, prayer of praise, body prayer, and so on. These prayer experiences can be incorporated into the catechetical gatherings of the catechumens. Prayer between catechumens and sponsors needs also to be encouraged.

Private prayer needs to be nurtured and encouraged. Rather than merely presenting prayer formulas to memorize, a balance between spontaneous prayer and some of the traditional prayer forms can be highlighted. Emphasis needs to be made on the importance of regularity in private prayer: perhaps encouraging the catechumens to designate a particular time of day for a specified period of time for prayer.

The issues and concerns of growth in the spiritual life will emerge naturally throughout the catechumenate process. Often they are addressed at catechetical gatherings, time with one's sponsor, or during opportunities to meet with team members. Days of recollection and retreat are excellent opportunities for catechumens, sponsors and team members to spend quality time reflecting on their experience of God.

Sometimes a catechumen will want additional support and guidance in the spiritual life. With the assistance of the team, the catechumen may discern the need for a spiritual companion or spiritual director. This may not be the case for everyone, and often the intense formation process of the catechumenate is sufficient support and direction for many catechumens. Opportunities for spiritual direction need to be made available for those who desire additional support and direction. Later in chapter thirteen, we will explore the art of spiritual direction in Christian life, and, specifically, in the RCIA.

LITURGICAL FORMATION

The rite also provides ample opportunities for the catechumens to enter into the public prayer and worship of the community. This liturgical formation is intimately connected with the catechetical, spiritual and apostolic formation dimensions of the RCIA. They flow from each other.

The liturgical rites celebrated during the period of the catechumate are often called intensifying rites. Their purpose is to highlight and focus the experience of God in the community through catechesis, service, and prayer. The intensifying rites of the catechumenate include celebrations of the word of God, blessings, anointings, minor exorcisms, and the presentations of the Creed and the Lord's Prayer.

Celebrations of the Word of God (RCIA, n. 81): The catechumens are to gather regularly with the parish community to hear the word of God. Usually, this happens prior to dismissal catechesis.

Blessings (RCIA, n. 95): To bless is to acknowledge God's presence. It is the recognition that in this person, this meal, this community we come to know God. Blessing is a form of recognition and thanksgiving.

The rite offers nine different blessings that a designated catechist can pray with the catechumens. These blessings can be ample and frequent, heightening the awareness of the catechumens of the graciousness and abundance of God's loving presence.

Anointings (RCIA, n. 98): To anoint is to pray for the strengthening and healing of the other. Anointings are prayers of support and encouragement. As with the blessings, there can be numerous opportunities for anointings during the catechumenate: period of great stress, time of personal illness or loss, or a time of encouragement.

Minor Exorcisms (RCIA, n. 44): An exorcism is a prayer that acknowledges the darkness or void of sin, calling upon the very presence of God to breathe life where there is only death. Once properly explained, minor exorcisms can be especially effective following a catechetical gathering during which time a great deal of pain and anguish was uncovered. Unlike the blessings and anointings, however, too frequent a use of minor exorcisms can have a negative effect on the catechumens. Frequent use may give the imbalanced impression that life is rooted in evil. The rite provides eleven different exorcism prayers.

Presentations (RCIA, n. 104): The presentation of the Creed (RCIA, n. 157–162) and the Lord's Prayer (RCIA, n. 178–183) are celebrations designated during the period of purification and enlightenment. However, they may be anticipated during the period of the catechumenate, especially because the period of purification is already filled with the preparation, celebration and reflection on the scrutinies.

The presentations are the gifts of the community to the catechumens. The timing of the presentations will need to be the result of discerning the catechumen's readiness to welcome and receive these gifts of faith from the community. It seems reasonable to celebrate these presentations closer to the celebration of election. Usually, the presentation of the Creed and the Lord's Prayer is celebrated only with the elect. However, they can be celebrated with the candidates for full communion who have had limited prior catechesis. In this regard, the presentations would serve as expressions of the faith celebrated at baptism, and now serve (as they do with the catechumens) as catechetical resources for deepening in faith and understanding.

The presentations are not written documents given to the catechumens. The manner and style of presentation needs to highlight that these are foundational proclamations of the community's experience of God, and that the community willingly shares these treasures with the catechumens. At the very least, the presentations need to include the verbal proclamation of the community of either the Creed or the Lord's Prayer.

The presentations as gifts of the community require their celebration with the community. If the parish celebrates gatherings for prayer other than the eucharist, such as communal morning praise or evensong, then these could be good times to incorporate the presentations.

While they can be celebrated with the catechumens and sponsors and the RCIA team, the presence of the community is a stronger symbol.

There can be a variety of modes of presentation: liturgical dance and gesture, song, incorporating the use of slides or video, or movement to different centers in the church. The needs of the local community need to be an important factor in constructing the celebration.

APOSTOLIC FORMATION

The great mystics of our tradition have always reminded us that the fruit of the experience of God, especially that nurtured in prayer, are lives molded in charity and justice. There can be no authentic expression of faith that is not rooted in justice and charity for all men and women. To suggest otherwise is something private, but not the Christian gospel.

Apostolic formation — living lives of discipleship — is not something that can be dictated. Throughout the catechumenate experience, the demands of fidelity to the gospel and authentic human living are raised again and again liturgically, catechetically, and spiritually. At some point, the catechumen stops and recognizes that the gift of God's love is most fully actualized when it is surrendered and expressed in lives of charity and justice. That awareness, however, cannot be given to someone. It emerges from the process of conversion.

Hence, it would be inappropriate to assign service projects to the catechumens. The most prudent and caring thing to do is simply to wait. Throughout the catechumenate process the issues of justice and peace, and living lives of discipleship, are raised, examined and prayed about. Then we wait. At the right time, the catechumen will be grasped by that awareness and will come to the team seeking help in discerning an appropriate work of service and justice. The decision rises from the conversion experience; it is more authentic.

Often the movement toward apostolic service comes later in the catechumenate process. That's fine. Often people need to enter into a safe environment of care and trust before they recognize that in order to fully embrace love, they must be servants. When the catechumen begins to embrace the life of disciple who is servant, then the initial discernment for election has begun.

7

Second Step:
The Rite of Election
or Enrollment of Names

INTRODUCTION

The catechumens have gathered with the bishop at the cathedral with the other catechumens in the diocese. After reflecting on the word of God, the bishop has called the catechumens forward to declare their intention. Based on the witness of sponsors, godparents and members of the community, the bishop invites the catechumens to sign the book of the elect. He then proclaims: "I now declare you to be members of the elect, to be initiated into the sacred mysteries at the next Easter Vigil" (RCIA, n. 133).

The rite of election brings to an end the period of the catechumenate and inaugurates the period of purification. The act of election by the bishop — the proclamation of admission for reception of sacraments — is a significant turning point in the catechumenate process. It celebrates the transition in the life of the catechumen from one who is seeking to one who is ready to stand firm in a commitment (while remaining a seeker). The election is the announcement that the community has discerned the catechumen is indeed ready to celebrate the Easter sacraments. This transitional rite is usually celebrated on the First Sunday of Lent.

The appropriate place for the rite of election is at the cathedral church, celebrated by the bishop. Some dioceses celebrate the rite of election in regional gatherings throughout the diocese, especially in those dioceses that cover a large geographical region. The 1988 ritual edition for use in the United States also provides, in addition to a combined rite for the unbaptized and the baptized seeking full communion, a parish rite to send catechumens for election by the bishop.

This ritual action is not a graduation. Nor is it merely a gesture. The election by the bishop acknowledges, among other things, the ecclesial and incarnational dimensions of sacramental life and commitment. We do not choose sacraments. Rather, we are chosen by God to experiences of God's love embodied in sacraments. Sacraments cannot be merited or earned. At the same time, they are not private affairs. Sacraments are one expression of the mystery of God present in human experience. They are ecclesial, rooted in the community called church that helps mediate the experience of God, and incarnational, rooted in the awareness of God present and inviting us into fuller life.

Our contemporary experience leads us to a different sense of election. For us, election is the democratic process of appointing someone to an office or position. It is the setting aside of someone who is deserving of an office. We are also familiar with the notion of "the elect" in some Christian strains of thought that suggests a certain group of people set apart and, as it were, appointed by God for salvation, thus excluding others from God's salvation (however holy one is, if the person is not part of the elect, that person is not saved). The notion of election in the RCIA is very different from these. Sacramental election is focused on what God has done and is doing in these people's lives. It is the public pronouncement that the individual is ready to enter the covenant relationship established through participation in the sacramental life.

DISCERNMENT FOR ELECTION AND RECOGNITION FOR FULL COMMUNION

The catechumens have undergone an intense period of formation throughout the period of the catechumenate. Stirred by the word of God and the life of the Catholic community, they have experienced the call to a new way of life again and again. At some point in the process, the catechumens, along with their sponsors and the team, discern their readiness to live faithfully the commitment of the sacraments they will celebrate with the Catholic community.

The discernment for election for catechumens and for recognition for candidates takes place slowly during the weeks prior to the Lenten season. The rite suggests the criteria to judge and discern the readiness for the Easter sacraments (RCIA, n. 120):

■ *Conversion in mind and in action:* Has the catechumen come to know God in this community? Has he or she been open to receive the word of God? Has he or she responded to the word both in prayer and in a life of service? Does he or she struggle with the demands of the word?

- *Sufficient acquaintance with Christian teaching:* Does he or she welcome the insights of the Catholic community in its teaching about how to follow the gospel? Has he or she been exposed to the best in Catholic thought on the fundamentals of the Christian life?
- *Spirit of faith and charity:* Does he or she seek God in prayer, with confidence and trust? Is there growth in the individual's capacity to give and receive love? Is there a personal relationship with God?
- *Acknowledged intention to receive the sacraments:* Has the catechumen found this community to be a place of welcome and support? Does he or she desire to contribute to the growth and development of this particular community? Does he or she desire to receive the gift of freedom and salvation (and all its demands) from God in Christ through the Spirit. Or, if baptized already, does he or she desire to deepen the freedom God generously gives in Christ through the Spirit? Does he or she recognize himself or herself as a child of God?

The discernment for election and recognition is not a discernment for canonization and final perfection. Nor is this the "final exam," the test of religious knowledge. Rather, our posture needs to be of welcome, of waiting, of listening to the catechumen's willingness to embrace fully, with all his or her limits and gifts, the way of life of the gospel within the Catholic communion. We are inviting the catechumen to recognize God's stirrings and the response of faith. For some people, the time is not right. There is more growth, more challenge, more of a response that is needed before the commitment of the sacraments can be made. One needs honesty and courage to make any decision at this point. There is no right decision, just good decisions. The catechumen, sponsor, team and pastoral staff will suffer with (i.e. be compassionate toward) God's promptings.

The decision for election ultimately rests in the hands of the community, as represented by the pastor, to make their recommendation to the bishop. If the catechumenate process has been honest and willing to respect individual conversion, then the catechumen will most probably be able to respect whatever decision is made. Recommendation to celebrate sacraments (and the commitment that entails) or to continue in preparation demands a trust forged by respect and concern for the catechumens.

GODPARENTS

Godparents are companions for the Christian life for the catechumen. Unlike sponsors whose role it is to better acquaint the catechumen with the community and offer initial support and care, the godparents serve the catechumens by helping them integrate into the Catholic community by offering on-going support, care, and the sharing of faith.

Godparents assume their role in the RCIA at the rite of election when the catechumen is formally recognized as ready for the Easter sacraments (RCIA, n. 123). Candidates for full communion do not choose godparents.

The godparents are chosen by the catechumen. Usually they are friends or close acquaintances who honestly struggle to live the values of the gospel in the ordinary of their daily lives. If there is one godparent, then he or she must be a fully initiated member of the Catholic Church. The godparent cannot be a parent; spouses are discouraged. A godparent from another Christian community may witness for the catechumen, but there still needs to be at least one Catholic godparent.

Some formation and support needs to be given to godparents prior to the rite of election, as well as during the period of enlightenment and purification. Many godparents will be unaware of the RCIA process and the expectations of them in the life of the catechumen. Providing the necessary support will help alleviate any confusion for them.

DAY OF PRAYER

At some point prior to the celebration of the rite of election, it would be beneficial for the catechumens to gather to prayerfully reflect on the significance of this transition. They have already struggled to come to a decision with their sponsors and the team regarding election. That had been done within the context of prayer. Now it is time to spend some initial reflection on the meaning of this call to the sacraments.

The format for this day of prayer can be very simple. It should be an opportunity for the catechumens and their godparents and sponsors to spend time together in prayer and reflection. Following are suggestions of basic components that can be part of this period of reflection.

■ *Private and Communal Prayer:* The time together needs to be balanced between private, quiet time for personal prayer and reflection, and communal prayer experiences.

■ *Proclamation of Scriptures:* The period of reflection could be focused around the scripture texts that will be proclaimed at the rite of election and rite of recognition.

■ *Initial Reflection Period:* The first part of the day could be time alone, reflecting in various ways on the components that went into the discernment for election: conversion of mind and action, familiarity with Christian teaching, spirit of faith and charity, and the desire to celebrate the sacraments. This could be done through a guided imagery prayer experience on the call to discipleship, followed by a guided reflection on conversion during which the invitation can be given to reflect back to life prior to entering the RCIA and life now: How has it changed? How am I different? How would I describe myself then and now? The tensions of the various dimensions of conversion discussed earlier (moral, intellectual, affective, etc.) could be raised for further reflection.

The elect and candidates could also be given a reflection sheet for their use during the day. Following are some possible issues that could be raised.

— Spend some time in quiet and silence, asking God to help you be present to God's Spirit.
— Think back to when you first came to the catechumenate. Try to describe how you felt about yourself, about God, about others. What words or symbols describe this time in your life?
— What were the turning points for you in the process? Who were the significant people along the way?
— Reflect about yourself now — your sense of self, your sense of God, your relationships with others, your relationship with the church. What insights or images do you have to describe this period in your life?
— How are you different now? How have you changed? What is the cause of this change in your life?
— What has God done in your life?
— What do you need from God in order to grow more, to discover more the richness of your person and of this community?

If the elect have kept personal journals during the catechumenate process, they can be encouraged to bring them along for review, reflection and prayer.

■ *Reflection on Election:* Later in the day, the catechumens could pair off with their godparents and sponsors and discuss why they want to receive the Easter sacraments. The questions for discernment outlined in the previous section might be helpful for discussion. This reflection period, as well as the numerous other times together, will help the godparents and sponsor to offer honest and authentic testimony at the rite of election.

■ *Preparation for the Rite:* Before ending the time together, you may want to briefly discuss the significance of the rite of election, i.e. it is a transition rite that brings them to a new period of preparation. You will not want to discuss the particularities of the rite beforehand. However, you will need to remind them of any plans for travel to the cathedral.

■ *Gathering with Sponsors and Godparents:* After the catechumens have left, the sponsors and godparents will need to discuss the rite. This could be done within the context of discussing the day of reflection.

— How was your experience today with your catechumen?

— Did you learn anything new today about him/her?

— Did you learn anything new about yourself?

— Discuss the focus of the witness given at election with the sponsors.

— Review the rite, perhaps using a guide sheet for their reference.

— Together go to the worship space and "walk through" the rite of sending.

THE RITE OF SENDING

Because election does belong to the bishop, the parish may celebrate a rite of sending (RCIA, n. 106–117, 530–546) to the election at the cathedral. The structure of the rite of sending will depend on how the rite of election is celebrated at the cathedral.

Day of Celebration: Since the rite of election is normally celebrated on the First Sunday of Lent, the rite of sending will need to be celebrated at a time prior to the cathedral celebration. A recommended time would be the day of election, at an earlier Mass in the parish community. Following the rite, the catechumens could then leave to travel to the cathedral. Circumstances of time and travel will, however, dictate to some degree the appropriate time of the rite of sending. The Sunday before the rite of election seems to be the earliest time it could be celebrated.

It has been suggested that there be two separate celebrations of sending, one for the candidates for full communion and one for the catechumens. This would continue to highlight the distinction between the two groups. This would also serve as an affirmation of the baptismal commitment already made by the candidates, as well as serve as a challenge to the baptismal commitment of the parish community. If the parish opts for two separate celebrations, the rite of sending for the candidates could occur on Ash Wednesday, the rite of sending for the catechumens on the First Sunday of Lent, and then all of them go to the cathedral rite of election and rite of recognition.

The model below will provide for one integrated celebration. The same concerns, however, can be adapted for celebrating separate rites of sending.

Time of Celebration (RCIA, n. 109, 536): The rite of sending follows the homily at the community's worship (or at a liturgy of the word celebration).

Presentation of Catechumens (RCIA, n. 111, 537): The RCIA coordinator speaks to the community concerning the readiness of the catechumens to celebrate the Easter sacraments. Having been part of the discernment process, the coordinator may choose to highlight some of the dimensions of conversion experienced by the catechumens while maintaining confidentiality.

The catechumens can then be called before the community (preferably one by one), accompanied by their godparent (and, if desired, their sponsor).

Affirmation by the Godparents and Assembly (RCIA, n. 112, 538): The presider now requests some testimony from those responsible for the formation of the catechumens. The presider may also witness at this time if the presider had been part of the discernment process.

The godparents (and sponsors) are the first to be invited to give witness regarding the readiness of the catechumens. They can complete their witness by recommending to the community that the catechumens be welcomed to the Easter sacraments.

Catechists are also encouraged to offer witness and testimony. Hopefully, the catechumens have had a rich experience of the community. Therefore, the presider may invite anyone from the community to come forward to give testimony.

Examination of Catechumens: There is no public pronouncement by the catechumens in the rite. Their presence is itself a statement of their intention. However, the presider may want to address the catechumens, asking them to make public their intentions regarding the celebration of the sacraments of initiation. Each of the catechumens could be given the opportunity to respond in his or her own way.

Recommendation and Enrollment: If the book of the elect is to be signed at the cathedral liturgy, then the presider affirms the recommendation to election by the community. However, because of the large numbers of catechumens, the signing of the book of the elect is happening more and more at the parish celebration. This would then be the appropriate time to invite the catechumens to sign the book of the elect. The godparent witnesses the signing of the book and may be asked to sign the book with the catechumen (RCIA, n. 113, 539).

The process of affirmation, optional examination, and enrollment may be done individually for each catechumen. While the catechumen signs the book of the elect, an antiphon can be sung by the community. The second possibility is that the affirmations are given for all the catechumens, followed by the optional examination of all the catechumens, followed by an individual signing of the book of the elect.

Presentation of the Candidates for Full Communion (RCIA, n. 540): The candidates for full communion are now recognized by the community. The RCIA coordinator commends the candidates to the community, as was done earlier with the catechumens. It is possible to present both catechumens and candidates at the same time at the beginning of this rite as long as the necessary distinctions are made. In order to maintain the distinction, the subsequent witness and affirmations need to be done separately.

Affirmation by Sponsor and Assembly (RCIA, n. 541): The sponsors are then invited by the presider to give witness as to the readiness of the candidates to enter into full communion with the Catholic Church. These affirmations can be followed by testimony from the presider, the catechists, and other members of the community.

Examination of Candidates: As with the catechumens, the candidates could be given the opportunity to express their readiness for the celebration of full communion.

Recommendation (RCIA, n. 542): In light of all the testimony, the presider then recommends the candidates to the cathedral where the bishop will formally receive them into the final period of preparation for full communion. There is no signing of the book of the elect, since this is a symbol acknowledging admittance into the community through baptism. Although the community may wish to symbolize this recommendation for the candidates in another way, the simplicity of the rite may itself be sufficient.

Acknowledgement by the Community: It would be appropriate for the presider to ask the community to affirm the decisions that were ritualized today. The community may applaud or respond with an appropriate song of praise and thanksgiving.

Intercessions for the Catechumens and Candidates (RCIA, n. 543): The community prays for the catechumens and candidates. The liturgical ministry, especially the ministers of music, may want to adapt the text provided to meet the needs and circumstances of the catechumens and candidates. This will include some previous awareness of their journey, which can be discovered either through participation with the catechumens and candidates or through dialogue with the RCIA team.

Prayer over the Catechumens and Candidates (RCIA, n. 544): The presider gathers all these prayers together in a prayer over the catechumens and candidates, adapting it to include the specifics of the group.

Dismissal (RCIA, n. 545): The catechumens and candidates are now dismissed from the assembly to journey to the cathedral for the rite of election. It would be an appropriate sign for the presider to present the RCIA coordinator with the signed book of the elect to be presented to the bishop at the cathedral.

THE RITE OF ELECTION FOR CATECHUMENS AND THE CALL TO CONTINUING CONVERSION OF CANDIDATES WHO SEEK TO COMPLETE THEIR CHRISTIAN INITIATION

The rite of election and the call to continuing conversion is celebrated by the bishop at the cathedral church or in regional gatherings. As mentioned earlier, the numbers of catechumens often dictates that the spontaneous witnessing by godparents and the community and the signing of the book of the elect take place at the parish celebration held prior to the cathedral liturgy. Because of the nature of this celebration, it would be more appropriate that the rite of election be celebrated during a liturgy of the word service rather than during a eucharistic liturgy.

Presentation of the Catechumens (RCIA, n. 130, 551): After the homily, the catechumens are presented to the bishop for election. If there are large numbers of catechumens from many parishes, one person may speak on behalf of all gathered. The catechumens may then be called forward (or asked to stand at their place) by parish rather than individually (a program booklet for the celebration could include the individual names of the catechumens), presuming this has been done already at the parish celebration.

Affirmation by Godparents (RCIA, n. 131, 552): It would be wonderful if the godparents could give spontaneous testimony concerning the catechumens. This could be followed by testimony from people from around the diocese. However, because of the large numbers, it probably would be more appropriate for the bishop to seek the godparents' affirmations by their general consent to a series of questions concerning the catechumens' readiness.

Invitation and Enrollment of Names (RCIA, n. 132, 553): The bishop then addresses the catechumens, asking them to publicly declare their intention. This is followed either by the signing of the book of the elect or the presentation of the signed book of the elect by the RCIA coordinator.

Election (RCIA, n. 133, 554): The bishop then reflects on the significance of the enrollment. Following this, he pronounces the words of election. He continues with words of encouragement to both the catechumens and their godparents (godparents may wish to place their hands on their catechumen's shoulder or somehow exhibit support through touch).

Presentation of the Candidates for Confirmation and Eucharist (RCIA, n. 555): As with the presentation of the catechumens, the candidates are presented to the bishop. This could be done at the same time, keeping the distinctions clear between catechumens and candidates.

Affirmation by Sponsors (RCIA, n. 556): The sponsors are invited to give testimony, as well as the entire assembly.

Act of Recognition (RCIA, n. 557): The bishop then formally recognizes the call to the sacraments of eucharist and confirmation of the candidates. He also instructs the sponsors with words of support.

The ritual could be adapted to celebrate the presentations and affirmations at the same time — first the catechumens, followed by the candidates. Then the bishop could call forward the catechumens for the act of admission or election, followed by the call to the candidates for the act of recognition.

Intercessions (RCIA, n. 558): The community then prays for the elect and the candidates.

Prayer over the Elect and Candidates (RCIA, n. 559): The intercessions are followed by a prayer of blessing by the bishops.

Dismissal (RCIA, n. 560): Following the blessing over the elect and candidates, the bishop then dismisses the entire assembly to celebrate the great Lenten retreat we are all called to observe.

The unbaptized are now named the elect. Those who are candidates for full communion continue to be called candidates. All of them, however, have been formally recognized as ready and willing to celebrate sacraments at the Easter vigil. Their preparation during these final weeks will shift in its focus.

Throughout this process, the parish community has been enriched and challenged by these men and women. The parish community, too, now enters into a new period of prayer and reflection: the Lenten retreat. The book of the elect, enthroned in the community's worship space, will be a good reminder for all of the call to a baptismal spirituality.

CATECHESIS FOLLOWING THE RITE

The experience of the elect and the candidates for full communion will be very different. Previously in the rite of acceptance and welcome, the basic movement of the rite was similar. Now the distinction between the two is made very clear. This becomes a good opportunity to discuss the dignity and respect of baptism in the Christian tradition (and hence why we make the distinctions ritually and catechetically).

The focus for catechesis needs to be the word of election and recognition by the bishop. This is the significant turning point in the entire process. After hearing the testimony of the community, the bishop proclaims the readiness for the celebration of the sacraments. Not only has the status of these people changed, but the focus and direction of catechesis will shift dramatically.

If the rite of sending was celebrated, the connection between the parish and the larger church will need to be made. Often the rite of sending is more powerful and personally effective for the elect than the cathedral rite because of the large numbers. However, we need to be careful not to underestimate the impact of the cathedral liturgy. The graciousness of the bishop will help bring together the experience of hospitality and welcome they have experienced in the community.

PREPARATION REMINDERS

- Make sure you know the date of the rite of election to be held at the cathedral, and then plan your rite of sending accordingly.
- The community needs to know what is going on. Some announcement in the parish bulletin can alert them to the rite of sending.
- Godparents need to be contacted early enough so they can plan to participate in the rite of election. Opportunities for formation and support of godparents need to be arranged.

- Sponsors need to be informed and consulted in the discernment for election and recognition.
- Godparents and sponsors need to know the basic direction the witnessing will take at the rite of election. In addition to reviewing the ritual, it would be helpful to give them guide questions from which they can formulate their reflections.
- Consultation with the liturgists and liturgical musicians needs to happen well in advance so they can adapt the ritual and provide acclamations that emerge from the experience of the catechumens.
- The final ritual text — with all its adaptations — needs to be housed in a binder or folder that clearly indicates this ritual is important.
- The book of the elect needs to be retrieved and ready for the rite. Scrapbooks and similar diary type books fail to represent the importance of this rite. You can purchase a leather-bound book of the elect through most liturgical supply stores.
- On the day of the rite, be sure the book of the elect and a few pens are in place.
- If at all possible, the group can travel to the cathedral liturgy together. Arrangements will need to be made for transportation to the cathedral.

8

Period of Purification and Enlightenment

INTRODUCTION

The period of purification and enlightenment is a time of intense spiritual preparation that occurs during Lent (RCIA, n. 138–139). The focus of this period in the RCIA is twofold: the proximate preparation of the elect for the Easter sacraments through prayer and penance, and the challenge to the local community to enter more deeply the cycle of the paschal event through the witness of the elect and their conversion journey. During this period there are certain rites that help bring about this purification and enlightenment: scrutinies, presentations of the Creed and Lord's Prayer, as well as the preparation rites for initiation.

Three scrutinies are celebrated on the Third, Fourth, and Fifth Sundays of Lent. The scrutinies are meant to help uncover and heal all that is sinful in the life of the elect, as well as raising up and strengthening all that is good in the life of the elect. The scrutinies are celebrations of healing and strengthening (RCIA, n. 141). Normally, the elect, along with the catechumenate team and their godparents, will have spent quality time beforehand reflecting on their areas of unfreedom, as well as their gifts. These reflections serve the liturgical ministers in incorporating the specific needs of the elect into the scrutiny celebrations.

The scrutinies are celebrated during the liturgy of the word, after the homily. Each year the texts and readings for the scrutinies come from cycle A of the lectionary because they help expose our growing need for God: the gospel of the Samaritan woman for the first scrutiny, the gospel of the man born blind for the second scrutiny, and the gospel of Lazarus in the third scrutiny. The assembly and the elect are called to silent prayer to reflect on their sin and need for God's freedom. This silent prayer is followed by intercessions that address the areas of sin and unfreedom addressed both in the scripture text and in the reflection of the elect. After this recognition of sin, the celebrant continues with the exorcism. As mentioned in the section on the period of the catechumenate, the exorcisms are prayers for freedom and strength for the elect, that God's Spirit may breathe life where there was once death due to sin. After the prayers of freedom (exorcism), the elect are then dismissed and the community continues with the liturgy of the eucharist.

The presentations of the Creed and the Lord's Prayer occur during the Third and Fifth Weeks of Lent, unless they have been anticipated during the period of the catechumenate (RCIA, n. 147). Often the presentations are anticipated because of the relatively short time of the period of enlightenment. Whenever the presentations are celebrated, it is essential that they be celebrated with the local community. The community now presents to the women and men chosen to celebrate the Easter sacraments the most treasured gifts of the community's faith and prayer: the Creed and the Lord's Prayer. The Creed is the foundational proclamation of the Christian faith, a summary of the truths experienced by the Christian community. The community passes on its faith to the elect, asking that they commit the Creed to memory, not only of the head, but of the heart. The elect will later publicly recite it at the preparation rites. The Lord's Prayer is the prayer of those who experience themselves as daughters and sons of God. The community expresses its deep desire to share that life with the elect through its gift of the Lord's Prayer. At the Easter sacraments, the elect will recite the Lord's Prayer with the community for the first time as full members of the Catholic Church.

The RCIA also gives various rites which can be celebrated as immediate preparation for sacramental initiation on Holy Saturday: recitation of the Creed, ephphetha rite, and the choosing of a baptismal name.

CATECHESIS DURING THE PERIOD OF ENLIGHTENMENT

The goal and focus of catechesis during the period of enlightenment is different than the period of the catechumenate. During the period of the catechumenate, the focus of catechesis was immersion into the fullness of the Christian community as expressed in the Catholic tradition — scripture, doctrine, worship, community and service. The period of enlightenment presumes such immersion and the readiness to make the commitment of baptism. Now the focus is akin to a retreat. The elect and candidates, firm in their resolve to embrace the gospel, experience a time set apart for deepened reflection on this gospel way of life, seeking the prayers of the community during these final days of preparation (RCIA, n. 139).

If there are both elect and catechumens, the period and process for catechesis will be different. Each group is to be dismissed from the assembly, but they should gather in separate places because the content of catechesis is different. Ideally, the catechumens (i.e. those who have discerned that it is not the right time to move to the commitment of the Easter sacraments) could be dismissed from one Mass while the elect are dismissed from another Mass.

This, then, is a time of prayer and reflection. This is not the time to cover materials that may have been forgotten during the catechumenate period. Rather, it is a time of focusing on God's gifting presence, and how that presence uncovers and reveals attitudes and lifestyles that are contrary to relationship with God — namely, sin — as well as raising up those attitudes and gifts that deepen the relationship with God.

The content of the catechesis for the first few weeks will be on the experience of election and the beginnings of this intense period of reflection, using the ritual text and the lectionary as the basis for reflection and prayer. The prayer becomes more focused when the elect celebrate the scrutinies. The experience of the scrutinies provides the material for the remaining catechesis.

The 1988 ritual edition provides a rite of reconciliation for the candidates for full communion rather than the scrutinies. However, the rite reminds us that the scrutinies are for the community as well as the elect. Hence, the value of the scrutiny experience can be as transformative for the candidates for full communion. It seems appropriate to include them in the celebrations as part of their own preparation for full communion. The direct result of these celebrations can then be the celebration of sacramental reconciliation for the candidates for full communion (as will be discussed in chapter eleven). Using the scrutinies to distinguish between the elect and the candidates for full communion seems to be an unnecessary distinction.

THE SCRUTINIES

As mentioned earlier, the scrutinies are celebrated on the Third, Fourth and Fifth Sundays of Lent. The scrutinies take seriously the profound love of God and the desire of God to bring all people to full freedom and salvation. As one deepens in one's awareness of the graciousness of the gift of God's love, one also becomes more sensitive to the barriers that keep this love from transforming and recreating life: the barriers of sin and evil.

The scrutinies raise up and expose whatever keeps the transforming love of God from liberating all forms of oppression. Some of those barriers are freely chosen, the result of personal sin. Others are the result of systemic evil: racism, sexism, ageism, and other forms of discrimination and oppression. Whatever the cause, none of them are rooted in the reconciling and healing love of God. The scrutinies unmask the deception of evil and sin for what they really are: robbers of true and authentic life.

The scrutinies also raise up those dimensions of life that welcome the loving presence of God, thus encouraging full life. These virtues and gifts of God stand as witness to a new way of living in the midst of the destructive dimensions of sin and evil.

Thus, the focus of the scrutinies are toward life, toward freedom, toward salvation. They take very seriously the transforming love of God. And precisely because they do take this love so seriously, the scrutinies also take seriously the reality of sin and evil. But sin and evil is neither the first word of creation nor the final word of destiny. The scrutinies are one expression of the first and final words of transforming and saving love.

PREPARING FOR THE SCRUTINIES

The best preparation for the celebration of the scrutinies is to help the elect identify and name their areas of strength and weakness in relationship to life with God in order that the community may pray with them. The rite clearly indicates that the prayers of intercession during the scrutiny may include the particular needs and concerns of the community (RCIA, n. 153). Thus, the community will pray for the elect rather than some general notions about the elect.

There can be many ways to prepare the elect for the scrutinies. Preparation does not mean rehearsal or even instruction about the experience of the scrutinies. Allow the scrutinies themselves to be formative, providing a period of reflection and integration after the celebration. Already the period of purification has been focusing on the need for honesty in naming one's relationship with God and others. It would naturally flow from this that the elect be led through a reflection process of specifying those areas of their life that need to be raised up for support or healing.

One way of doing this could be to provide a retreat experience with the elect during which time the issues of their life could be raised and addressed. Another possibility would be to provide a prelude reflection experience for each scrutiny. This would provide the elect with the opportunity to discern their need from different perspectives, i.e. the symbols of the scrutinies: living waters, light for the world, new life.

Following are reflection pieces to help prepare the elect for the celebration of each of the scrutinies. Like the other models presented in this resource, they are meant to serve exclusively as examples of how you can create your own preparation process. The needs of the elect will be very different depending on personalities and circumstances. Hence, adopting these reflections will not be of service because they do not take into account your elect. Instead, allow them to help you to design reflection pieces for your elect.

PREPARING FOR SCRUTINY I: LIVING WATER

- Water is a powerful and life-giving resource in our life. Reflect on experiences in your life when water was very important. Write out some images of your experience of water.
- Often when we think of water, we think of thirst. What does it mean for you to thirst?
- We thirst for something in life. What is it that you thirst for?
- Read the gospel text for Sunday: John 4:5–42, the woman at the well. What are some of the images and feelings that stir within you as you hear this text?
- How are the gifts in your life helping you to fulfill your basic thirst — perhaps not totally, but at least you are beginning to drink from life. Name those gifts that you pray can be strengthened.
- What keeps you from quenching your thirst? What holds you back? Often what holds us back — our sin, our demons, — can be discovered in our personal life (such as my refusal to really trust God and other people) and in how we experience life (such as the pain experiences due to sexism or racism). Name your sin, your demons, those things both within you and in society that keep you from a full life.

PREPARING FOR SCRUTINY II: LIGHT OF THE WORLD

■ Recovery comes with a cost. Recovery makes us responsible. Recovery demands that we witness to a new way of life. What are some of the "risks" of recovery?

■ Recovery can be the restoration of vision. Perhaps we have distorted vision. Perhaps we can't really see, and, thus, this blurred vision keeps us irresponsible. What are some examples of blurred vision in our culture (i.e. not seeing things honestly, authentically, with wholeness)?

■ Reflect on your own life. Where do you now experience darkness? What obstacles block the light? What do you need to be "in the light"?

■ Guided prayer experience based on Sunday's gospel text: John 9: 1–41, the man born blind.

— Recognize that this is a time of prayer. Be mindful that you are in the continuing presence of God.

— Take a few moments to relax, to quiet down. Breathe deeply and allow your worries and concerns to roll away, acknowledging that you will address them later.

— Focus on a word or phrase that recollects you, such as Jesus or holy. Repeat the word, slowly, again and again, allowing it to help focus and center you.

— Imagine yourself sitting along the roadside. You are tired, cold, feeling worn out. The road is a dirt road; you know this because you inhale the dust as people pass by. You are blind. Because you are blind, people think you're a sinner, and therefore reject you, cast you aside. Other people take advantage of you, or push you around, or rob you. You are blind, you are poor, you are an outsider. And as the day begins to end — you feel the early evening chill as the sun sets — you begin to worry again: Where will I go? Will I be safe?

— Suddenly you sense a large crowd gathering nearby. You hear the noises of people rushing, the voices, the excitement. What can this be? All you know is that people keep pushing you around.

— Without any notice, two people pick you up and rush you through the crowd. You struggle, you resist. You are frightened. Who are these people? What do they want with me? Will they hurt me? Fear grips you, holds you. Then, suddenly, there is silence. You feel the crowd move away from you. The two people are still holding you up, and then you hear them say: "Teacher, who sinned — this blind one or the blind one's parents?" Shock. Surprise. Resentment. Embarrassment. All these feelings begin to run rampant within you. You have been brought in front of everyone — a sinner. And now you feel ashamed, you want to run. The teacher responds but you really don't hear him. You simply want to run away.

— The hands holding you drop. You sense someone standing before you. The person touches you, holds you up. But this time it is different. You know the hands that push you, that hurt you, that rob you. These hands are strong but gentle. These hands tell you that you can relax, you can trust.

— You hear the voice of the stranger, filled with care and concern, "Who are you? What is your name?" You respond. The teacher then says to you, "My name is Jesus."

— Jesus. You have heard about the great teacher and prophet. You have heard stories about how he has helped people, loved people. But what could Jesus want with you?

— Jesus continues. "What is your blindness? Where is there darkness in your life?"

— "What keeps you blind, in the darkness?"

— "Do you want to see? What do you need in order to really see?"

— Jesus begins to pray for you. Listen to what he says for you.

— Then you feel something warm and soft on your eyelids. Jesus is massaging mud on your eyes. As he does this, he continues to pray for you.

— Then Jesus says to you, "If you desire to see, go to the waters of Siloam, to the waters of those who are sent, and wash yourself."

— To be able to see. Life can be different. But do you want life to be different, do you want to change? Sight will change you, free you, make you more responsible. You need to decide if you will go to the waters or back to the roadside.

— Once you decide, you go and do what you must do. Whatever you choose, you are aware that Jesus walks with you. Whatever the choice, he will not abandon you.

— At your own time and pace, return to this place and time.

■ Reflect on the prayer experience. Write for yourself any thoughts, images, feelings that capture and express the experience.

■ How have you been moving "into the light"? What gifts do you have from God that strengthen you to overcome the dark areas of your life?

- What keeps you blind? What is your blindness? From what do you need the saving and healing love of God?

- Disappointments. Rejections. Broken dreams. Life isn't always what it can be, should be. Reflect on your own experiences of brokenness and loss. What images or words describe these experiences?
- These experiences are experiences of death. Left as they are, they rob us of full life. What are some of the deaths that happen to us, personally and as a community?
- How have I experienced life from death? How has this affected me?
- Read and reflect on Sunday's gospel: John 11:1–45, the raising of Lazarus.
- What is it all about, this thing called life? How do I know life? What is meaningful to me?
- How has the experience of coming to the Catholic Church been an experience of death? Of life?
- Give everyone strips of paper, suggesting the wrappings on Lazarus. What holds me in bondage? What are the wrappings made of that keep me in death? Write these on the strips of paper.
- What do I need from God? Write those on the wrappings.
- At a later time — preferably after the scrutiny — return to the strips of paper and destroy them, acknowledging the movement toward fullness of life.

PREPARING THE INTERCESSIONS FOR THE SCRUTINIES

Throughout the period of preparation for the celebration of the scrutinies, the elect have had the opportunity to reflect on the areas of their life that need to be strengthened so they can be faithful to their commitments, as well as the areas of sin and bondage that keep them from truly being free. The team, with the help of the parish liturgists and musicians, can then construct the prayer of intercessions based on these reflections.

If the preparation for the scrutinies happens prior to each scrutiny, the intercessions can be formed based on the discussion and reflection. If the preparation happens during an extended retreat experience for all the scrutinies, then the content of the experience will need to be used for all three scrutinies. The images of the scrutinies — living waters that quench our basic thirst, light for our blindness, and the gift of the fullness of life — suggest an intensification in the prayer of the community that can be reflected in the wording of the intercessions.

What might these intercessions look like? The rite provides us with a model text for each of the three scrutinies. The preparer will need to read the scripture text, the scrutiny text — with special note of the intercessions — and then listen carefully to the experience of the elect. Based on the need of the elect, and integrating the intercessions provided in the rite, the cantor can develop intercessions that reflect the experience and prayer of the elect and of the community. For example:

From the blindness of greed and possessiveness, we pray, Kyrie eleison. KYRIE ELEISON.

From the blindness of success at all costs, we pray, Christe eleison. CHRISTE ELEISON.

From the blindness caused by a distorted image of a God of wrath, we pray, Kyrie eleison. KYRIE ELEISON.

While preserving the spirit of the scrutiny intercessions, the intercessions need to reflect the particular needs of a particular group of elect at a particular time and place. Therefore, the intercessions could never be reused by another community, or even by another group of elect within the same community, because their needs and concerns will be very different each time.

The rite suggests approximately eight intercessions. The listing of intercessions, however, can be extended (perhaps twenty or twenty-five) so that a rhythm and movement in the intercession prayer can be maintained. The decision to extend the intercessions is based on the desire to heighten the experience for both the elect and the community. As the litany is proclaimed, people wrestle with their own sin and sense of gift. This needs time and prompting.

CELEBRATING THE SCRUTINIES

The basic structure for the scrutinies is the same for all three scrutinies. Therefore, we will explore that basic structure, raising some concerns for celebration.

Readings: It is suggested that the readings for the scrutinies come from the lectionary texts for the Third, Fourth and Fifth Sundays of Lent, Cycle A: the woman at the well, the man born blind, and the raising of Lazarus (RCIA, n. 146, 150, 164, 171). The argument that repeating these readings each year limits the exposure of the community to the full lectionary pales in comparison to the powerful effect the readings can have for both the elect and the community. If for some reason during cycles B and C the corresponding readings are used, the texts for the scrutinies will need to be rewritten to highlight the focus of those texts.

Homily: In addition to exploring the issues that emerge from the scriptures proclaimed, the homily serves as a preparation for the scrutiny that follows. Hence, the preacher will need to incorporate the value and purpose of the scrutiny in the preaching.

Call of elect and candidates (RCIA, n. 152, 166, 173): The elect and candidates, accompanied by godparents and sponsors are called forward so the community can pray for them.

Invitation to silent prayer: The presider first invites the community to pray in silence for the elect that they may have a true spirit of repentance. Then the elect are invited to pray. At this time, the elect may kneel or bow their heads.

Intercessions for the elect (RCIA, n. 153, 167, 174): After an appropriate period of silent prayer, the intercessions — based on the needs and concerns of the elect — are prayed. This is an extremely powerful moment in the ritual. Simply reading the intercessions may not necessarily create the mood that the rite is calling for at this time. It would be more effective if a cantor sang the intercessions in litany style. The response could be Kyrie eleison, Christe eleison, or Lord, have mercy. A slow, deliberate, ascending movement for the intercessions can, in itself, be a signal that we are praying for freedom. The godparents and sponsors can hold the shoulders of the elect to convey support and acceptance during these intercessions.

Exorcism (RCIA, n. 154, 168, 175): The exorcism is the prayer of God's presence. In response to the intercessions that named the darkness, the void, the emptiness of sin, the exorcism is the acknowledgment of the breath of God being welcomed into those areas that lack life. The exorcism also acknowledges the power of grace over sin. The exorcism is a prayer for freedom.

There are three movements to the exorcism prayer, a trinitarian movement. First, the presider invokes the power and presence of the Creator God to free and protect the elect from sin. Following this prayer, the presider calls upon the power and presence of the Spirit through the ancient symbol of the imposition of hands. Slowly, the presider lays hands on the head of each of the elect, continuing the prayer for freedom. This symbol can be expanded to include the RCIA coordinator and the godparent/sponsor in joining the presider with the laying on of hands. The third movement is the prayer invoking the power and presence of the Christ. The worshiping community can be invited to extend hands over the elect during this final movement.

Dismissal (RCIA, n. 155, 169, 176): The elect are then dismissed from the assembly with words of support and encouragement.

CATECHESIS FOLLOWING THE SCRUTINIES

The experience of the scrutinies is usually a very powerful and moving one. There will be ample material from the experience itself to help the elect integrate and experience empowerment because of the scrutiny. There is a bi-directional focus: the reflecting back on the experience, and how the elect are freed for the on-going reflection on conversion that the scrutiny demands.

Inevitably, if the intercessions were constructed with the needs and concerns of the elect in mind, the elect will begin to discuss how they heard their issues, their blockages, their sin named and prayed for. Often this brings about a deepened awareness of God's forgiving love and the level of commitment one is called to in following the gospel.

One would think that after going through one scrutiny, the power and effect of the subsequent scrutinies would diminish. However, if the scrutinies are prepared carefully and honestly, the opposite effect often happens. The elect begin to take even more seriously the need for God and the desire for freedom. The roots of sin — rather than sinful acts — begin to become exposed for what they are. The elect begin to release the illusions and fears that keep them from living full lives. Somehow the excuses that provided comfort and convenience before — "That's just the way I am," "I'm not *really* prejudiced," "I can't give any more than I have already," "I don't have time to worry about those people" — prove to be inadequate, uncomfortable, lies.

The period of catechesis following the scrutinies is primarily a time of support and care for the elect, helping them see God's love operative in the midst of the painful naming of sin. The focus is on God's love, not on our sin. This is not the time to be preoccupied with wretchedness (in fact, there is no wretchedness). Rather, it is the time to be preoccupied with the freedom of being called a child of God, and anything that keeps us from living that vocation to its fullness.

Some parishes celebrate a litany of prayer similar to the scrutinies at each of the community's liturgies on the prescribed Sunday. Therefore, even though the elect may be gathered at one Mass, all of the community will have had the chance to struggle with their call to freedom. Following the scrutinies (or the litanies at Masses without the elect present), an invitation can be given to the worshiping community to spend time after Mass to reflect on the experience and look at some of the implications of the prayer of exorcism. Often parishioners experience great discomfort and confusion about the scrutiny experience. This would provide an opportunity — similar to the catechesis following the scrutinies for the elect — for the parish to process and reflect on their experience.

THE PRESENTATIONS OF THE CREED AND THE LORD'S PRAYER

The rite places the presentations of the Creed and the Lord's Prayer during the period of purification and enlightenment. However, as people begin to implement the rite, they recognize that the experiences of the scrutinies are more than ample reflection and prayer for the Lenten retreat. The rite also recognizes this and gives the opportunity to anticipate these presentations during the catechumenate period (RCIA, n. 147).

In chapter six, we explored the presentations as intensifying rites for the period of the catechumenate. However, if the decision is made to celebrate the presentations during the period of purification and enlightenment, a few reminders are in order.

■ The presentations are not to be celebrated at the same liturgy during which one of the scrutinies will take place. The focus of both ritual movements is very different. Merging the scrutinies and the presentations lends itself to confusion and clutter. Each ritual of itself is rich in meaning. Keep them separate and distinct.

■ The presentations are celebrated separately. The presentation of the Creed happens during the week following the first scrutiny (Third Week of Lent) and the presentation of the Lord's Prayer occurs during the week following the third scrutiny (Fifth Week of Lent).

■ The presentations are celebrated primarily with the unbaptized. While the previous reception of the Creed and the Lord's Prayer may wish to be affirmed in the same celebration for the already baptized, we do not celebrate the presentations with them unless there has been no prior catechesis at all. In those situations, it would be appropriate to entrust the presentations to these candidates for full communion, thus providing them with a stronger foundation for their Catholic Christian life.

■ The presentations are best experienced in the midst of the community. Private ceremonies make clear statements about the value of the ritual, as well as expressing an implicit ecclesiology.

CELEBRATING THE PASCHAL TRIDUUM

The liturgical life of the community, as well as its basic sense of identity, is focused toward the stirrings of the great waters of baptism. On this night of nights, men and women are immersed into the death and resurrection of Jesus the Christ, and the community is also immersed more deeply into this saving event. It is a solemn and holy night. It is a night that empowers for the call to service.

The Lenten period ends on Thursday of Holy Week. The paschal triduum — the three days — begins with the Mass of the Lord's Supper on Holy Thursday and continues through the Easter evening prayer. The entire Holy Week needs to become a period of final preparation for the elect and candidates. Already they have entered into the period of Lent in a spirit of prayer, repentance, and sincere listening to the word of God. All of this is heightened for them as they enter this sacred season of the church.

There are no specific rites for the elect during the liturgical services on Holy Thursday and Good Friday. This does not diminish their inclusion and witness in these liturgies. Because of the importance of these liturgies for the life of the community, there is often concern expressed as to how appropriately and to what extent are the elect to be included in these worship experiences. Following are some suggestions that may be helpful.

■ If possible, the time of the triduum can be a period of retreat for the elect. They need to be encouraged that this is both a special and necessary time of final preparation for the vigil service. If possible, they can be encouraged to take vacation time from work so they can be focused in their prayer over these next few days. Sometimes this cannot reasonably happen. In those cases, encourage the elect to make every effort to be present with the community for prayer. For those who are able to be available throughout these days, you may want to provide a space for their own reflection and prayer — a meditation room of sorts. Their sponsor, godparent, spiritual director, or someone from the team may want to be available to them at various times over the days for support and shared prayer.

- The elect will need to know well in advance that their active presence at the community's worship on Holy Thursday and Good Friday is needed even though there is no specific ritual that includes them.
- Regarding Holy Thursday, some people choose to allow the elect to remain for the entire worship because of the catechetical dimension of this feast. While there are no barriers to such a decision, it would seem inconsistent with the value placed on dismissal to change this practice at this time. There will still be the tension of allowing the elect to remain at the table they are not yet initiated into. Emphasis would seem to be placed on the objective action and words rather than the active participation of the community, which includes sharing in communion. The texts for Holy Thursday, the preaching, and the experience of the mandatum (the call or mandate to service as symbolized in the washing of the feet) are powerful and potent sources for catechesis. The message conveyed with dismissal, even at the Mass of the Lord's Supper, is far more formative and important to the community and the elect than choosing to allow them to stay.
- It is often customary for parishes to have a period of adoration of the Blessed Sacrament following the transfer of the eucharist at the end of the Mass of the Lord's Supper. The elect may be invited to spend time in prayer with the community. However, they need some preparation for the experience. The eucharist is reserved after the Holy Thursday liturgy for the sick and for the Good Friday service. The Blessed Sacrament is understood as the sacrament of the church; present here is the transforming presence of God and the transformed commitment of the community. Eucharist does not make sense apart from the community within which it is celebrated. The team will need to be careful in its presentation so as to convey not a reified ("thingness") eucharist — something we adore, we get, and so on — but rather the active presence of God transforming the community in its very self identity.
- The period from the Holy Thursday liturgy through the vigil has always been traditionally observed as a period of fasting and prayer. The elect are to be encouraged to spend time in prayer and fasting in preparation for the vigil.
- There has been some discussion about celebrating reception into full communion (the candidates) at the Holy Thursday celebration. There may be some value to this in terms of keeping the appropriate distinction between the elect and candidates. However, it may complicate what needs to be a rather simple liturgy. The clarity of the

focus of this night in relation to the entire triduum might be lost. It seems more appropriate to celebrate the completion of initiation at either the vigil or on Easter Sunday. The Holy Thursday eucharist would be the appropriate time, however, to receive back into the full life of the community those who have been enrolled in the order of penitents.

■ On Good Friday, the parish will celebrate a number of services to commemorate the passion and death of the Lord Jesus. Often this will include some form of the liturgy of the hours (morning prayer, for example), a service of the stations of the cross, perhaps an ecumenical service, and the parish liturgy or celebration of the Lord's passion. The elect need to be encouraged to use the various periods of prayer throughout the day to provide a rhythm for them in their prayer and fasting. It is appropriate to expect the elect to be gathered for the celebration of the Lord's passion with the community. Because the communion rite is not central to this liturgy — and there is some informal discussion among some liturgists who would prefer to see the communion rite at this service eliminated altogether — there is no need to dismiss the elect from the assembly at this time. Depending on time, a period of reflection and catechesis might be appropriate following the service. If this cannot happen, don't worry. There is plenty in the liturgy itself to awaken and stir the hearts of the elect.

■ For the liturgies of both Holy Thursday and Good Friday, the presence of the sponsors with the elect is extremely important.

DAY OF PRAYER

The rite encourages that the elect set Holy Saturday apart for prayer and reflection (RCIA, n. 185.1). The team may choose to use this opportunity to gather for the day with the elect (and sponsors, whenever possible). Rather than having a structured day of prayer, provide the elect with the opportunity to have a quiet space for the day. Godparents can be alerted to touch base with the elect to take care of any needs they may have at home during the day. For most of us, if we are not taken from our homes and given the place to pray and rest, we won't. There will be so many distractions for the elect at home — and so many preoccupations.

The parish community may gather together on Holy Saturday morning for morning prayer. This would be a good opportunity to incorporate the preparation rites for the elect with members of the community gathered. Following the preparation rites, the elect can then remain at the parish center — or in another designated place — in prayer and reflection. The texts from the vigil readings can be used for reflection. At lunch time, the elect and sponsors can share a simple meal — soup, cheese, bread, fruit — with their godparents, team members and parishioners. The afternoon can include more time and space for private prayer and reflection. Midday, all the elect can gather for a prayer experience and faith-sharing, and then return home for the final preparations before the vigil service.

Some people react to the notion of asking the elect to stay for most of Holy Saturday with the team in prayer and reflection. However, numerous members of the elect who have done just that have been positive and supportive of the idea. Most admit that they would have found it difficult to create this space in their own home. They felt relieved of anxieties and could focus on the true meaning of the vigil experience. There wasn't time to worry, only to pray and to keep watch with God.

PREPARATION RITES: HOLY SATURDAY

The RCIA provides various rites that begin the initiation ritual: presentation of the Lord's Prayer if it has been deferred, the recitation of the Creed, the ephphetha rite, and the choosing of a baptismal name. Depending on need and pastoral discernment, any or all of the rites can be celebrated (RCIA, n. 186). The preparation rites are only celebrated with the elect.

The structure of the preparation rites is a liturgy of the word service. It can easily be integrated into the morning prayer of the parish community on Holy Saturday morning. After the homily, the rites chosen are celebrated.

Recitation of the Creed (RCIA, n. 193-196): The recitation of the Creed is not only a "giving back" of the Creed to the community, but is a preparation for the profession of faith that will be proclaimed at baptism. Hence, it is a catechetical moment. Note that the recitation of the Creed should only be done if there was a presentation of the Creed earlier in the period of enlightenment or catechumenate.

It is customary for the elect to recite the Creed from memory. While there is no statement in the rite one way or the other, it would seem appropriate that the words that symbolize the life of the community are engraved in the heart and mind of the newly initiated. Of course, if the elect is too nervous to recite from memory, a copy of the Creed can be provided.

Ephphetha Rite (RCIA, n. 197–199): The ephphetha rite (see Mark 7:31–37) is an appropriate complement to the scrutinies. Throughout the period of purification, the elect have prayed for freedom from sin. The ephphetha is the prayer for God to open the ears of the elect to truly hear God's word and to open the mouth of the elect that they may proclaim it. The rite focuses on the fact that the very ability to hear and respond to God's word is grace and not something we can earn or manipulate.

If both the recitation of the Creed and the ephphetha rite are to be celebrated at the same ritual, then the ephphetha rite precedes the recitation of the Creed (RCIA, n. 194). Symbolically, it is the grace of God that empowers one to hear the message of the gospel and then to proclaim it. The Creed that is proclaimed flows from the experience of God's grace.

Choosing a Baptismal Name (RCIA, n. 200–205): In some circumstances, the elect may opt to choose a new name expressive of the baptismal experience. This is not a common practice in North America where most names tend to have Christian origins already.

If the elect are to choose new names, the presider will need to reflect on the importance of being named by another. Naming denotes some sense of relationship and intimacy. It suggests that one knows another. To give another a name expresses the transformative quality of the relationship. The same is true of our experience of God, especially in baptism. We are transformed in the experience of baptism.

As mentioned, it is more likely that the elect will keep their given name. If the presider wishes to reflect on the importance of naming in this context, it would be appropriate to also include the meaning of each of the names of the elect.

It seems rather "busy" to celebrate all of these preparatory rites at the Holy Saturday morning prayer experience. The focus is lost. The choosing of a Christian name can be anticipated at the rite of acceptance into the order of catechumens (RCIA, n. 73, 200). There can be a natural connection between the ephphetha rite and the recitation of the Creed. All three rites, though, become cumbersome.

Whatever rites are chosen, the liturgy team planning the parish morning prayer experience needs to be informed about the direction and concerns of the preparatory rites. Then the accompanying readings and psalmody (if used) can appropriately express and connect these rites within the larger picture of the triduum.

9

Third Step: Celebration of the Sacraments of Initiation

INTRODUCTION

The sacraments of initiation — baptism, confirmation, and eucharist — are usually celebrated at the Easter vigil. As the parish community gathers to celebrate the central mysteries of our faith, the paschal event, the community also welcomes men and women into the power and life of Christ's death and resurrection. Through the celebration of the Easter sacraments, the elect receive the forgiveness of sin, celebrate their identity as daughters and sons of God, share in the mission of Jesus, and become full members of the Catholic communion.

The celebration of baptism follows the service of light and the liturgy of the word during the vigil. After an appropriate procession to the baptismal font, the celebrant invites the community to pray for the candidates who are asking for baptism. After silent prayer, the community sings the litany of saints, a symbol of the communion of the church that extends beyond all space and time. Following the litany, the baptismal waters are blessed, recalling the great deeds of God and invoking the power and presence of the Trinity. The candidates for baptism are then invited to a renunciation of sin and to make a profession of faith in the paschal mystery into which they will be baptized, thus publicly affirming their intention to live the new way of life of the gospel. Immediately following the renunciation of sin and profession of faith, the elect come forward for the baptismal washing, the water rite — either through immersion or by the pouring of water — and the proclamation of the trinitarian formula: I baptize you in the name of the Father, and of the Son, and of the Holy Spirit. The newly baptized are then clothed with the baptismal garment (usually a white robe) and presented with a candle lit from the Easter candle, both symbols of their new way of life.

The celebration of confirmation follows the baptismal rite. After the invitation to silent prayer for the outpouring of the Holy Spirit, the celebrant continues with the laying on of hands, the ancient symbol of invoking the power and presence of the Holy Spirit. The laying on of hands is done over all the candidates followed by the anointing with chrism, the sealing of the baptismal commitment. After the celebration of confirmation, the renewal of baptismal promises by the community follows, and those who are newly baptized and confirmed are led to their places within the gathered community. These new members of the community are now called neophytes, the "newly planted."

During the celebration of the eucharist, the neophytes participate fully for the first time in the prayer of the community. They are welcomed to the table of the eucharist and share in the body and blood of Christ, thus being strengthened for this new way of life they have accepted.

THE EASTER VIGIL

The great liturgy of the Easter vigil is the climax of the life of the community: we come together to baptize and be baptized into the saving death and resurrection of the Lord Jesus Christ. At the waters of baptism, along with those immersed for the first time, we enter into the mystery of redemption. Together we celebrate the victory of Christ over sin and death.

Briefly, we will review the basic movement of the vigil liturgy in order to place the baptismal liturgy within its proper context.

The vigil is celebrated after nightfall on Holy Saturday night. It is a time of prayer and celebration, a time of welcome to those who will be baptized, confirmed and share in the eucharist. It is also a time for the community to rededicate itself to the mission of the reign of God. Communities that do not have women and men who will enter the waters of baptism during the vigil will have a more difficult time of exposing themselves to the power of these symbols.

There are four basic movements to the vigil service: the service of light, the liturgy of the word, the liturgy of baptism, and the liturgy of the eucharist.

THE SERVICE OF LIGHT: The service of light needs to be celebrated in a place where the community can gather. It serves little purpose to celebrate the service of light in the church vestry where no one but the ministers can be present. If there is no place to gather for the community, then the service of light needs to be adapted for the worship space of the community. The movement of the service is simple — and it is the simplicity of these rites that heightens the power for the symbols to speak. Fire is blessed. The Easter candle is blessed and lighted. In the darkness of the night, one light shines bright, shattering the darkness, offering hope. The candle is carried in procession through the community with the proclamation: "Christ our Light!" Candles lit from the great candle begin to be passed among the assembly as they solemnly process into the worship space. The Easter candle is enthroned and usually incensed. After the community has assembled, there is silence. With only the light from the Easter candle — and its extension to the candles held by the community —the Easter proclamation is sung. The Exultet is a prayer of blessing and thanksgiving.

THE LITURGY OF THE WORD: Following the Easter proclamation, the community sits for the liturgy of the word. Environment and mood are created with dim lighting, allowing the burning Easter candle to stand as witness to the proclaimed texts.

There are a total of nine readings prescribed for the vigil. In the early church, the community kept vigil all night, recalling the great deeds of God and of God's love in the community. They told the stories of salvation. While the community remained in prayer and proclamation all night, the elect were gathered in the baptistry for their initiation. Thus, the newly initiated — when brought to the community who had been praying and listening to the scriptures all through the night — became the concrete enfleshment of God's continuing salvation in our midst.

Many parishes have reduced the number of readings for the vigil. The instruction in the lectionary states that at the very least two readings from the Hebrew scriptures (one of which must be the Exodus account) and the two prescribed texts from the Christian scriptures are to be used. With the renewed interest in the vigil liturgy, especially because of the central focus of initiation, more and more parishes are beginning to restore the full vigil experience. One way of doing this is to begin with the Easter fire and then move into the cycle of readings. Perhaps a new text could be proclaimed every half hour, with the intervening time for a response and private prayer. The community can be alerted to this, and people can arrive at various times. Done in this way, the vigiling can extend over a period of three to four hours. Then, at a prescribed time, there can be the proclamation of the Exodus, Romans and gospel text, preceded by the Exultet.

THE LITURGY OF BAPTISM: The 1988 ritual edition for use in

the United States provides a "combined rite" for celebrating sacramental initiation at the Easter vigil for the elect and the candidates. As with the other rituals, it is important to make clear the distinction between the two groups. Following are some reflections on the movement of the liturgy of baptism during the vigil.

Presentation of the Candidates for Baptism (RCIA, n. 219, 568): The liturgy of baptism follows the homily and is celebrated in full view of the community. If the baptismal font is not situated where the community is able to participate, then a portable vessel will need to be used in the sanctuary.

If the liturgy of baptism will be celebrated at a different place in the church, there is an appropriate procession to the baptismal font (again, presuming the font is in view of the community). The Easter candle is carried in the procession while the litany of the saints is sung. The minister of baptism and the elect with their godparents and sponsors gather around the font.

The elect are presented to the community with a few words of witness by the RCIA coordinator.

Invitation to Prayer (RCIA, n. 220, 569): The presider invites the community to pray for the elect as they prepare to enter into the waters of baptism. There follows a period of silent prayer. If the litany of the saints becomes an extension of this prayer, it would be appropriate to ask the elect to prostrate themselves in prayer.

Litany of the Saints (RCIA, n. 221, 570): The litany of the saints is sung unless it has already been used during the procession to the baptismal font. The litany can be adapted to include other petitions: names of patron saints of the parish community, the elect, and the candidates; names of our brothers and sisters of the covenant at Sinai such as Abraham, Sarah, Jonathan and David; names of other members in the communion of saints not yet formally recognized such as Thomas Merton, Dorothy Day, or John XXIII; and names of holy men and women from other religious affiliations (strong ecumenical flavor) such as Martin Luther King, Jr. The litany should move and not be dragged out.

Blessing of Water (RCIA, n. 222, 571): The rite prescribes that the presider sing the blessing of the water. This may cause a concern for presiders who cannot sing. In those instances, it seems appropriate that the blessing be sung by a cantor or schola. If the presider should choose to recite the blessing (although the text does seem to be a hymn and not a pronouncement), an appropriate antiphon could be sung by the community at various points during the blessing.

The blessing of the water recounts the various uses of water in the history of salvation. After asking God to unseal the fountain of baptism, the presider lowers the Easter candle into the still waters. This rather graphic and deliberate gesture seems to have ancient roots — the impregnation of the primordial waters with new life, breaking open the waters with fertility. The symbol of the candle breaks the seal of the water with the enlivening grace of God's Spirit so that all who enter these waters can be filled with this same Spirit. We now have the first stirrings of the water — the waters will move again when the bodies of those to be claimed in baptism are immersed in them. Thus, these men and women will become the bearers of this new life. Though the movement of the symbol — the immersion of the Easter candle into the waters, stirring them up — may be subtle (or even lost if done poorly), it makes a powerful statement of the sacramental dimension of life.

Profession of Faith (RCIA, n. 233, 572): The presider then invites the elect to reject sin (RCIA, n. 224, 573) and make a profession of faith (RCIA, n. 225, 574). Depending on the number of elect, the presider may choose to question all of them as a group or individually. During the baptism liturgy of the early church, the elect turned and faced the west, the darkness, and rejected sin and evil. They then were instructed to face the east, the rising sun, and to accept the new life of baptism. The elect can similarly be involved in the turning from west to east. The presider can ask them to face the west, the direction of darkness, and begin to question them on their desire to renounce sin and evil. Then they can be invited to turn (with the assistance and support of their sponsors and godparents) to face the east, the rising sun and morning star, and profess faith in Christ Jesus. The profession of faith can either be as a group or individually, and usually takes the form of responses to a series of inquiries: Do you believe in God, the Father Almighty . . . ?

Baptism (RCIA, n. 226, 575): The baptism follows immediately after the profession of faith. If the profession of faith is made individually, then the baptism follows prior to the next person's profession of faith. If the profession is made as a group, then the individual baptisms follow.

The rite offers three options for baptism: full body immersion, immersion of the head only, or the pouring of water over the head of the elect. It seems reasonable to suggest that full body immersion most fully expresses the symbol of the water bath in baptism. The elect will enter into the fullness of the death and resurrection of the Lord. They are dying to the old in order to embrace the new. They enter into the waters of life and death in order to emerge transformed by God's Spirit. The power of that symbol — for the one being baptized as well as for the baptizing community — is best expressed with full body immersion.

Some churches have constructed baptismal pools in the entrance-way of the church — a clear reminder of the responsibility of the baptized. Usually the baptismal pools are of two types: either one with running waters, or one that can be covered with a brass plate. For those churches with baptismal pools, the choice for baptism is obvious. However, all churches (in fact most churches) do not have baptismal pools. Still, there are some options that can be explored.

If the community desires baptism by whole body immersion, a container such as a hot tub can be rented for the vigil service. The hot tub needs to be appropriately decorated (and disguised) so as not to appear to be a symbol of middle-to-upper class wealth and values but a water bath. Then it will be very easy to have full body immersion.

If this option cannot work, then a child's plastic pool can be decorated for immersion of the head only. The elect would kneel in the pool and then bend over into the water, guided by the presider.

The last option is to have a vessel for the pouring of water over the head into a bowl or font. If this option is used, the gesture of pouring needs to be large, and ample amounts of water need to be used.

Whatever option is used — again, with the preference for full body immersion — the presider baptizes the elect in the name of the Trinity with each invocation followed by either the immersion or the pouring of water. The abundance of water used should make the elect gasp for air each time — filling themselves with the newness of life.

Explanatory Rites (RCIA, n. 227, 576): Following the baptism, there are a series of rites that help expand and explain — through symbol — the meaning of the baptism experience. If there will not be a celebration of confirmation during this celebration, the baptism is followed by an anointing with chrism, similar in intention to the anointing in infant baptism (RCIA, n. 228, 577).

The neophytes ("the newly planted") then are clothed with the baptismal garment — usually a white robe, although it can be of a different color depending on local custom (RCIA, n. 229, 578). Then their godparents present the neophytes with candles lit from the Easter candle.

In the case of baptism by immersion, the decision will need to be made as to when to send the neophytes to change from their wet clothes into their Easter clothing. They could possibly leave now with their godparents and return for the confirmation rite. However, they would miss the witness of the community as it renews its own baptismal promises. Or they could remain through the confirmation rite, and then leave to change. The community could have an extended period of music and prayer prior to the procession of gifts, which should include the neophytes.

Renewal of Baptismal Promises (RCIA, n. 237, 580): The community, having witnessed the baptism of the neophytes, is now called upon to renew its own baptismal promises through a renunciation of sin and a profession of faith. If the neophytes turned toward the west and east in their renunciation and profession of faith, it would seem to overwork the symbol to repeat it again. If they did not, perhaps this could be included at this time.

Sprinkling with Baptismal Water (RCIA, n. 240, 583): Following the renewal of baptismal promises, the presider sprinkles the community with the blessed water. Prior to the service, an appropriate branch can be cut for use at this time. The presider may wish to test out the branch prior to the ritual. While we do not want to drown people, we do want them to experience the waters of baptism. A slight mist of water does not convey the message.

Another option would be to invite the community to come forward to the baptismal pool and to sign themselves with the baptismal waters. This procession to the waters need not be organized. In fact, it should have the quality of spontaneity. Some people will sign themselves, others will touch the water, and others will actually dip part of their body into the water. During this time, an appropriate hymn can be sung.

CELEBRATION OF RECEPTION INTO THE FULL COMMUNION OF THE CATHOLIC CHURCH (RCIA, n. 584): Following the community's renewal of its baptismal promises — which includes the renewal by the candidates — the presider invites the candidates and their sponsors to come forward and make a profession of faith within the Catholic community. The candidates for full communion can either recite individually the formula for profession of faith (RCIA, n. 585), or the presider may ask in question form the essential dimensions of the profession (as in the baptismal renewal) and candidates can individually respond. The presider then approaches the candidates and personally welcomes each one, receiving them into the Catholic Church (RCIA, n. 586).

CELEBRATION OF CONFIRMATION: Confirmation should follow the baptisms and reception into full communion. In the absence of the bishop, the minister of baptism and of reception into full communion is authorized to confirm (RCIA, n. 232, 588).

Invitation (RCIA, n. 233, 589): If the neophytes have left the community to change, they should return at this time to celebrate confirmation. The neophytes and the newly received, along with the sponsors and godparents, are instructed in the meaning of confirmation and its association with baptism. Following this, the community is invited to pray in silence for the neophytes and newly received.

Laying On of Hands (RCIA, n. 234, 590): The presider then extends his hands over the neophytes and newly received and says a prayer of invocation, asking God to send forth the Spirit in a new way in their lives.

Anointing with Chrism (RCIA, n. 235, 591): The laying on of hands is followed by the anointing with chrism, the sealing of the sacrament. This sealing — traditionally associated as the indelible mark of the Spirit — sets the neophyte and newly received apart for service for the mission of the reign of God. They are now, as it were, branded or marked for charity and justice.

The chrism used for the confirmation and the action of confirming needs to be visible to the community. A simple but elegant procession of the chrism prior to the celebration of confirmation could help focus this part of the ritual. Or the chrism could be carried in by liturgical dancers who then gracefully present the chrism to the presider. The chrism, which can be carried in a crystal container, can then be poured by the presider into a glass bowl for the confirmation rite. During the anointing, the presider can dip his hand into the chrism and smear it liberally on the foreheads of the neophytes and newly received. The chrism should not be wiped away from the foreheads after the confirmation rite.

THE LITURGY OF THE EUCHARIST (RCIA, n. 241–243, 592–594): The neophytes and newly received now take part in the community's celebration at the table of the eucharist. They join, for the first time, in the community's prayer during the general intercessions or prayers of the faithful. Perhaps they may be part of the presentation of the gifts. They are mentioned during the eucharistic prayer.

Prior to the breaking of the bread, the presider may wish to briefly mention the importance of the eucharistic meal in terms of our sacramental initiation. The neophytes and newly received are then welcomed to the table to share in the community's communion with the Lord and with each other.

The community can continue the celebration of baptism and full communion with a reception and party following the Easter vigil. The parish community can have the opportunity to personally welcome the neophytes and newly received into the Catholic Church, as well as into this particular parish community.

CATECHESIS FOLLOWING INITIATION

The entire period of mystagogy will be given for reflection and prayer about the experience of initiation and the implications for living that makes on the neophytes.

SPECIFIC PREPARATION REMINDERS FOR THE LITURGY OF BAPTISM

- If immersion is used — either full body or immersion of the head only — the elect will need to know this ahead of time so they can dress appropriately and bring along a change of clothes. They can be advised to wear a simple outfit — one that can not be seen through when wet — and bring along their Easter outfit.
- Plenty of towels will need to be readily available for the newly baptized, especially if by immersion. A quick toweling of excess water is all that is needed at the time of the ritual. Standing dripping in the waters of new life is a rather strong statement to the community.
- Someone can be assigned for each of the people to be baptized to assist them with the changing of clothes after they leave the assembly.
- If baptismal robes are to be used, they will need to be ready for the vigil. A simple poncho-style robe would suffice.
- The vessel of chrism for confirmation can be carried into the community in a glass container for everyone to see. As with the gospel procession, there can be a procession or liturgical dance to carry in the chrism.

10

Period of Postbaptismal
Catechesis or Mystagogy

INTRODUCTION

Sacramental initiation does not end at the Easter sacraments. The RCIA provides for the final period, the period of postbaptismal catechesis or mystagogy (that is, reflection on the mysteries). The neophytes, along with the community, reflect together on the celebration of the Easter mysteries — the paschal event — and begin the process of making it a full and active part of their lives. The neophytes continue to gather weekly, supported by the community and their godparents, until Pentecost.

The Easter season, the season of feasting, is celebrated by the entire community. The neophytes gather at the Sunday eucharist with the community, witness to their experience of God for the community, and participate in the planning and celebration of the eucharist. They are leaven for new life in the community; they are the source of renewal for the community. Together, the neophytes and the community discern their gifts and recognize their responsibility to serve the mission of the reign of God. Mystagogy is the final period of the initiation process, but the beginning of the responsibility of discipleship.

A PAUSE DURING THE STORY

We are historical people and celebrate our unique identity as people who are becoming. We change and grow and develop. Each one of us and all of us together have a story that is not merely casual, teleological or determined, but open to vast possibilities. The RCIA respects this personal developing story and is an attempt to provide the tools needed to deepen one's commitment to one's story, and hence renew the community's story, through conversion to and experience of Jesus Christ.

Tertullian (d. 225) had pointed out that Christians are not born, but made. We cannot know the impact of an experience until we have moved through history and then stand back in wonder and remember. Such remembrance is not the deception of nostalgia but an active presence of self that evokes the fullness of the memory in such a way that one is participating in that reality again. Mystagogy is that: it is a pause in the story of the neophyte and the community with God to look with awe and wonder at the great deeds of God and believe more deeply, singing God's praise.

Unfortunately, it is precisely at this important period of integration and interiorization that many RCIA programs end — because they are programs. They have worked hard to prepare the elect for the Easter vigil, and now everyone is exhausted, or interest begins to wane. The initiation program was focused on Easter immersion rather than an RCIA process focused on serving the mission of the reign of God. The experience of sacramental initiation serves as the foundation for a life of service and commitment. The community has the responsibility to provide effective catechesis (in the form of mystagogy) for the newly initiated so they can bring together the various threads and dimensions of their initiation experience and recognize the empowering presence of God. To "close shop" and leave the neophytes on their own after the vigil would be irresponsible. Therefore, a parish's RCIA process needs to be developed out of their understanding of the role and vision of mystagogy, and not vice versa.

What does this mean, to develop our RCIA process based on mystagogy? The members of the community, and in particular the RCIA team with the pastoral staff, needs to articulate for themselves what it means to be servant of God, to be about the reign of God. Once there is this understanding of the Christian call, then the RCIA process is developed to help individuals to respond to God's invitation to a life of commitment, to this way of life (conversion). The initiation process is a response to a call to a particular gospel way of life.

The rite describes the period of mystagogy as a time for deepening the Christian experience, a time for spiritual growth, and a time to enter more fully into the life and unity of the Christian community (RCIA, n. 7.4). How is this done? The rite suggests through (a) meditation on the gospel, (b) sharing in the eucharist, (c) doing works of charity, and (d) the support and care of godparents, the community and pastoral staff (RCIA, n. 244). Furthermore, the rite highlights the period of mystagogy as a time to facilitate a fuller and deeper understanding of the gospel not only because of what the neophytes have already learned, but above all through their experience of the sacraments they have received (RCIA, n. 245).

It has already been mentioned in this resource that effective catechesis for sacraments prepares people for the sacrament without practicing the sacramental rite. Thus, the experience of the symbols is fresh and new. The simplicity and power of the symbol speaks to the individual rather than the information of what it should be like. Because of the nature of symbol — if indeed the experience of the symbols has been authentic and not manipulated — and a symbol's ability to evoke a level of universal experience, the articulation of the symbol experience is usually consistent with the tradition's articulation. Thus, we need to trust the power and message of symbols and symbolic experiences such as sacraments to effect their own message rather than trying to program a message prior to the experience.

How can we pastorally bring about this process of mystagogy? The rite calls for the period of postbaptismal catechesis to be done during the Easter season (RCIA, n. 7.4), using the lectionary readings of Cycle A (RCIA, n. 247). We need to bring our parish community back to the awareness that the oldest season of the church year is this period, commonly called the Great Sunday or the *Magna Dominica*, and should be celebrated as a time of feasting!

THE MYSTAGOGUE

Catechesis during the period of mystagogy takes on a different dimension than in the previous periods of the RCIA, although throughout the entire RCIA the catechesis is mystagogical, i.e. catechesis leading into rites and flowing from rites. Now the process is akin to theological reflection: the newly initiated are invited to stand back and see the whole picture in context. They are invited to: reflect on their experience of God mediated through the rich symbols of the community; discover how that experience is connected to, and at the same time roots, their previous exposure to the word of God, Catholic teaching, worship, service and community; and struggle to integrate all of this as empowerment for full active Christian life.

This form of catechesis is grounded in a sensitivity to symbols. The symbols experienced are opened and explored for deeper meaning, as well as for integration into daily life. The temptation to explain must be avoided; this is a period of wonderment in the presence of mystery.

The catechist, therefore, will need to be a mystagogue: someone who has given himself or herself over to the experience of mystery and will now guide the neophyte to an initial exploration of what that means.

MEDITATING ON THE GOSPEL

(a) The Sunday eucharist during the Easter season is the primary time for catechesis. The neophytes had regularly gathered with the community for many months, even years, to share in the community's faith. Finally, they were brought to the celebration of the Easter vigil with only their desire to enter into the death and resurrection of the Lord. Slowly and deliberately, the community led the neophytes from the darkness of sin into the light of Christ, immersing them in the waters of baptism, anointing them with the oil of the Spirit, and then leading them to the banquet table of the Lord's supper to share in full communion with the church. All of these symbols heightened and deepened their relationship with Jesus, though the neophytes may not have the words to adequately express the experience. Now, gathered with the community, they begin to hear what the symbols they experienced mean within the Christian community.

Cyril of Jerusalem (d. 386) captures this sense in his first of a series of postbaptismal homilies:

It has long been my wish, true-born and long-desired children of the Church, to discourse to you upon these spiritual, heavenly mysteries. On the principle, however, that seeing is believing, I delayed until the present occasion, calculating that after what you saw on that night I should find you a readier audience now when I am to be your guide to the brighter and more fragrant meadows of this second Eden. In particular, you are now capable of understanding the diviner mysteries of divine, life-giving baptism. The time being now come to spread for you the board of more perfect instruction, let me explain the significance of what was done for you on that evening of your baptism.

The preaching moment during the period of mystagogy is extremely important for the neophytes and for the community. While it is unreasonable to expect the preaching moment to explain and expand all the richness of the initiation experience, the preacher can continually interpret and connect the experience of initiation with the texts of the Easter season, thus providing a primary form of mystagogy. To facilitate this end, the RCIA recommends that the readings from Cycle A be used during the Easter season at the Masses celebrated with the neophytes because of the nature of those readings.

(b) The neophytes meet weekly with the catechetical team to uncover and explore the richness of the initiation commitment, as well as to begin to integrate themselves in the parish community. Though the primary experience of mystagogy is the community's breaking open and sharing of the word and eucharist (RCIA, n. 247), the continued weekly gatherings help the neophytes more explicitly "unpack" their experience.

With the help of the catechetical team, the neophytes can begin to internalize and appropriate the experience of initiation. They will need to reflect on the power and message of the Easter symbols. What was it like to stand in the darkness of the church with the one light of the Easter candle? What meaning did the stories of God's deeds throughout history have for you? How were you able to enter into the prayer with the entire church as sung through the litany of the saints? What was it like to go into the waters of baptism? How do you understand yourself now that you are sealed with the Spirit? What was it like to remain with the community for the eucharistic prayer rather than being dismissed? What meaning did sharing in the eucharist have for you?

The reflection on the mysteries — the experience of God in the sacraments, in the word proclaimed and in the community — can easily be integrated in the reflection on the Sunday texts, especially if Cycle A readings are used. The focus of catechesis now is integration and preparation for mission. Following are some ideas on how the texts during the period of the Easter season can be explored to include the issues of mystagogy.

EASTER SUNDAY: Acts 10:34, 37–43; Psalm 118; Colossians 3:1–4 or 1 Corinthians 5:6–8; John 20:1–9. *Possible catechesis:* The focus of the readings is the resurrection of Christ and the experience of the early disciples of the resurrection. The neophytes will need to reflect on their experience of the sacraments celebrated at the vigil, and their connection to the paschal event.

EASTER II: Acts 2:42–47; Psalm 118; 1 Peter 1:3–9; John 20:19–31. *Possible catechesis:* The readings focus on the life of the community formed in the death and resurrection of the Lord. This would be an appropriate time to further discuss the sacraments of baptism and confirmation: new life as children of God, members of the community of believers, forgiveness of sin, anointed and set apart.

EASTER III: Acts 2:14, 22–28; Psalm 16; 1 Peter 1:17–21; Luke 24:13–35. *Possible catechesis:* The readings highlight the appearance stories following the resurrection, with a special emphasis on experiencing the Lord within a meal context. The reflection on the Easter sacraments can continue, with a focus on the eucharist and experiencing the Lord in the breaking of the bread.

EASTER IV: Acts 2:14, 36–41; Psalm 23; 1 Peter 2:20–25; John 10:1–10. *Possible catechesis:* The readings point to Christ, the good shepherd, and our experience of relationship with Christ. The neophytes can continue their sacramental catechesis — reflection on encounters with the risen Lord — by exploring the remaining sacraments, using their previous catechumenate experience. The scrutinies of Lent will aid in a catechesis of reconciliation. The anointing with the oil of catechumens (for strength, etc.) will aid in a catechesis of the anointing of the sick. And reflection on their previous experience of mission throughout the process will enable them to reflect on the sacraments of mission or vocation, holy orders and matrimony.

EASTER V: Acts 6:1–7; Psalm 33; 1 Peter 2:4–9; John 14:1–12. *Possible catechesis:* The readings begin to turn toward the responsibility of the baptized toward service for the reign of God in the context of ministry. The neophytes can begin to discern with the team (and with other members of the community) their experience of giftedness for service.

EASTER VI: Acts 8:5–8, 14–17; Psalm 66; 1 Peter 3:15–18; John 14:15–21. *Possible catechesis:* The readings develop the central role of the Spirit in the development and expansion of the community and its ministry. Without the Spirit, there are no ministries, there are no sacraments. The neophytes continue to reflect on their mission, empowered by the Spirit, to live lives of love and justice.

ASCENSION THURSDAY: Acts 1:1–11; Psalm 47; Ephesians 1:17–23; Matthew 28:16–20. *Possible catechesis:* The Feast of the Ascension is a celebration of our call to embrace and serve the mission of the reign of God with Jesus. Throughout the readings, the image of the Spirit who empowers us for service is very clear. The focus of the feast moves us from looking away to the heavens for Jesus to looking for Jesus within the concrete way we live lives of the gospel, both personally and communally. The neophytes will need to grapple with moving from this "safe" environment (akin to looking up in the skies for Jesus) to life in the larger community, a life of service and commitment.

EASTER VII: Acts 1:12–14; Psalm 27; 1 Peter 4:13–16; John 17:1–11. *Possible catechesis:* The readings highlight the focus for all ministry and service: witness to the reign of God, as expressed and realized in the Christ event. Glory, truth, unity are all manifestations of this reign of God. The neophytes are encouraged to reflect on the role of their witness in the community to build up the body of Christ. Also, the central place of prayer in the life of the believer needs to be encouraged.

PENTECOST: Acts 2:1-11; Psalm 104; 1 Corinthians 12:3-7, 12-13; Sequence; John 20:19-23. *Possible catechesis:* The gift of the Spirit is the empowerment of individuals and the community for service for the reign of God. Women and men are transformed for witnessing to the good word of God's presence within and among us, a presence that liberates and redeems us. The neophytes will end their reflection on service and mission, recognizing their own call to proclaim by their lives the reign of God.

(c) The neophytes can be encouraged to read and pray the scriptures daily, if this is not already part of their lives. Resources for exploring the Sunday texts could be made available to them so they can begin to prepare for each Sunday's gathering of the community to listen to the word of God. Also, opportunities for varieties of prayer experiences can be made available to them — or, at the very least, information about different prayer forms can be given to them. Each neophyte will approach the experience of God in a different way because of the unique relationship with God, as well as the unique personality of the neophyte. Discerning appropriate personal and communal prayer forms with the neophytes will be a great service, as well as highlighting the on-going importance of liturgical prayer.

SHARING IN THE EUCHARIST

(a) The Sunday eucharist during the *Magna Dominica* is the place of mystagogy, beginning with the Easter Sunday celebration. But this can happen only if the neophytes feel part of the local community because the true catechist is the community. We must avoid minimalism, thus avoiding no change: this is an important period in the life of the whole church. The environment should be festive: fresh spring flowers, decorative wall hangings, rich vestments, incense and beeswax candles. The music should be rich — keep the Easter brass and strings to keep the Alleluia alive! Flood the senses: rich and bright sights, clear and joyful sounds, renewing and fragrant smells, fresh and appealing tastes, warm and embracing touch.

(b) The neophytes are encouraged to be a part of the liturgy planning during the *Magna Dominica*. Pastorally, this can be problematic because usually the Easter season is prepared well in advance of Easter.

However, as part of that preparation, the liturgy committee may choose to designate specific dimensions of the preparation to be taken care of by the neophytes, such as preparation of the general intercessions one week, or presentation of the gifts another week, or baking the eucharistic bread another week. Then the director of liturgy can participate with the neophytes during the catechetical gatherings to help better prepare them for liturgical prayer.

(c) The neophytes are introduced again to the community and welcomed. They are to be remembered by name during the homily and the general intercessions. They continue to wear their white baptismal albs and sit in their reserved seats without leaving after the liturgy of the word.

(d) One of the greatest gifts the neophytes give to the community is the witness of their presence. The community deepens its own awareness of God's loving concern and gift of salvation as it sees these new members of the community embrace the way of life of the gospel. The Easter Sunday eucharist is when the neophytes begin their witness to the parish by their presence as well as through witnessing. The neophytes can be given the opportunity after communion to strengthen the community by giving witness to the experience of God they have celebrated. Sponsors and godparents can also be included to witness before the parish. By Pentecost, each of the neophytes and godparents and sponsors will have had the opportunity to speak if any so choose.

WORKS OF CHARITY

(a) John Paul II in his 1979 World Day of Prayer for Peace said, "We are beginning to see that the parish catechumenate is a rich and fertile soil in which to plant the seeds of justice and peace." Hopefully the neophytes have discovered through their prolonged period of formation that the commitment to discipleship is a commitment to mission for the reign of God. Concretely, it is to stand in solidarity against oppression and announce the liberation of God with one's life.

(b) The neophytes are invited to discern how they have been gifted to serve the mission of God in this community and in the larger church and world. This discernment is aided by various presentations: experiential witness of the sacramental life by married couples, the ordained and other ministers; needs of the parish presented by the parish team and ministry development committee of the parish council; and reflections on personal and communal conversion to justice.

(c) The community also needs to discern its needs and how the community invites new people to serve the community. Once the community is able to articulate specific areas of service, representatives of the various organizations, such as the parish council, can invite the neophytes to consider using their gifts in service in these particular ways.

(d) The neophytes and the community need to learn the art of ministerial reflection in order to manifest the basic motivations behind their service. Unfortunately, charity and condescension become mixed in the same pot. Condescension is looking down on others, recognizing their need, and providing them with assistance — because they can't do it and we can. We give them what they need because there but for the grace of God go I. Sometimes our motivation is tainted by our own guilt and desire to free ourselves through contributing to others. As St. Vincent de Paul reminds us: May the poor forgive us for our charity to them (when this charity comes from motives of condescension and relieving of guilt).

Charity, on the other hand, recognizes the complexity of the human person and recognizes one's solidarity with the other person. It is not a case of "I have to give," but rather "We stand together in need." Compassion is knowing how to suffer with others in their true need: physical, psychological, and social. For charity and compassion to be authentic, it must include all three levels of solidarity. It is the willingness to truly stand with another, whatever the cost.

SUPPORT AND CARE OF THE COMMUNITY

(a) After the Easter vigil, the parish community can celebrate with a party to welcome the neophytes into the community.

(b) The sponsors and godparents continue to meet with the neophytes on a regular basis to help them become more acquainted with the parish community and the Catholic way of life.

(c) The neophytes can be invited to join new-forming and existing support groups in the parish to continue to share faith with others and to be assisted in living the gospel in the ordinary of their life: their families, neighborhoods, work, and the world.

(d) At some time during the Easter season, the neophytes gather with the other neophytes of the diocese around the table of the word and eucharist with the bishop.

(e) The neophytes are encouraged to continue to meet monthly during this first year to continue to be of support to each other. As early as the seventh century, it became the custom that the neophytes would meet yearly to celebrate the anniversary of their baptism.

PREPARING FOR MYSTAGOGY

The effectiveness of the period of mystagogy rests on how effectively the previous periods of the RCIA were implemented. If they were implemented with a focus toward mystagogy and life commitment, then the catechetical team will be able to retrieve these experiences and help the neophytes to effectively integrate them. However, if the rich experiences of word and symbol are missing, then the period of mystagogy will prove to be a difficult time.

The first place to look for preparing to implement the RCIA is in the period of mystagogy — what are its demands and how do we prepare people for this way of life? And for parishes that have already started implementing the rite, the process can be evaluated and strengthened based on the experience of mystagogy. Know how goes your mystagogy, and you will know how goes the rest of the RCIA implementation.

Following are some reflection questions to help prepare for the implementation of the period of mystagogy, and hence, the implementation of the RCIA.

1. How do you understand the reign of God?
2. Essential dimensions for catechesis are: word, worship, community and service.
   a. During the catechumenate, are there rich experiences of the word? Will they come to know God's presence in the breaking open of the word, both in the assembly and in their own gatherings?
   b. Are there ample experiences of worship with the community (such as Sunday morning liturgy of the word) and with each other as a group?
   c. Are there opportunities for the catechumens to meet and become familiar — both formally and informally — with the parish community (the sponsor's role is key here)?
   d. Are the catechumens encouraged to become actively involved in works of charity, service and justice throughout the catechumenate process, thus enfleshing their experience?
3. Are the scrutinies celebrated well so the elect have a profound

awareness of sin and the need for deliverance from sin? Will the experience of the scrutinies be rich enough for further reflection later during mystagogy, with a special focus on reconciliation?

4. Are there anointings and blessings during the catechumenate that will become the source for reflection on the sacrament of the anointing of the sick? Will the catechumens recognize the anointings as prayers for strength and healing amidst life's journey?

5. How do you celebrate the vigil? Can the catechumens come to an awareness of God's presence through the symbols — words and actions — of the ritual?

MYSTAGOGY: BEGINNING OR END?

Is mystagogy an end? Perhaps it is an end to this ritual of initiation. But it is a beginning for the rest of one's life — a model of how we need again and again to pause during our story and to remember, to renew and recommit, to be challenged and stretched because of our belief and trust in the gospel of Jesus Christ.

Part Three

Specific Pastoral Issues

11

Some Pastoral Issues

INTRODUCTION

A variety of pastoral issues emerge during the implementation of the RCIA: the question of annulments, financial support of the church, and ecumenical questions, to name a few. In addition to attending to the specific needs of the catechumens during the RCIA process, the catechumenate team will need to be sensitive to some of these issues. Following are some comments on areas of pastoral concern that seem to emerge regularly in parishes implementing the rite.

EVANGELIZATION

How do inquirers come to our communities? Do we advertise? Do we make direct contacts? What are the issues of evangelization?

Evangelization is bringing the message of the gospel to those who may not have heard this good news, as well as continuing to proclaim the gospel so it is heard in new ways by those already familiar with it. While this proclamation of the kerygma does happen through verbal witness, the most effective evangelization is the manner and quality of an individual's and community's lifestyle. People see how we live, how we relate, how we pray, and they begin to ask questions about it. This is the primary form of evangelization for the RCIA.

This does not exclude the possibility of inviting people to come and see our community, or running some kind of local advertisements. However, such attempts should be secondary to the community's own renewal and witness to the gospel. It is often the experience that communities expend great efforts at evangelization. People come forward and some enter the RCIA process. But when the process of sacramental initiation is completed, there is not much of a community for the neophyte to live in. The process of evangelization needs to be intimately connected with the vision of the parish community and its own call to conversion. What have we to offer as a parish? Why do we want people to join with us?

LITURGICAL MUSIC IN THE RCIA

The role and purpose of liturgical music is to assist the community in its prayer, and to enhance the experience of the prayer (some might call this "to pray better," but it is difficult to place such qualitative judgments on the experience of prayer — what does it mean "to pray better?"). "Music should assist the assembled believers to express and share the gift of faith that is within them and to nourish and strengthen their interior commitment of faith" (*Music in Catholic Worship,* n. 23). Liturgical music can do this in a number of ways: by adopting an attitude toward liturgical music as a ministry of service to the community, by corresponding with and reflecting the liturgical action, and by facilitating participation in the liturgy.

Adopting an attitude toward liturgical music as a ministry of service to the community. For too long and for too many, liturgical music (and musicians) have been viewed as the after-thought in liturgical planning and ministry. This attitude, unfortunately, has often been perpetuated by some musicians themselves. "Music should assist the assembled believers to express and share the gift of faith that is within them and to nourish and strengthen their interior commitment of faith" (MCW, n. 23). Musicians need to be part of the liturgy preparation. Music — and its performance — needs to be of a high quality. "The musician has every right to insist that the music be good" (MCW, n. 29).

Corresponding with and reflecting the liturgical action. Liturgical music is not an appendage attached to the ritual. Rather, it complements and flows from the liturgical experience. The criterion for selecting music and acclamations is not because we like the piece, or because we always sing this piece. Rather, it is because it reflects and brings the community to encounter the essential dimensions of the liturgical action. "Does the music express and interpret the liturgical text correctly and make it more meaningful? Is the form of the text respected?" (MCW, n. 32).

Facilitating participation in the liturgy. Liturgical prayer is not performance, either by the ministers of prayer or by the musicians. The Constitution on the Sacred Liturgy asks that "all the faithful be led to that full, conscious, and active participation in liturgical celebrations which is demanded by the very nature of the liturgy," thereby encouraging the community "to take part by means of acclamations, responses, psalmody, antiphons, and songs, as well as by actions, gestures, and bodily attitudes" (*Sacrosanctum Concilium*, n. 14, 30). Composition and choice of liturgical music needs to empower the worshiping community for full and active participation in the rites.

Throughout the implementation of the RCIA, the ritual experience is enhanced by the appropriate use of liturgical music. This presumes the active participation of the musician, to some degree, in the hearing of the journey of faith of the catechumens. The beauty of the rituals of the RCIA lies in their ability to disclose the conversion experiences of the catechumens and the community. The musicians need to be sensitive to this both in their own lives and in how this is manifested in the community.

ENVIRONMENT AND ART

In addition to music, the environment we create is an important communicator to both the catechumens and the parish community. This includes the sense of warmth and hospitality we offer to people who come to our community, as well as the basic decor of our worship space and the symbols of our celebrations.

The U.S. Bishop's Committee on the Liturgy published a statement in 1978 entitled *Environment and Art in Catholic Worship* as a companion piece to *Music in Catholic Worship*. In this statement, the bishops offer principles for preparing liturgical space for worship. It would be helpful to highlight a few of these principles as they apply to the RCIA.

The concern of environment and art is to draw people together to celebrate, not to distract or alienate. "The environment is appropriate when it is beautiful, when it is hospitable, when it clearly invites and needs an assembly to complete it" (EACW, n. 24). The place of worship will be an important evangelizer to those seeking a faith community.

The RCIA celebrations lend themselves to the use of rich and powerful symbols. Symbols evoke a response from various levels and dimensions of the person and the community. "[T]he liturgical celebrations of the faith community involves the whole person. They are not purely religious or merely rational and intellectual exercises, but also human experiences calling on all human faculties: body, mind, senses, imagination, emotions, memory" (EACW, n. 5). Signing of the sense and passing on of the cross, handing on the gospel book, the laying on of hands, the presentations of the Creed and the Lord's Prayer, the waters of baptism, the anointing with oil, the breaking of the bread, the light in the darkness, the community assembled, and so on: these symbols — gestures, word, art — need to be pronounced yet simple. They need to be easily recognizable. They need to also carry the message that this is important. "One should be able to sense something special (and nothing trivial) in everything that is seen and heard, touched and smelled, and tasted in liturgy" (EACW, n. 12).

Other forms of visual art are also appropriate during the RCIA. Wall hangings, banners in procession, liturgical vestments — all can change or detract from the celebration. The lighting during the vigil service, the mood created during the scrutinies, the decor around the water font for baptism, the flowers during the eucharist, the dancer who processes with the oil in a glass bowl, the simplicity of the Easter candle, the bread torn during the eucharist — all of these and more are art. All of these necessarily communicate certain attitudes about the ritual celebration. What we choose and how we choose it reveals something about the value we place upon it. Therefore, liturgy places two demands on art: quality and appropriateness (EACW, n. 19): "Quality means love and care in the making of something, honesty and genuiness with any materials used . . ." and appropriateness means that the work of art "must be capable of bearing the weight of mystery, awe, and wonder . . . and it must clearly serve (and not interrupt) ritual action which has its own structure, rhythm and movement" (EACW, n. 20, 21).

PREACHING

Sometimes we are of the misunderstanding that the catechetical gatherings are based only on the scriptures proclaimed in the assembly. These texts are formative and central. However, the preaching that builds and develops this proclamation is also very important. It is the whole liturgy of the word experience — which includes the preaching moment — that becomes the foundation for the catechesis.

For many people in our communities, the only *formal* moment of catechesis is the experience of preaching. People will often choose the Mass during which to celebrate depending on who is preaching. Unfortunately, the preaching moment has often been a weak link in the assembly's worship. The reasons for this vary: poor training, inability to keep theologically current, inability to keep socially current, lack of preparation time, and so on. As in the catechetical moment, the preaching moment is an attempt to integrate the proclaimed word of God in a meaningful and credible way in the ordinary lives of people. The preaching moment is a time of invitation and challenge.

Sometimes the preaching moment becomes an instructional moment — and when it does, when its concern becomes the transmission of information, then it is no longer preaching. Preaching is proclamation.

This would suggest, then, there can be an on-going working relationship between the preacher and the catechists. If the catechetical gathering flows from the experience of the word — both the text and the ensuing proclamation — then it would be a helpful resource for the catechist to know the basic direction and emphasis of the preaching. The issues and insights raised in the preaching moment could be expanded and developed in the catechetical moment. The passing on of information that is transformative can then be relocated in the catechetical moment and out of the preaching moment.

The integration of the preaching and catechetical moments are quite clear when the rituals of the RCIA are celebrated. The preacher is hard pressed to make a proclamation on the scriptures and the rite of acceptance and welcome if the preacher has not somehow shared in the experience of the candidates, even if only through conversation with the catechists. This becomes clearer during the scrutinies. The intercessions and exorcisms of the scrutinies need to build on the preaching moment if they are to be addressed to both the catechumens and the gathered community.

The "how" of working together — preacher and catechists — can only be determined by those involved. Perhaps a regular gathering — weekly or monthly — between them for prayer, sharing of faith and the initial development of the preaching-catechetical moments would be both a good discipline and service: discipline because it will force all involved to spend an appropriate period of time with the word, letting it make a claim, and service because both the preacher and the catechist will be able to glean insights from each other in preparing their respective part of the experience.

In some situations, it may not be possible to gather regularly to pray the scriptures and to prepare the preaching-catechetical moments (but when it does happen, it usually makes a remarkable difference in both moments). At the very least, there needs to be a commitment to find some time prior to the celebration of the liturgy of the word to discuss — even if only by phone — the issues that will be addressed in the preaching moment. When the two moments are not working together, we can suffer from a schizophrenic presentation. This is not to suggest that the preaching moment dictates the direction of the catechesis. However, it makes for a more integrated approach to work together.

ECUMENICAL SENSITIVITY

The Rite of Christian Initiation of Adults was restored for the sacramental initiation of unbaptized adults into the Catholic Christian communion. However, it has been the experience of most parishes that the largest number of adults seeking full sacramental initiation are baptized Christians in another ecclesial community. In light of this reality, the pastoral implementation of the RCIA demands a high level of ecumenical sensitivity.

We have already discussed the need to make explicit in the ritual celebrations the distinction between the unbaptized and the baptized in the RCIA process. Following are additional principles that can help inform initiation praxis.

- The process of celebrating full communion in the Catholic community needs to be a positive experience, respecting the experiences of baptism and formation which have already taken place. The posture is one of respect and welcome: respect for the individual's previous religious affiliation, and welcome into the continuation of their journey of faith in the Catholic tradition. Any manner of triumphalism is to be avoided (RCIA, n. 475.2, 479).
- The process of formation usually requires a prolonged period of preparation that corresponds to the one prescribed for the unbaptized (RCIA, n. 401, 402). Catechetical formation (doctrinal and spiritual preparation) needs to be coordinated with the liturgical year (RCIA, n. 408, 477), and includes the period of mystagogy (RCIA, n. 410).
- The previous formation and Christian life of the already baptized needs to be taken into consideration and will affect the length of the period of formation (RCIA, n. 400, 473, 474, 478).
- The community supports these men and women throughout the process (RCIA, n. 403). Sponsors from the community accompany them and give witness for them (RCIA, n. 404, 482).
- The various periods of preparation are marked by liturgical rites, similar to those for the unbaptized, yet clearly noting the distinctions (RCIA, n. 405, 406, 407, 478). "Anything that would equate candidates for reception with those who are catechumens is to be absolutely avoided" (RCIA, n. 477).
- Prior to the celebration of reception, the candidate, according to his or her conscience, may celebrate the sacrament of reconciliation. It is advisable that the candidate inform the confessor that he or she is a candidate for full communion (RCIA, n. 483).

- Reception into full communion is usually celebrated at the Easter vigil through a profession of faith and celebration of confirmation and the eucharist (RCIA, n. 409). The priest who presides at the celebration of full communion has the faculty for confirming the candidate (RCIA, n. 481). If celebrated at another time, it is preferred that the reception into full communion occur within the celebration of the mass (RCIA, n. 475, 476).
- Baptism is not to be repeated. Only in the case of reasonable doubt concerning the fact or validity of the baptism should baptism be administered conditionally, and only after a full explanation is given to the candidate (RCIA, n. 480).

CANON LAW

At some point during the catechumenate process, the question of the appropriate role and function of canon law will need to be addressed, if for no other reason but that it is a reality in the life of the church.

The Code of Canon Law makes explicit reference to the RCIA in various sections. It will be helpful to see, within the context of the law of the church, the responsibility of the church to provide a full and adequate formation process.

- Full Christian sacramental initiation requires the celebration of baptism, confirmation, and eucharist (canon 842 par. 2, 866).
- Adults desiring baptism are to enter the catechumenate process (canon 851 n. 1). They are to be prepared through liturgical rites, instructed in the truths of the faith, and formed to a life in accordance with gospel values (canons 788 par. 1 and 2, 851 n. 1, and 865 par. 1).
- Children of catechetical age preparing for baptism are to follow the same process (appropriately adapted) as adults (canon 852 par. 1).
- Sponsors must be fully initiated members of the church who are leading the Catholic way of life (canon 874 par. 1).
- A sponsor or godparent of another Christian denomination may be admitted as a witness only if there is also a Catholic sponsor or godparent (canon 874 par. 2).
- A catechumen has the right to a Christian burial (canon 1183 par. 1). When two catechumens are married, or when a catechumen marries an unbaptized person, the appropriate rites are to be used (cf. RCIA

n. 47, *Rite of Marriage,* nos. 55–66, "Rite for celebrating marriage between a Catholic and an unbaptised person").

- Those who are fully in communion with the Catholic Church are those baptized persons who express this intention within the structures of the church through profession of faith, participation in the sacramental life, and adherence to ecclesiastic governance, i.e. union with the hierarchy (canon 205).
- The Code does not specify procedure for those already baptized and preparing for full communion. The norms established in the 1986 ritual edition of the RCIA are to be invoked. Their baptism in another Christian community is to be recognized and respected (canon 869 par. 2).
- Those already baptized can be admitted to the sacraments of penance, eucharist and anointing under certain circumstances (canon 844 par. 3).
- The norms established with the rites of the church retain their force unless they are contrary to the Code (canon 2). Hence, the liturgical norms established and approved in the RCIA are supported by the Code of Canon Law.

CELEBRATING THE SACRAMENT
OF RECONCILIATION

The period of purification and illumination has as one of its goals the purification of the minds and hearts of the elect. The scrutinies help reveal the attitudes and actions that inform the heart. Inevitably the experience of and reflection on the scrutinies raises the question of sin and evil. For the elect, the experience of baptism will be, among other things, an experience of the forgiveness of sin. The candidates for confirmation and eucharist, who also share in the scrutinies or in a penitential rite similar to the scrutinies, also deal with the question of sin and evil, especially within the context of their fidelity to their baptismal covenant.

Candidates for confirmation and eucharist are encouraged to consider the possibility of celebrating the sacrament of reconciliation prior to their completion of sacramental initiation. If they choose this option, some basic catechesis for the sacrament will need to be done in order to help prepare the candidates. They can be encouraged to participate in a parish communal penitential service so they can experience and reflect on the communal dimension of sin and forgiveness. When they participate in private confession, they can explain to the confessor that they are preparing to celebrate confirmation and eucharist. After the experience of sacramental reconciliation, the candidate will need the opportunity to reflect back on the experience and discover some of the richer dimensions of the sacrament that can only be experienced. This reflection can be done with the group (although not everyone will have had the experience), with one's sponsor, or with a member of the catechumenate team.

PREPARING FOR INITIATION AND MARRIAGE

The process for sacramental initiation is an intense period of formation in faith. Often people come to the RCIA because of their intention to marry a Catholic and the desire to share a common faith. The process of preparing for marriage, just as with the RCIA, is a long and intense formation process. Marriage preparation makes a great deal of demands on the couple — explicitly and implicitly. Explicitly, there are the variety of arrangements ranging from participation in marriage preparation sessions, working out various dimensions of the married life (such as budget, where to live, and so on), and the arrangements for the wedding itself. Implicitly, there are a variety of changes and challenges that the couple — as individuals and as a couple — need to deal with prior to the formal marriage ceremony. The demands of loving, sharing life, surrendering some dimension of autonomy, and the necessary growing that happens as love deepens to the level of a life commitment — all of this is rather intense and demands a lot of time and energy.

Both experiences, preparing for full sacramental initiation and preparing for marriage, require a high level of commitment, time and dedication to the formation necessary to prepare oneself for the witness of celebrating the sacrament. Therefore, it seems pastorally prudent not to enroll individuals in the RCIA process who are also preparing for marriage. As we discourage children from preparing for reconciliation and eucharist at the same time — albeit for different reasons — the same fundamental insight that each sacramental celebration demands the necessary time and focus for preparation also holds true here. Often the experience of preparing for marriage and full sacramental initiation is overwhelming. In such circumstances, it seems more helpful to the individual to encourage that he or she give fully to the process of preparing for marriage, and then, after having had a chance to celebrate God's presence in matrimony, begin the process for full sacramental initiation.

ANNULMENTS

One of the difficult dimensions of the catechumenate process is working with members of the RCIA who will need to enter into the annulment process. This is difficult because it requires entering into what is often a painful discussion early in the relationship. Once the formal annulment process has begun, however, it oftens becomes a period of healing for the individual. If the individual is a catechumen (i.e. unbaptized), then the possibility of the Pauline or Petrine privileges (to be discussed below) might apply. These are dissolutions of the marriage bond in favor of the practice of the faith.

It is helpful for team members to be aware of some basic issues concerning annulments. An annulment is the formal declaration that a marriage was never a sacramental union. It does not claim there was no marriage — but that there was no sacramental marriage. Therefore, this does not affect the children; they are now not suddenly illegitimate. In order for someone to petition for an annulment, he or she must have already received a civil divorce.

People who are divorced and remarried (without the previous marriage being annulled) are not excommunicated from the church. This penalty, which originated in 1884 and existed only in the United States, was removed by the United States bishops in 1977.

The pastoral minister will need to place the annulment question within the larger picture before beginning the process with the catechumen. Is the person already remarried? Does the person plan to enter into a new marriage, especially in the near future? How recent was the experience of the divorce? It seems pastorally sensitive to give the catechumen the time needed for some preliminiary healing from a recent divorce. Unless it is absolutely necessary, the annulment process can be addressed at a later time.

Without diminishing the uniqueness of the marriage relationship, there are some basic situations that can help the team determine the need to discuss the necessity for an annulment. An annulment of a marriage will be needed before the individual can enter into another marriage (or, in the case of one who is already involved in a second marriage, for that marriage to be recognized as valid) if there was a previous valid marriage (from which there is a civil divorce). The annulment process helps to determine if the marriage was indeed valid and, hence, still binding. The Catholic Church acknowledges all valid marriages — civil or religious — to be binding. The marriage between Christians is considered potentially sacramental. Therefore men and women who are divorced and plan to remarry (or are remarried) who are entering the Catholic community, either through baptism or a profession of faith, will need to enter the annulment process.

The following situations can help clarify whether there will be the need to begin the annulment process for a particular individual. Of course, it is presumed that the individual is presently divorced. However, for clarity's sake, we will list the situations in terms of the previous marriage relationship. The first spouse mentioned will be the catechumen or candidate.

Unbaptized person married to unbaptized person: Annulment needed. The catechumen could also investigate the possibility of the Pauline privilege. The Pauline privilege, a privilege of the faith, is when both parties are unbaptized (and hence there is no sacramental marriage because a sacramental marriage presumes baptism). This bond can be dissolved in favor of the newly baptized person entering into a sacramental marriage (cf. Code of Canon Law, canons 1143–1147).

Unbaptized person married to baptized Christian (not Catholic): Annulment needed. The catechumen could also investigate the possibility of the Petrine privilege. The Petrine privilege, another privilege of the faith, refers to the marriage between a Christian and an unbaptized person. If the marriage is consummated after the unbaptized person becomes a Christian, then this cannot be invoked. If the conditions exist for the dissolution, however, then the case has to be sent to Rome.

Unbaptized person married to Catholic in Catholic service: Annulment needed.

Unbaptized person married to Catholic in other than Catholic service (with no permission of bishop): No annulment is needed because there never was a valid marriage in terms of Catholic "form." Catholic form is a marriage in the presence of a delegated Catholic priest before two witnesses. The only exception to this is when the bishop grants permission to be married before a minister, usually during what is called an interfaith marriage. If this form is lacking in a marriage where one or both partners is Catholic, there is no valid marriage.

Baptized person married to unbaptized or baptized Christian (not a Catholic) in either a civil or religious service: Annulment needed.

Baptized person married to Catholic in Catholic service: Annulment needed.

Baptized person married to Catholic in other than Catholic service (with no permission of bishop): No annulment is needed because there never was a valid marriage in terms of Catholic "form" (see the discussion above on Catholic form).

The grounds for an annulment fall into four basic categories: formal cases, documentary cases, privilege or dissolution cases, and other general grounds that don't fall into the previously mentioned categories. It will be necessary for the individual to dialogue with a member of the pastoral team to determine initially the probability of the annulment process. However, the team should always feel free to contact the tribunal for guidance in cases that seem complex. Eventually, all petitions for annulments are handled by the diocesan tribunal.

The grounds for annulment through formal cases prove that there never existed a sacramental union in the marriage. These fall into three categories: psychological, simulation of consent, or force and fear. Psychological grounds attempt to show a lack of due discretion or of due competence. Some examples include: lacking in sufficient use of reason; intoxication, alcoholism or drug addiction at time of marriage; and immaturity. Simulation of consent is the conscious decision at the time of the marriage to place conditions on the marriage consent, such as entering marriage only to avoid the draft or to give a child a name. Other examples include the expressed intention of not remaining faithful to one's partner or the refusal of children. Force and fear would limit the ability of the individual to make a free and full consent — for example, the typical "shotgun" wedding, or someone choosing to get married at an early age because she is pregnant.

The second set of grounds are called documentary cases. These fall into two categories: defect of form and previous bond. Defect of form refers to the lack of the proper Catholic form for the marriage. This only applies to weddings that include at least one Catholic. The necessary procedures can be handled locally. Previous bond means that if it can be proven that the spouse had indeed entered a valid marriage prior to the marriage in case, then the marriage in case is invalid (and no annulment is needed).

The third set of grounds is called dissolution and is invoked either through privileges of the faith or because of nonconsummation. In terms of privileges of the faith, there presently exists two options: the Pauline privilege and the Petrine privilege. Both of these have already been described above. Nonconsummation — that the marriage was never consummated in sexual intercourse — needs to be petitioned through Rome.

There are other grounds for annulments: lack of the age of consent, impotence, forced marriage, one person in canonical orders or vows, murder of former spouse to marry the present one, fraud, and so on.

One final note. When helping a catechumen apply for an annulment, it is often in the best interest of the catechumen not to petition for the annulment under any specific grounds. Then the tribunal will be forced to evaluate the case only in terms of those petitioned grounds. Rather, allow the tribunal to assess the case and propose the appropriate direction the case needs to go. Whatever the situation, however, the pastoral minister will need to be sensitive to the various avenues for healing available through the pastoral care of the church.

VALIDATION OF MARRIAGE

The validation of a marriage (or, more technically correct, the convalidation) is the act of making valid a marriage union. There are two situations wherein the need to convalidate a marriage would affect a catechumen or candidate for full communion. The first is if the spouse of the catechumen or candidate is Catholic but they were not married in a Catholic service (or had received the permission of the bishop for an interfaith service). The second is if the catechumen or candidate is in a second marriage and the first one is annulled. The annulment nullifies the previous bond and allows the present marriage to be recognized as valid.

FINANCIAL SUPPORT OF THE CHURCH

Should the catechumens and candidates contribute to the financial support of the church? Do we enroll them in the "envelope" system? What is at question here is not whether we should be asking the catechumens to give money (after all, they leave before the collection basket is passed) but how we help facilitate appropriate expressions of tithing.

Tithing is larger than giving money. It is one dimension of responsible stewardship. Stewardship is the manner in which we integrate two key Christian concepts: all that we have is gift from God, and the responsibility to care for the little ones in the world community. Stewardship is the responsible use of our resources — time (probably today the premium resource), talent, and treasure — that reflects these basic Christian values. Stewardship recognizes that all we have is given for the full body, for the whole human community. In particular, it is meant to help those marginalized — the little ones — who have no power, few resources, and are dependent only on God for their life. Stewardship is a concrete enfleshment of the preferential option for the poor.

It is no secret that the structures of life have become more complicated. Time is the premium resource we can offer to others. Often monetary assistance is the way to avoid giving of my valuables — myself and my time. Such giving of money is not necessarily tithing. Tithing is giving from one's want, from one's substance, not one's surplus. Tithing is not a matter of convenience. It is a matter of sacrifice.

Thus, we need to turn the question around. Is it appropriate to encourage stewardship in the catechumenate? Yes. The specifics of that stewardship will differ for each person. Within this context, however, it makes sense that one dimension of this stewardship will be financial tithing to help support the works of the parish community.

One last reflection. If tithing is a value for the individual Christian — one dimension of responsible stewardship — and the Christian community (or parish) is one locus of formation for Christian life and celebration, then it seems appropriate that the parish itself become a tithing parish. We teach and form people by the way we live life. If the parish is generous not only from its surplus, but also from its substance, then we will be making a clear and direct statement about the value and place of tithing. As we are inviting the catechumens to experience a church larger than their RCIA gatherings, we as parish need to recognize the needs of the church and the world larger than our parish community.

DEVOTION TO MARY AND THE SAINTS

Devotion to Mary and the saints is a part of the life of the Catholic community. At various times in our history — and for various reasons — this devotion has been distorted with grave implications. Without appropriate guidance and direction, devotion to Mary and the saints can shift to God-like proportions. Mary becomes the primary focus of prayer and devotion. The saints become the primary mediators of grace. Something is fundamentally wrong when the consciousness of God's presence and love is dwarfed by a piety that is fixated on Mary or the saints.

With Vatican Council II, there has been a dramatic shift in the church's understanding of Mary. Mary is seen as a symbol or type of the church, the pre-eminent member of the church. In the Dogmatic Constitution on the Church, the council declares that Mary belongs *in* the church and not be treated as a separate doctrine that says she is *above* the church. With a return to the ancient sources of the community, the council declares Mary as the symbol of Christian discipleship. (cf. *Lumen Gentium,* n. 8 and Chapter VIII). In the Constitution on the Liturgy, the council declares that the church sees in Mary that which the church desires and hopes to be (*Sacrosanctum concilium,* n. 103).

Pope Paul VI, in his 1974 apostolic exhoration on Mary entitled *Marialis Cultis,* gives five sets of principles that should govern our understanding of and devotion to Mary — and, by extension, to the saints: theological, biblical, liturgical, ecumenical and anthropological.

Theological: This falls into three basic categories: trinitarian, christological, and ecclesiological. Marian devotion must have a trinitarian reference or else Mary assumes God-like proportions. It must place Mary in a subordinate role to Christ who alone is the savior and mediator. And, lastly, it must never disconnect Mary from the church, for she typifies the church and discipleship.

Biblical: Marian piety must be rooted in an authentic biblical witness that proclaims the reign of God. While the Christian scriptures tells us little about Mary, one thing is clear: she hears the gospel proclaimed to her (the annunciation) and accepts it. When we look at the ministry of Jesus, we discover that the disciple is the one who hears the word of God and keeps it. Mary is described as one who does this. The testimony of the Christian scriptures gives witness to Mary's faith as a disciple.

Mary is also a singer of the song of justice. When we turn to the beautiful Magnificat, we hear placed in Mary's mouth the proclamation of God's justice to the poor as one of the poor.

Liturgical: In terms of all piety and prayer, the liturgy is the norm. We remember Mary and the saints — and the wider church — in the eucharistic prayer, and then praise God in their company. Devotions are extra and secondary to the liturgical life of the community. Devotions to Mary are only important if they lead to fuller discipleship.

Ecumenical: The practice of faith is to God alone. In the midst of this, there is solidarity in the church — the communion of saints — by whom we are accompanied on this journey of faith. In this context, we call upon Mary to accompany us. The focus remains on God.

Anthropological: This raises the question of the changing role of women, as well as a critique on the traditional image of Mary as passive which has been used to reinforce the passivity and domesticity of women. We need to recast the symbol of Mary within her biblical roots so she can be model of discipleship for both men and women. When we turn back to the biblical literature, Mary gives an active and responsible assent in the annunciation. She is intelligent enough to ask questions. She very vigorously proclaims God's justice for the oppressed. And she is imaged as a woman who is courageous in many situations, especially the cross. There is no timidity or submissiveness in Mary. She is a woman of strength and suffering; she lives life as a pilgrimage of faith.

The natural time to include catechesis on Mary and the saints would be at the time of the great feasts of Mary (Mary, Mother of God, the Assumption, the Immaculate Conception), and various celebrations of the saints, such as All Saints. A "saint of the week" reflection could be included regularly during the catechetical gathering (perhaps as part of the prayer) to highlight the life of a saint whose feast will be celebrated during the week.

INITIATION OF CHILDREN

The RCIA provides a model of initiation for unbaptized children who have reached catechetical age (RCIA, n. 252f). The ritual follows the process for adults with appropriate adaptations for children. Following are some principles that may prove to be useful in forming a process for the initiation of children.

- Although the term RCIC has become popular (Rite of Christian Initiation of Children), technically it is incorrect. The rite entitled "Christian Initiation of Children Who Have Reached Catechetical Age" is one rite within the larger RCIA. Therefore, the theology and vision of the RCIA informs the praxis for children.
- Provision is made for the joint celebration of sacraments for unbaptized and baptized children completing sacramental initiation who are in the same catechetical group (RCIA, n. 308). This presumes that the children preparing for baptism are enrolled in a catechetical program with peers in addition to the catechesis for sacramental initiation.
- Prior to enrollment in the catechumenate process, the coordinator will need to meet with the parents or guardian of the child. They will need to know the expectations and responsibilities of parents in preparing children for sacraments. This may become a "teachable moment" for the parents. They can be encouraged to take advantage

of adult enrichment and formation programs available in the parish.

- The sponsors and catechists will need to be carefully chosen. It is important that they have a familiarity with the initiation process, as well as an ability to effectively communicate with children.
- Children preparing for initiation need to gather for catechesis appropriate to their age. This would suggest that when there is a large difference in age — such as children who are seven or eight and children who are twelve or thirteen — it might be helpful to them to work with them separately. One possibility is to have all the children together for part of the catechetical gathering, and then break off into age groups for a period of integration.
- As with the adults, the children can be dismissed from the Sunday assembly for their own experience of breaking open the word of God. If the Mass the children are attending is not focused for children, perhaps it may be appropriate to dismiss the children for a children's liturgy of the word and catechesis.
- The structure of the initiation process is similar to adult initiation. There is the acceptance into the order of catechumens. Oddly enough, the rite of election is listed as optional, which raises some theological questions. During the period of final preparation, the rite gives guidelines for celebrations of penitential rites. These penitential rites are similar to the scrutinies. They are constructed, however, to include baptized children preparing for reconciliation, the celebration of which follows the dismissal of the catechumens. The final step is the celebration of the initiation sacraments of baptism, confirmation and eucharist.
- Sensitivity and care must be used when preparing the public rituals. If children are prepared for ritual celebration — and part of that preparing is appropriate and effective ritual celebrations during catechesis — then it is more often the case that they will be comfortable celebrating the rites of initiation during the community's celebrations.
- The language of the ritual text provided will need to be adapted for the particular age group of children, as well as their particular circumstances.
- Celebration of the sacraments of initiation takes place at the Easter vigil. However, for pastoral reasons — such as the time of the vigil or the number of adults being initiated — the pastoral team may determine to shift the time of initiation for the children to Easter Sunday morning.

INITIATION OF ADOLESCENTS

The initiation of adolescents, while similar to the process for children and adults, needs to be done separately because of the age and circumstances of the adolescents. They are too old to be affiliated with the children's process, and too young to appreciate the adult formation process. It is recommended that, with their peers, the issues of adolescence can be more effectively integrated within the Catholic vision of life. The incorporation of a peer ministry as well as other youth ministries is appropriate during this process. The ritual texts will need to be adapted for these adolescents. If the decision is made to celebrate the rituals with either the children or adults, the preference should be made for celebration with the adults.

INFORMATION FOR SACRAMENTAL BOOKS

Sometime during the catechumenate process, it will be necessary to get the information needed to be recorded in the sacramental books of the parish. While this may not seem terribly necessary in the scheme of things, this information will be useful at a later time for the catechumen when a copy of the baptismal certificate is needed for some reason or another.

The following information is usually needed for the register for baptism (this would be for the catechumens). A notation needs to be included that they celebrated all the sacraments of initiation.

Full name:
Date of birth:
City of birth:
Present residence:
Father's name:
Mother's maiden name:
Godparent 1:
Is Godparent 1 Catholic?:
Godparent 2:
Is Godparent 2 Catholic?:

Candidates for full communion in the Catholic Church will need the same information (though instead of godparent, they supply the sponsor information) with the following addition:

Date of baptism:
Church of baptism:
Location of church:

EVALUATION

Evaluating the RCIA experience is important feedback for the RCIA team. Periodically, there can be evaluations by participants regarding the catechetical gatherings, the experience of the rituals, and the catechesis on the rituals. The various ministries can also spend some time evaluating their experience of the RCIA.

All of these evaluations (preferably written ones) can then be reviewed by the RCIA team periodically for future planning and development. The evaluation process needs to be a regularly scheduled dimension of the process.

12

Presiding at Prayer

INTRODUCTION

One of the many important developments which has come from the implementation of the Rite of Christian Initiation of Adults has been the number of lay women and men who have assumed roles of leadership in prayer. Days of prayer, catechetical sessions, presentations of the Creed and the Lord's Prayer, scrutinies — all of these are examples of the prayer settings in which catechists and coordinators of catechumenate programs find themselves serving the community as the presider of worship. Yet many lay leaders consider themselves unprepared to serve the community in this capacity. There is an honesty and wisdom in such reservations. We can all recall presiders who distracted rather than drew us into the experience of prayer. The ministry of presiding at prayer is, in a special sense, an art.

These reflections are intended to offer some guidelines for presiding at prayer, especially for lay women and men who have not had the opportunity for formal training in liturgical celebration. Along with concrete suggestions, these reflections hope to raise some of the underlying attitudes we bring to celebration. Simply knowing the actions and words does not necessarily constitute leadership in prayer. There is another level of awareness where the art of attentiveness to the Spirit is cultivated.

PERSONAL EXPERIENCE

One of the richest resources we have for developing the art and ministry of presiding can be found in our own experience of prayer. Take a few moments and reflect on these questions:

■ Recall a good experience of celebration. What were the qualities of the leader of prayer?

- Recall a poor experience of celebration. What words or images describe the style of the presider?
- What are the gifts you bring to leadership in prayer?
- What are your areas of concern, areas which need to be developed?
- What are your fears?
- What do you need to help you in this aspect of your ministry?

Naming these qualities, gifts, fears, and needs can help you begin to focus on the question of presiding at prayer and aid your own development as a minister of prayer.

SOME FOUNDATIONAL ISSUES

Presiding at prayer is a ministry of responsibility, not a right or privilege one attains. This service to the community demands some basic skills and, more importantly, a basic awareness of one's role within the context of the community. We will address three important foundational issues which can either educate or prejudice our attitudes toward celebration: ministry, personal identity, and the role of presider.

(1) *Ministry:* The majority of our experience of leadership in worship is from ordained clergy. And that is appropriate since one of the primary roles of the ordained clergy is to lead the community in worship. However, one disadvantage to this may be the development of a view that leadership in prayer is the exclusive role of the ordained. We are all too familiar with people who believe the church is primarily the direction given by the clergy. The RCIA, however, gives us a different vision of church: all the initiated are called to serve the mission of the reign of God. It is the entire community, with its levels of differentiation, which is named church. And it is from this sense of mission, this sense of commitment that we recognize the diverse ministries in the community. It is the community who is the celebrant at worship. This is facilitated by appropriate pastoral leadership. In some instances, this leadership will not be from an ordained person.

(2) *Personal Identity:* Christian personal identity is rooted in the Christian revelation of God. God-present-with-us: empowering, forgiving, ennobling. Leadership in prayer calls the presider to be rooted in this gifted presence of God, to be at home with who he or she is, to be a prayerful person. True self-knowledge stands at the heart of the spirit-

ual life. Such self-knowledge is also important for leadership in prayer. Our service to the community as leaders of prayer reflects our honest struggle as praying people. There is a transparency to the experience of presiding. There needs to be some relationship between what our words and actions say and our experience of God. This relationship will be evident to the community. It is the honest awareness of one's giftedness and limitations that enables one to lead prayer rather than perform prayer.

(3) *Role of the Presider:* One important dimension of Christian revelation is this: God is always faithful. When we gather for prayer or to celebrate sacrament, God is present. Our concern, then, is not with God's side of the experience because we know of God's fidelity. Rather, our concern is with our side of the experience, our response in faith. The presider's role is to help the community respond to the presence of God. The presider serves the community by raising the questions, highlighting the journey, and gathering our prayer. It is God who invites us to give that which we thought we could not give, not the presider. The presider is servant, but servant with an important responsibility. Having relevant rituals is not enough. Presiding is the art of calling forth the community's awareness of God-present-with-us. The following guidelines for presiding at prayer are intended to help develop this art.

SOME GUIDELINES FOR PRESIDING AT PRAYER

I. PLANNING THE PRAYER

1. The liturgical rites and prayerbooks provide a framework and structure for the prayer. Time with the texts provides the necessary enfleshment of the words. The presider at any worship needs to plan with the texts well in advance of the celebration. Going in cold is a disservice (and betrays a certain attitude). This planning includes having a general sense of the movement, structure and flow of the entire service.

2. Know the meaning of the texts. This can only come by spending time with the texts. The presider need not be glued to the book when leading prayer. Sometimes we suffer from a rigid literalism when it comes to liturgical texts. It is more important to know the movement and structure of the prayer experience.

3. Adapt the text to meet the pastoral circumstances. Again and again in the RCIA we read the words "adapt to local circumstances" (cf. RCIA, 35). So, by all means, adapt. Adaptation does not mean change for change's sake. Adaptation means being aware of the needs of the gathered community and then working with the texts to serve that community. Adaptation does not mean minimalism ("They're not ready for this yet") but does mean sensitivity to what will call and challenge the community beyond the status quo.

4. Incorporate planned spontaneity. Spontaneity in prayer leadership does not mean "winging it" during the celebration. The longest, least intelligible, and often most boring prayers come from leaders of prayer who make up the prayer on the spot. If you are choosing to diverge from the prepared text, prepare for it. This does not mean memorizing new texts or becoming a slave to the new prayers you wrote. But it does mean having a sense already of the direction of the prayer and the essential elements of the prayer. In spontaneity, brevity is your best ally.

5. Know your space. Whenever possible, it is helpful to spend time walking around the worship space. Get a sense of where you will be, where others will be. Arrange the worship space to enhance community, not isolation. The focus of worship is God-present-with-us, not the presider. Remember that when you plan where you will be during the prayer. Take the time to acquaint yourself with the speaker system. Don't let the worship time be the first time you've heard yourself using the microphones. Learn the best way to be heard in the space provided.

6. Know the people. Much of what has been said presumes some basic knowledge of the people you will be praying with. The RCIA demands the leader of prayer to have a personal awareness of the conversion journey of the catechumens in order to honestly incorporate their stories into the ritual. Good liturgical leadership demands good pastoral presence.

7. Plan with other ministers. The RCIA rituals will include the ministry of sponsors, catechists and the community. Perhaps there will be liturgical dance, or a symbolic interpretation of the Creed. You will need to know the music and how it holds the worship experience together. As leader of prayer, it is your responsibility to coordinate the various ministries during the prayer experience. You need to know who is doing what, when and where. And you need to know this well in advance of the celebration so you can include this in your attempt to create a wholistic vision of the prayer gathering before you call the community to prayer.

II. PERSONAL AWARENESS

1. The presider needs to be aware of personal limitations and gifts. And she or he must utilize those gifts for the community.

2. It can't be said enough that the personal perception of one's role as presider will dictate how one presides. The presider is a facilitator, an enabler, a sustainer of renewal, and, most importantly, one of the community.

3. Presiders who have given ample time to preparing for the prayer experience can be confident in their prayer leadership. Confidence, however, does not mean freedom from stress. One rarely ever becomes totally comfortable in prayer leadership. There is always some nervousness or anxiety. These stressors provide the cutting edge for creative worship. The energy present can heighten our presence with the community. Yet it is also important to recognize when these stressors become debilitating. At that time, one will need to reevaluate the appropriateness of liturgical leadership.

4. The presider needs to have a basic awareness of what is happening inside of himself or herself. Prayerful time needs to be spent to recognize and name feelings and concerns which construct our personal awareness at a particular time. If it is possible, the presider can strive to come to some resolution of conflict before the prayer experience. Realistically, that is not always possible. However, being aware of one's own agenda keeps one from imposing it on others. Leadership in prayer, especially if it includes some homily or meditation reflection, is not the place to burden the community with one's own concerns and issues. Of course, there are exceptions to this, and the leader of prayer knows when it is appropriate to disclose personal issues which enhance the building of the community.

5. The leader of prayer needs to be familiar and comfortable with his or her body. This includes an awareness of one's voice: cadence, inflection, tone, and volume. Other factors to be mindful of are one's hands and how one uses them, gestures, posture, eye-contact, how one walks, and so on. Christian prayer is incarnational: it recognizes God who became flesh. Good leadership is incarnational: it recognizes God present in the full person.

6. Know how to use your body. Practice gestures. Walk through the prayer experience. Practice raising the lectionary without hitting the microphone. Become comfortable extending your arms in prayer. Watch yourself in a mirror. Practice being graceful with body gestures.

7. Pray the ritual out loud several times. Hear how your voice plays with the poetry of the prayer. Sense the rhythm. Sing the text. Try

it a number of ways. Experiment with a variety of presentations. These exercises also help you to become more familiar with the texts.

III. DURING THE CELEBRATION

1. Personal grooming and appearance are very important. Allow yourself the necessary time so that you don't look as though you just ran in off the street (and, hopefully, you haven't). Liturgical dress may be appropriate during certain RCIA rites, such as presentations or scrutinies. There are some who prefer lay leaders of prayer not to vest. Others hold that since the alb is a baptismal garment, it is an appropriate vestment for lay leadership in prayer. However you dress, be tasteful so as not to distract by drawing attention to yourself.

2. Your body (and how aware you are of your body) is an important communicator. Use simple gestures, but be sure they are full and graceful. People will need to see you from a distance. When signing your body with the cross at the beginning of prayer, do just that. While you may think your gestures are exaggerated, the person in the back of the assembly will be grateful to see them. Allow your body to help create an atmosphere of prayer. When you sit, sit attentively rather than slouching in the chair. When you stand, avoid swaying back and forth. Don't rush your movements. At various times you may want to calm yourself through deep breathing.

3. How you use your voice will be an important factor in the prayer experience. Therefore, in order to be intelligible, you will need to speak slowly, clearly and loudly. Experimentation earlier with the speaker system will help you to gauge your volume and closeness to the microphone. Familiarity with the texts will help with the flow of your speech. Avoid the two extremes of being monotone and of extreme variations in speech.

4. How you are present during the prayer is important because of your role of leadership. When there is singing, sing (but not into the microphone). When there is a reading, watch the reader and listen. When there is a witnessing, be present to the person. During periods of meditation, give yourself the permission to do just that. Spending the necessary time planning before the prayer experience should free you up to be present to the prayer experience.

5. As presider, you help establish the sense of hospitality and welcome within the community. Worship, while sacred, does not have to be (and should not be) sterile and somber. Throughout the prayer experience, consciously choose to help create a warm environment of hospitality and prayer by what you say and do. When you lead prayer,

respect the participants by looking at them. The same goes for preaching. There is nothing in the rituals that says the presider must appear
somber. In fact, looking into the eyes of the community can enhance
your leadership.

6. The ritual prayers and readings need to be housed in books or
folders that tell the community: "This is important." A leather-bound
folder can serve nicely to hold your written prayers. Fumbling through
missalettes or having loose papers around sends a clear message to the
community. You can facilitate the flow of worship by having the texts
clearly marked, in order, and neatly contained.

7. In the midst of it all, surrender to the prayer. Allow yourself to
simply be in the prayer with the community. The first times at presiding
are the most difficult times. We are self-conscious, nervous, wanting to
make sure everything is just so. Eventually we all learn that the ritual
has a life of its own. We help navigate, not control. Good navigation,
however, means knowing the map beforehand.

13

Spiritual Direction
and the RCIA

INTRODUCTION

An important question that is being raised again and again in catechumenates is this: Do we encourage the catechumens to engage in spiritual direction? As we will briefly explore, the ministry of spiritual direction is an important (and, I believe, essential) dimension of Christian life. The recent shift in the renewal of spirituality and lay ministry formation has unveiled the large numbers of people who are seeking companionship in the spiritual life through the process of spiritual direction. Yet the catechumen already has developed unique relationships of companionship with the catechumenate team, sponsors, godparents, and the local community itself. In light of this, what is the role of spiritual direction in the RCIA?

Do we encourage the catechumens to engage in spiritual direction? The answer, as with many questions on the catechumenate process, is yes and no. The decision for spiritual direction is a personal choice on the part of the individual catechumen; it cannot be forced (unlike the prevailing model in ministry formation situations which require the candidates to engage in spiritual direction). For some catechumens, the formational process of the RCIA provides the adequate guidance and support the individual needs at this particular point on the journey. Others will desire to explore in more depth their questions and searchings. For these individuals, a spiritual director may be a helpful complement to the RCIA formation process.

It is strongly encouraged that the team raise the issue of spiritual direction for the catechumens, either individually or as a group. This would help the catechumens to know that there is additional support for the journey if they would desire some at this time. More importantly, it would help to prepare the catechumens for their full life in the community. The gift of spiritual direction needs to be available for all members of the community. The RCIA process has already begun to orient the catechumen in a particular way emphasizing the importance of personal prayer, reflection, discernment, and action. Spiritual direction serves as one formational dynamic to continue that process. The questions and concerns about spiritual direction, in many ways, are also applicable to the team and sponsors.

The following reflections are an expansion of one definition of spiritual direction. They are meant to provide material for the catechumenate team to understand more clearly this particular ministry in the church and the potential applications in the catechumenate process. Additionally, these reflections will help establish a particular posture or life agenda for both catechumens and team members concerning the importance of on-going companionship in the spiritual life.

CHRISTIAN SPIRITUAL DIRECTION

Christian spiritual direction has always held a special place in the Christian tradition. The letters of St. Paul can be seen in this context of spiritual guidance and formation. People followed the great "abbas" and "ammas" of the desert tradition in order that they might be enlightened by them. Bands of men and women gathered around charismatic figures — Benedict, Francis of Assisi, Clare of Assisi, Dominic, Catherine of Siena, John of the Cross, Teresa of Jesus, Ignatius Loyola, Francis de Sales — looking for direction, insight, hope for a deepened awareness of God. The same is true today. Men and women are seeking the face of God with the supportive guidance and insight from those gifted for the journey, spiritual directors.

WHAT IS SPIRITUAL DIRECTION? ONE DEFINITION

Christian spiritual direction (or accompaniment) is a dynamic and formative relationship in which an individual directee (or group) entrusts himself or herself to a director — a gifted, authentic and praying person who is honestly grappling with true life. The spiritual direction process develops in an atmosphere of trusting vulnerability where the director helps the directee to interpret and draw out deeper meanings from his or her life experience, thus helping the directee to sift through and come to some sense of a life direction in dialogue with God. This process, to be truly Christian, is rooted in the living Christian tradition and inevitably invites one to surrender in obedience (i.e. active listening) to God's gift of true freedom.

The need for spiritual direction is rooted in the Christian belief in God's continual self-revelation to all people. Spiritual direction is not the privilege of the few but an invitation for all to nurture this life-giving relationship with God. The process called spiritual direction serves to help one come to a heightened awareness of God's gifting presence, which calls each person to fuller personhood, to respond to one's fundamental vocation. Spiritual direction helps give focus to all the areas of one's life: Who is God for me in this and how do I experience myself in relationship to this God?

Spiritual direction is a dynamic process. One is always invited to explore more deeply the promptings of the Holy Spirit. As in all life, there is the ebb and flow, the intense moments and the stirrings, the crisis and the ordinary. All these moments potentially hold an invitation from God. Some of these moments require heightened awareness or attunement to the gift of life being offered. The question of frequency of visitation with another in the spiritual direction process will necessarily be a very individual question. There are periods of one's life which demand that the individual spend more time in direct accompaniment with a spiritual friend. At other times, one experiences less the intensity that calls forth such a relationship and is able to "sit with" her or his life experience of God. One must be cautioned, however, not to associate spiritual direction with crises. Rather, spiritual direction can be about all the seasons of one's life. Even in the calm of the mid-day, we are prone to self-deception. Sometimes, when the sun is at high noon, we are more in need of spiritual friendship because we can fail to see our shadow, we can fail to struggle for true self-knowledge.

UNPACKING THE DEFINITION: ELEMENTS OF SPIRITUAL DIRECTION

I. **"A Dynamic and Formative Relationship . . .":** The Christian tradition offers a wide variety of images and models of spiritual directors. Some of these images include father, mother, gardener, friend, mentor, companion, confessor, and guide. Such multiple and diverse images respect the wide variety of persons who are engaged in the spiritual direction process. Yet all of the images speak of some form of interpersonal relationship, suggesting the importance of the spiritual direction process emerging within the context of relationship and not as a passive acceptance of information by the directee. The images suggest some investment and involvement in the directee's life.

II. **"Entrusted to a Director, i.e. a Gifted, Authentic, Prayerful Person . . .":** The spiritual direction relationship is not a casual meeting of friends, though in such gatherings of friends much insight into the spiritual life can be gleaned. But our discussion has led us to see spiritual direction as a particular kind of relationship. Not all people are disposed to teaching, or administration, or management. The same is true for spiritual direction. While charity and good will provide a grounding for such accompaniment, the responsibility of the spiritual direction process necessitates that one be qualified to serve as a director.

What are the qualities of a spiritual director? Certainly, one will look for different things in people depending on one's particular life situation and life season. However, there seem to be some fundamental qualities that serve as a foundation for the spiritual direction process. We have already mentioned basic charity and good will as necessary gifts of a director. To complement these, a spiritual director must be committed to living life on all levels: physically, emotionally, psychologically, intellectually, and spiritually. In addition to this, the spiritual director must be a man or woman of prayer and the spiritual life. Because the director knows the struggle to articulate one's experience of God, she or he will have the sensitivity and care to walk slowly with another, knowing that the ways of God are rarely clear though always enriching. Such a director walks with compassion. The compassion comes not from knowing the ins and outs of the spiritual life but rather from a dedication to surrendering oneself to that very process. To complement this experiential dimension, a director needs to be informed of various academic disciplines that aid in the spiritual process: a good foundational theology, a healthy appreciation for the human sciences (in particular psychology), some exposure to a theology of prayer and spiritual development, some exposure to classical literature in spiritual development, and some basic listening skills with which one can facilitate another's struggle to articulate his or her relationship with God. This emphasis on training is not meant to bring spiritual direction into an elitist category. However, a human being lives in a complex web of relationships that demand a director to have at least some awareness of various way he or she can help the individual to articulate the presence of God in the midst of his or her life.

III. **"Develop in an Atmosphere of Trusting Vulnerability . . .":** There are no qualifications for one seeking spiritual direction other than a personal desire to come to an articulation of God's activity in one's life. However, there are certain elements that create an atmosphere that facilitate and enhance the spiritual direction process. Of special interest here are those elements which reflect the posture of the directee.

(1) MUTUALITY: The spiritual direction process is one of complementarity, of balancing, and not one of dominance or submission. The directee comes to the recognition that his or her search for God elicits certain gifts from the director to facilitate that journey.

(2) OPENNESS AND TRUST: A key dimension is the openness and trust that the director fosters in the relationship, helping the directee to be more vulnerable and self-disclosing. Various factors contribute to this establishment of trust, ranging from the physical environment of the gathering place to the care and consideration exhibited by the director. In this caring environment, the directee is free to entrust his or her experiences, fears, hopes, dreams, and questions — all that contributes to the fabric of one's life. An incarnational theological perspective affirms the importance of all dimensions of life as being moments of God. The directee comes to experience the reverential respect given to his or her life by the director and, as a result, slowly becomes willing to further break open areas of his or her life for deepened reflection.

Another important facet of trust and openness is insight into self-deception. A director helps to bring focus, to raise the God questions that a directee often fails to recognize. A directee needs to ask himself or herself the hard questions when he or she chooses not to disclose certain areas or issues of life. Spiritual direction is not psychotherapy or counseling. However, the same "stuff" of one's life needs to be raised and explored from the distinct dimension of the God-focus in order to come to know God's stirrings. Such honest and frank disclosure also helps the director to situate the isolated moments of a directee's life within the context of the larger story of one's life.

(3) CONFESSIONAL: There is a confessional character to the spiritual direction relationship, especially for the directee. However, this confession is not to be confused with the popular and narrow sense of confession associated with the sacrament of reconciliation. That understanding of confession is usually a list of sins and grievances for which the penitent is sorry and seeks forgiveness. The focus is on the sinfulness. Rather, the confessional character of spiritual direction is more in keeping with the root meaning of *confessio:* to give praise. Augustine's *Confessions* are a good example of this richer understanding of this dimension of spiritual development. The *confessio* is the deep recognition of one's life (attitudes, orientations, actions), of true self-knowledge leading to the awareness of one's giftedness and one's

failure to be responsible for those very gifts to enable loving relationships, especially with God. This posture is coupled with the reverent awareness of God's forgiving and all-consuming love. This leads to gratitude, to thanksgiving, and to praise: the confession may be in the stillness of silence or may be given voice. In whatever form, the *confessio* is a sacrament-moment. In the process of spiritual direction, the directee oftens comes to this moment of holy insight.

IV. **"Helps the Directee To Interpret and Draw Out Deeper Meaning . . .":** The director has an interpretive role in the direction process. He or she is open enough to receive the gift offered by the directee, to allow it to speak within the context of the individual's life history as well as to explore the invitations to a deepened sense of God and self, and then to reflect back such insights to the directee. Hopefully, this process enables the directee to make connections, to address certain questions and issues, and to glean new insights. The director is not offering new advice or encouraging his or her own particular pattern of spiritual development. Rather, the director listens to the deeper truths that emerge from the directee's life, dreams, hopes, concerns, fears, and prayer. In short, the director is helping the directee pay attention to God.

The director, then, provides the directee with some form of interpretation. The director listens to the patterns being formed, the connections being made (or not being made), and suggests possible meanings in the statements or reflections of the directee. Indeed, spiritual direction is an art that needs the same care and patience as any art. The director desires to free the directee from a myopic vision of his or her life in order to see the larger picture. The director helps the directee to stand back from the painting of his or her life to see the various colors, textures, and movements within the larger context. The director's task is to help the directee to rewrite the story of his or her life from a new focus — to see and explore the movement of God within the total weaving of one's life — and thus to come to a new sense of self in relationship to God.

V. **"Sift Through Life To Come to a Life-Direction in Dialogue with God . . .":** One facet of the spiritual direction process is spiritual discernment. Discernment is basically the sifting through of life experiences and options in order to come to some fundamental perception of a life direction (i.e. who is God calling me to be and how can I best respond?). This process necessitates that one probe his or her heart to find the true self (the person we are gifted to be by God) and then to make choices that are authentic to that self. Discernment, then, is about making choices. True discernment leads one to an honest choice for life, for deeper congruence. Yet we can also use the term discernment to speak of the daily process of life decision-making.

VI. **"Rooted in the Living Christian Tradition . . .":** The spiritual director does not stand on his or her own authority. Rather, he or she is empowered for ministry through the gift of the Holy Spirit, mediated within human experience and, in particular, the Christian community and tradition. Therefore, the spiritual director cannot stand as a private interpreter, an individual sage or guru who stands apart from the community. The spiritual director needs to confirm the authenticity of his or her testimony with the orthodoxy and orthopraxis of the Christian tradition.

The Christian tradition is a living tradition and, hence, the spiritual director views his or her ministry from the perspective of active and dynamic involvement in the relationship between God and God's people. A spiritual director needs to be grounded in the community's articulation of this relationship. Scripture serves as the foundation. A director desires to know intimately the movement of God with God's people as witnessed in the scriptures. She or he desires to root her or his own life in the gospel of Jesus Christ; this is an active event of choosing the word as focus and not merely having intellectual knowledge of the text.

A director also desires to complement his or her scriptural rooting with a sound theological base. A healthy appropriation of the theology that has emerged from Vatican Council II is essential if one is to be faithful to the tradition. The documents of Vatican Council II are our most recent articulation of the church's understanding of its self-identity. It is both a privilege and a responsibility for spiritual directors to have a working theological foundation in our heritage. Because of the nature of spiritual direction, it is most appropriate that a director develop a practical theology that holds in dialogical correlation human experiences and questions with foundational theological themes.

A third dimension of the tradition that is essential for a spiritual director is being in conversation with the various spiritual traditions of prayer and religious living (e.g. Carmelite, Franciscan, Benedictine). Each religious tradition offers a particular perspective and emphasis within the whole of spiritual development. The classical texts and sources for these traditions are an invaluable tool for the spiritual director as she or he helps bring to light the religious dimension of another's experience. A resourceful director is less apt to quote the classics and more likely to glean the necessary wisdom from the traditions that can be applied to his or her discovering with another.

VII. **"Surrender and Obedience to God's Gift of True Freedom"**: Perhaps the most difficult issue to address in terms of spiritual direction is the question of obedience. Obedience and spiritual direction have always been closely aligned throughout the tradition. However, with the contemporary thrust toward self-determination and autonomy, obedience has been regarded as suspect. One reason for the suspicion of obedience has been the misinterpretation of obedience. For many, obedience conjurs up notions of submission, blind control, denial of self-will, and a passive acceptance of another's commands and desires.

Obedience comes from the Latin *ob audire,* to listen to, to be attentive to, to be able and willing to hear. The spiritual direction process is one of attentive listening to God's loving invitations to life, as well as listening to those areas of blockage that keep us from experiencing God as life-giver. Obedience is not about forming impotent and irresponsible "yes-men-and-women," but rather is a calling to responsible stewardship for one's very life. Together the director and directee listen to the stirrings that speak of God, and then discern life directions. One gradually learns to set aside (more often, to be purged from) one's wounded self-centeredness that demands the bright lights and attention of center stage in order to mask the true fears of loneliness, alienation, and loss of love. Attentive listening to the already-given Spirit of truth empowers one to allow God to emerge as the true center. Obedience is the discipline of stripping away the false self.

Therefore, obedience requires a relationship grounded in trust. Sometimes we are deaf to God's invitations. Sometimes we choose to harden our hearts — and not because we are evil, but more often than not because we are limited, if not totally blind at times, in our vision. The trust established in a spiritual direction relationship enables one to let another help take off the blinders. Obedience in this concrete situation is the ability to listen to the director as one given by God to help establish true freedom. This may be made manifest in a pentitential practice, or in a particular perspective offered on an issue, or in a simple invitation to change a certain dimension of how one lives.

SPIRITUAL DIRECTION AND THE CATECHUMENATE: CLOSING REMARKS

It is clear that the spiritual direction process is a special relationship. As mentioned earlier, many catechumens will choose to seek out a spiritual director to accompany them in their journey of faith. The RCIA team needs to make competent and gifted spiritual directors available for the catechumens. On the other hand, it will be of no service to anyone if catechumens are forced to work with a spiritual director. That is what it will become: work. Rather, the team may encourage and help raise the question for the catechumens. But the choice needs to be theirs.

14

Discernment

INTRODUCTION

The RCIA, when fully implemented, respects the unique journey of faith of the individual within the structures provided by the rite. A key dimension of this balance between individual conversion and the structured periods of the catechumenate is discernment. Prior to each transition to a new period of the process — marked by a ritual celebration — there is a prolonged period of discernment to help the catechumens identify their readiness to make the commitments required of the next period of formation.

Throughout this resource, we have reflected on the specific concerns and issues of discernment proper to each period of the RCIA. At this point, it would be helpful to examine the art of Christian discernment in general in order to situate the particular focus that discernment has in the RCIA.

A CONTEMPORARY APPROACH TO DISCERNMENT

Life is full of decisions. And there is never a guarantee that the decisions we make will indeed be the right decisions. However, one can be opened to a posture of decision-making that reflects a God-focus. One can enter into the process of discernment. The word "discernment" comes from the Latin *discernere* and means "to separate out," "to distinguish," "to recognize what is distinct and different." Discernment is the art of clearing away what is not worthwhile and life-giving from that which is indeed authentic and life-promoting. Discernment is about recognizing and responding to God's invitation to continually embrace the reign of God.

It is important to distinguish two types of discernment. The first type is moral discernment. Basically, moral discernment deals with issues of right and wrong, explicit good and evil. Our discussion presumes that one has developed the ability to discern between good and evil in this way.

The second type of discernment is life-centered discernment. This type of discernment is usually between two apparent goods, between two (or more) viable options or choices. This type of discernment struggles to hear God's invitation to a fuller experience of life. Sometimes the choice is between good and evil, but it is a very subtle form of evil (as opposed to the obvious distinction in moral discernment). It is this life-centered discernment that will be the focus of these reflections.

THEOLOGICAL PRESUPPOSITIONS

A contemporary understanding of discernment needs to be rooted in a fresh and invigorating theology. Our discussion on discernment presumes the following theological concepts:

- Revelation is the active process of God's self-communication, our response in faith, and the ensuing change in our lives or conversion.
- An important center of God's revelation is human experience, i.e. the religious depth dimension of human experience.
- God's will or plan, as articulated in Ephesians 1:9–10 and affirmed in *Dei Verbum,* chapter I, n. 2, is that all creation be drawn up into God's eternal embrace of love. The fulfillment of this plan is when Christ is the all in all.
- Since God's will is to bring all creation into God's embrace of love, God desires the well-being of all creation, especially the human community. Whatever facilitates authentic love can be seen as being in accord with God's will.
- Such a notion of God's will, then, is dynamic and takes seriously the particularity of the human experience. It eliminates the notion of a pre-defined blueprint or map of God's will. Rather, God is actively involved in the *now* of our life, inviting us to fuller life.
- Furthermore, the human person is created for God, open for fulfillment only by infinite love.
- The fulfillment of human desire is God. A theology of grace articulates God's self-gift of love to us. God's love empowers us to seek the truly authentic and valuable. Hence, we strive for true self-transcendence through self-sacrificing love.
- God's free gift of self — grace — empowers us to make decisions congruent with responsible living. Therefore, the decisions and

choices we make need to be situated within the responsibilities of our present state in life.

■ An understanding of discernment, therefore, is an exploration into the wonderful mystery of God-present-in-love. In that sense, it is messy. There are no clear-cut answers, no pre-set agendas. It is the continual awakening to God's invitations to deepened love and authentic life in our concrete, historical situation.

DISCERNMENT: RIGHT OR WRONG?

Before exploring some basic criteria for a contemporary discernment, it is necessary to address the question of the "right" judgment based on a discernment process. Discernment is not a foolproof set of directions one follows in order to come to the perfect solution. Rather, it is a surrender into a process of coming to fuller self-knowledge and responding out of that experience. While the practical judgment one makes is of definite value, it is the whole process of trust and surrender which is of greater importance. Such a process affirms the basic theological assertions mentioned earlier in this study: God's loving presence within the human person, and the human person's striving to come to a sense of wholeness and congruence with the gifted presence of love already given. We will never achieve fullness of all we are and can be while we are pilgrims on the way to God. There will always be an element of incompleteness. Therefore, we can never know if the decisions we make are "right" decisions because we see now "only as in a glass darkly." However, we can know if we have made a "good" decision if we have been faithful to the demands of the discernment process.

FOOLISH EXPECTATIONS

It will be helpful to discuss briefly what the discernment process is not before considering some contemporary criteria for discernment.

Discernment does not occur only through gut-level responses such as feelings or emotions. This is not to belittle the role and importance of affectivity in the discernment process. But rather it is to affirm that affectivity, however integrated, cannot be the sole criterion for a discernment. A case in point: someone feels good after a period of prayer during which time the individual has asked for God's guidance in a life-direction. The person presumes God's guidance in the warm feeling and makes a decision based on that confirmation of God's will to be done. So the person enters religious life, or considers marriage based on this gut-level instinct. But what happens when the "feelings" are gone?

Discernment does not in essence happen through a systematic and logical process, a step by step approach whereby a clear, correct and precise answer can be guaranteed because of faithful "following of directions." Such a notion is simply a new form of secular decision-making. Discernment is more than decision-making. It is an adventure that faces the mystery of God's stirrings. While there is order to God's movement, such order is wholistic and not totally rational and logical.

Discernment, in most cases, does not occur through private revelations to an individual. We are men and women situated within a world community and, more specifically, within the Christian community. Private revelations are prone to self-deception and therefore need the corrective of the community's confirmation. God's revelation is within human experience. Such revelation is always interpersonal, and calls forth the necessary guidance and support from the larger community. Otherwise, one would feel justified in establishing a privatized religion with a privatized God. Prophets (which may appear to be of the "private revelation" vein) always remained situated within the community, even though it was often to this very community the prophet spoke the difficult word of God.

GUIDELINES

It has already been mentioned that there is no clear-cut method to follow for a correct discernment. Such an "easy" method would be a welcome sight for many of us. However, such a method would negate several fundamental Christian beliefs: the uniqueness and individuality of each man and woman; the inability to determine another's "level" of spiritual development (i.e. we do not know the hearts of others); the impossibility to grasp the fullness of God's love and justice; and the resistance to a domestication of God, faith and the spiritual life (i.e. making it ever so neat, organized, controllable and, ultimately, boring).

However, there are certain guidelines which have emerged from the Christian community's struggle to be faithful to God's call that can be used as a measuring stick to our experience of discernment. Again, such guidelines will not assure an infallible response but help serve as a barometer of sorts. These guidelines are not listed in any order of importance. No attempt has been made to prioritize any of them for fear they will become a new set of "easy rules" to follow. Hopefully these guidelines will offer a balanced and more complete approach to the process of discernment.

- An important center of God's continual revelation is our concrete historical situation. Therefore, discernment is the art of finding meaning in our daily lived lives as it reflects God's revelation. Discernment is about a new quality of vision. It is not about seeing new things but seeing things in a new way. Discernment, therefore, is rooted in the revelation of God in Jesus, the Christ. Of the many things we could say about such revelation, one key dimension is the question of relationship. Jesus reveals a God who is deeply involved in the life of people. The God of Jesus is not a removed and distant observer. The life-praxis of Jesus illustrates the level of commitment one must be willing to embrace in order for the values of this already-near God to emerge. The question becomes "What is God inviting me to do and how do I respond to this invitation?"
- Often the ways of God can be discerned through the use of common sense supported by informed and prudent judgment. The use of common sense may also serve as a preliminary moment in the discernment process. Caution needs to be exercised, however, as to the extent of the use of common sense. The drawback lies in the extension of common sense: we sometimes presume to be experts in areas we only have basic knowledge of. We overextend our competency, and therefore blind ourselves to the need for further investigation and consultation.
- Discernment is a wholistic process: intellect, psychological state, affectivity, spiritual, volitional, physical. All elements of our embodied person can play a role offering cues. For example, the intellect can gather and sort the necessary data. One's psychological state affects the process: if one is under duress or experiencing high levels of anxiety, one can suspect the origin of the process. Feelings, though not absolute indicators of discernment, contribute to the process by signaling either uncomfortableness or a sense of congruence. From a spiritual perspective, the person enters into mystery beyond human comprehension, a journey of faith. The volitional dimension, or will, affects the discernment in how one eagerly accepts and responds to the decision as "ringing true." The body also plays a significant role: if the mind is saying "yes" but the body is breaking down, one needs to reconsider the process in light of what the body is saying. Discernment, like conversion, affects the various dimensions of one's life.

- One recognizes that the gift of God's love centers the person, and therefore one can approach this process with confidence that God will guide us in our faithful searching. Such a level of trust presumes a developing relationship between the individual and God. Discernment is not the "quick fix" solution to life's worries: you "fill up" with God and run around until you reach empty, and then you "fill up" again, stopping in at the garage whenever you have a problem. The great mechanic God solves it all for you. Discernment presumes the rigors and joys of willingly entering into relationship with the one who is greater yet chooses to love us. We acknowledge that we are often unfaithful in this relationship. And yet God continues to come to us where we are and forgive us, love us, reconcile us to renewed relationship. Such a relationship demands vulnerability, risk, the "leap" into the darkness of faith truly believing that the arms of God will hold us and embrace us. When one lives in this mystery ever so near yet ever so much more, when one gives oneself to love, one fosters a level of trust and confidence that believes that God's desire is truly the good of all. One can then freely submit to the rigors of striving, searching, sometimes wandering because the Beloved is always there, even in apparent absence.
- One also must be comfortable with the possibility of a wrong decision. However if one is faithful to the process of discernment, one can rest in the certitude of a *good* decision, knowing that God will use whatever our falterings are to bring about good.
- Time is an important dimension to discernment. We can differentiate between time as *chronos* and time as *kairos*. *Chronos* is measured time, the time of a clock. It is our accustomed way of keeping time, of "clock-watching," of knowing when someone is early or late. Such measured and calculated time is human time with human expectations. *Kairos* is God's time, the appointed time, the time that best serves the building of God's reign. God's time breaks in silently like a thief in the night, or a master returning from a feast. It is not calculated and cannot be measured except in terms of the fidelity of the night watch. It takes trust to allow God's time to emerge, to know the right moment and not rush into any discernment.
- The process of discernment leads one to a sense of true detachment, i.e. to remove ourselves enough to be able to accept whatever is asked of us. Without the pressure of calculated time, one can allow God's Spirit to emerge and invite us toward the greater good. Such detachment teaches one to make room to welcome whatever is given. We learn to accept all as gift. We are not a stingy heart, but rather a heart that is opened with room for all God asks of us.

■ The posture of one in discernment is the posture of obedience and surrender. Obedience means to truly listen to the words of life, and then respond to such words. Surrender means to turn over private expectations and desires for the greater gift which can be received if one opens his or her heart to God. Both are active postures based in trust.

■ Discernment should always be approached with a contemplative posture, i.e. a heart opened to God's stirrings and movements. Such a heart is listening in love to all inner impulses. This posture is most enhanced through prayer. It is important to note that simply because a person has prayed is no guarantee that the decision made is correct and reflective of God's will. Another important dimension is not only that one pray, but also how one comes to this prayer. We have already discussed the posture of obedience, surrender and loving trust which is necessary to attune one's heart to God's call.

■ The place to begin in discernment is true self-knowledge. One must be continually willing to search his or her heart and confront the illusory and celebrate the gifted dimensions of the self in order to facilitate invitations to deepened awareness of the self. The path to self-knowledge, however, is not simply an intellectual exercise. It is an exercise of both the head and the heart. This dynamic tension gives a depth and breadth to one's self-understanding. As Pascal says: "The heart has reasons reason does not know." To speak of the heart, one must refer to the symbolic and affective dimensions of the person. Imagination and memory are important vehicles for coming to this level of self-knowledge. But one cannot stop there. In order for conversion to continually take place, one must let the story of Jesus have an impact on the individual's story, transforming the imagination and personal symbols.

FOUR MOVEMENTS

The discernment process itself can be characterized by four movements: deliberation, reflection, insight, and decision and action.

(a) *Deliberation:* There are two forms of deliberation one needs to be available for in order to give balance to a discernment. The first deliberation or consultation is to oneself. One needs to take seriously the call to true self-knowledge, which help one come to terms with one's gifts as well as with one's limitations. Secondly, one needs to consult with others. When looking for someone to consult, certain qualities are important. One needs someone who will help the individual work (and talk) the discernment through — someone who is objective (doesn't have personal gain at stake or is too personally involved), and someone who leaves the individual free to ultimately make his or her own decisions, even if they are poor ones. In addition to another person, one needs to consider consulting other authorities: the scriptures, tradition, books and articles.

Deliberation includes the acquiring of the necessary information to make an informed decision, assessing one's current situation honestly, and visioning the resolution. Additionally, it includes hearing all sides of the issue, weighing the pros and cons, and honestly surveying the possibilities.

Some helpful reflection questions: Am I open to consult other persons in this process, especially my spiritual director? Do I consult with my legitimate authorities for feedback and direction? Do I find time for silence and solitude in this decision-making process? Can I bring this decision to my prayer?

(b) *Reflection:* There are at least two types of reflection. One type implies certain expectations. One has already made up his or her mind, has already decided what meanings will be discovered. The individual's own desires, goals, and needs dictate what will be discovered because the individual already knows what he or she wants to discover. Such an individual closes his or her eyes to anything which might threaten the planned meaning. One imposes meaning on life rather than uncovering the meaning that emerges. Such reflection does not sponsor an honest discernment.

The second type of reflection is quite the opposite. During this type of reflection, an individual tries to see and accept whatever meanings that emerge. One does not protect oneself from the uncomfortable. Rather, the individual is opened to the truth in whatever way he or she can at a given moment. Such a posture demands that one not be possessive or frightened; rather, one is able to trust divine providence and can wait.

During an honest discernment, an individual will allow the issues and ideas raised during the deliberation to begin to work from the inside out. Slowly and respectfully, the discerner will listen to the word of truth and value that emerge, whatever the cost. There is a level of disinterested involvement: one gives oneself over to the process without making a previous claim on the vision that begins to take shape.

Some helpful reflection questions: Where is God for me in all of this? How does this relate to my life in community? How will Christian love be advanced? Can I recognize the limits as well as the possibilities in the decision? How does the decision promote Christian values? Is this a responsible course to take?

(c) *Insight:* The theologian Bernard Lonergan claims that insight is the release of the tension of inquiry. One gives himself or herself to the discernment process, opening oneself to whatever gifts that will be given to him or her because of the process. One slowly purges oneself of any urgency or desire to "short-cut" and simply can *be* with the process. On a deeper level, something is happening. Images are being transformed, symbols reinforced, awareness of self made more explicit. All of this can happen because the self has received the message from the individual that he or she respects and reverences both the process and the person. Such an individual can wait through the labor of birthing. It is the gift of the Spirit.

Some helpful reflection questions: Do I give this time to settle, to seep into my person? What feelings do I have while making this decision? How might these affective responses influence my choice? How is this related to my life — my history and my vision for the future? Whom do I experience myself to be in relationship to God in this process of decision-making? Is there a sense of inner peace and quiet with the decision? Can I honestly say that this decision "fits" with my true sense of myself?

(d) *Decision and Action:* After prayerful reflection and consultation, one can come to a posture of liberation and hence decision. This decision will affirm and promote gifts given for the building of the reign of God. One should resolve to follow the decision made until evidence presents itself that the decision needs to be re-evaluated.

EVALUATION OF DISCERNMENT

True discernment leads to the truth, and from the truth into freedom. St. Paul offers some criteria for discerning the presence of the Spirit in Galatians 5:22–23 in his discussion on the fruits of the Spirit. We can broaden such an interpretation to include those who have made life-centered discernments in response to the Spirit's promptings. The presence of the Spirit can be recognized through the Spirit's fruits: love, joy, peace, patience, kindness, goodness, faithfulness, gentleness, and self-control. Paul also lists in Galatians 5:20–21a the works of those who do not walk with the Spirit: fornication, impurity, licentiousness, idolatry, sorcery, enmity, strife, jealousy, anger, selfishness, dissension, party spirit, envy, drunkenness, carousing and the like. One who lives by the Spirit and the decisions of the Spirit will reflect in his or her way of life the fruits of that same Spirit.

DISCERNMENT AND DAILY LIFE CHOICES

Discernment, we have discussed, is about making choices. True discernment leads one to an honest choice for life, for deeper congruence. Yet can we use the term discernment to speak of the daily process of life-decision-making or is it specified for fundamental choices?

A healthy perspective on men and women would affirm that the small choices of daily life are rooted in a more radical sense of choice. They come together to form a collage, a mosaic of one's basic life-direction. Yet one would be rendered impotent if one entered the discernment process (as described throughout these reflections) for every decision one made. Rather, the more formal discernment process is best suited for major decisions, transition moments, periods of self-evaluation. As one is faithful to honest discernment, one begins to cultivate a certain awareness or posture to life's choices which starts to affect even daily choices. Hence, the virtue of good decision-making begins to emerge, the virtue of discretion. Discretion is the ability to choose daily life with some sense of congruence with one's gifted identity. However, one can be deceived, and thus a period of self-consciousness examen can help situate one's daily choices more concretely within the greater pattern of God's loving activity.

Thomas Aquinas defines virtue as follows: "Virtue is a good quality of the mind, by which we live righteously, of which no one can make bad use, which God works in us, without us" (*Sum. theo.* Ia IIae, q. 55, art. 4). Our use of the term virtue comes from the Latin *virtus,* which basically means excellence, worth, goodness, courage. A virtue is an acquired disposition. It is a manner of living life which reflects wholesomeness and integrity. The life of virtue is the choice to accept the invitation to be courageous, to be fostering good, to move toward excellence (not in the achievement sense, but in the sense of human fulfillment).

The virtue of good decision-making reflects an attitude of centered living. One knows from whence the source of life comes, and continually lives out of that same source or center. The quality of one's life changes, and one begins to face the world with an awareness of God's presence. Classical language has always referred to this as the conversion process: the turning about in order to see things as they really are through the eyes of God. When one accepts the conversion invitation, when one allows the shape of his or her life to be formed by the hands of God, then one is awakened to a new sensitivity. One instinctively responds to life from a gospel value-perspective. Such is the virtue of good decision-making. One places all decisions within the context of the reign of God.

The emphasis is not on the how of making daily decisions, but on the way of becoming more human and more Christ-like. The how of decision-making flows from a converted heart.

DISCERNMENT AS POSSIBLE HERMENEUTIC OF SELF

Discernment often happens with the context of a spiritual direction relationship. However, this is not always the case. Yet, in whatever context discernment occurs, it is clear that a form of hermeneutics (i.e. interpretation) is taking place. One listens attentively to the story of one's life: one's past, present and future hopes. One reaches into the depths of self to uncover and allow to stand the "root metaphors," the foundational images and symbols of self which articulate how one experiences oneself at this moment of life. All of this is allowed to emerge and stand on its own, to speak its own truth. One then takes that horizon and faces the horizon of the possibilities offered, the choices in discernment. Through a process of detachment and scrutiny, one allows the choices to emerge on their own, to speak their own truth. Eventually there is a fusing of the two horizons: the horizon of the individual and all he or she experiences himself or herself to be, and the horizon of the new decision. Both serve as a text, in the technical sense. Both have a truth to speak. Both are now radically changed as a new sense of self and a new sense of the choice emerges in their union. The decision-making process now no longer has merely a past (the process, the pre-understandings, the basic horizons) but also a meaningful present and future. The choice, which seems congruent to God's will as understood and one's own sense of true self, breaks forth into new action, a new sense of living in the world.

The process of discernment is a process of coming to meet and accept the person I am gifted to be. It is a process of reading the "text" of my life. This process reveals myself to myself in a new way. It offers an interpretation of my past and the person I have come to know myself to be. The hermeneutic task is just that: to open up the text to allow the truth to emerge and speak its message to a new day. Discernment helps lead one to such a new day.

CONCLUSION

Christian discernment is concerned with the quality of life. Christian discernment is intimately connected with the conversion process. It is impossible to move through the process of discernment without truly allowing oneself to experience on-going conversion. Discernment is the sorting out of God's call; conversion is the responding and allowing God to change us.

Throughout the RCIA, the candidate and team, along with the parish staff and community, are called upon to discern the various movements and invitations from God to enter into the commitment of sacramental initiation. In addition to assisting the catechumen to come to an honest decision, the team can also help the catechumen develop a basic life posture of discernment that is rooted in the providential love of God. This is accomplished through the modeling offered throughout the RCIA, but most especially at the manner and style of the discernments at the various periods and stages of the RCIA.

Resources

There are a number of resources available that will assist the pastoral minister in the implementation of the RCIA. Some of the resources deal specifically with the RCIA, its theology and history. Others are useful for exploring specific theological, catechetical or pastoral dimensions of the implementation of the rite. Following is an introductory listing of available resources that can assist the team and other ministers in the RCIA. The listing is not exhaustive, nor does it mean to be. Rather, it serves to introduce some helpful reference material for further study and exploration of the Rite of Christian Initiation of Adults.

RITE OF CHRISTIAN INITIATION OF ADULTS

Amandolare, Ronald, Thomas P. Ivory, and William J. Reedy, eds. *Resource Book for the RCIA*. New York: Sadlier, 1988.

Barbernitz, Patricia. *RCIA: The Rite of Christian Initiation of Adults: What It Is, How It Works.* Liguori Publications, 1983.

Barbernitz, Patricia. *RCIA Team Manual: How To Implement the Rite of Christian Initiation of Adults in Your Parish*. New York: Paulist Press, 1986.

Bourgeois, Henri. *On Becoming Christian. Christian Initiation and Its Sacraments*. Mystic: Twenty-Third Publications, 1982.

Boyack, Kenneth. *A Parish Guide to Adult Initiation*. New York: Paulist Press, 1980.

Duffy, Regis. *On Becoming a Catholic Christian. The Challenge of Christian Initiation*. San Francisco: Harper & Row, 1984.

Dujarier, Michel. *A History of the Catechumenate. The First Six Centuries.* New York: Sadlier, 1979.

Dujarier, Michel. *The Rites of Christian Initiation. Historical and Pastoral Reflections.* New York: Sadlier, 1979.

Dunning, James B. *New Wine, New Wineskins. Exploring the RCIA*. New York: Sadlier, 1981.

Ellebracht, M.P. *The Easter Passage. The RCIA Experience.* Minneapolis: Winston, 1983.

Field, Anne. *From Darkness To Light. What It Meant To Become a Christian in the Early Church.* Ann Arbor: Servant Books, 1978.

Hinman, Karen. *How To Form a Catechumenate Team.* Chicago: Liturgy Training Publications, 1986.

Johnson, Lawrence, ed. *Initiation and Conversion.* Collegeville: The Liturgical Press, 1985.

Kavanagh, Aidan. *The Shape of Baptism: The Rite of Christian Initiation.* New York: Pueblo Publishing Co., 1978.

Kemp, Raymond B. *A Journey in Faith. An Experience of the Catechumenate.* New York: Sadlier, 1979.

Lewinski, Ron. *Guide for Sponsors,* revised edition. Chicago: Liturgy Training Publications, 1987.

Lewinski, Ron. *Welcoming the New Catholic,* revised edition. Chicago: Liturgy Training Publications, 1983.

The Murphy Center for Liturgical Research. *Made, Not Born. New Perspectives on Christian Initiation and the Catechumenate.* Notre Dame: University of Notre Dame Press, 1976.

O'Dea, Barbara. *The Once and Future Church.* Kansas City: Celebration Books, 1980.

Reedy, William J. ed. *Becoming a Catholic Christian.* New York: Sadlier, 1979.

Rite of Christian Initiation of Adults: An Annotated Bibliography. Washington, D.C.: Federation of Diocesan Liturgical Commissions, 1983 (1987 addendum).

Study Text 10. Christian Initiation of Adults: A Commentary. Washington, D.C.: USCC, 1985.

Wilde, James A. ed. *A Catechumenate Needs Everybody: Study Guides for Parish Ministers.* Chicago: Liturgy Training Publications, 1988.

Wilde, James A. ed. *Commentaries on the Rite of Christian Initiation of Adults.* Chicago: Liturgy Training Publications, 1988.

Wilde, James A. ed. *Finding and Forming Sponsors and Godparents.* Chicago: Liturgy Training Publications, 1988.

Wilde, James A. ed. *Parish Catechumenate: Pastors, Presiders, Preachers.* Chicago: Liturgy Training Publications, 1988.

CONVERSION

Conn, Walter. *Christian Conversion. A Developmental Interpretation of Autonomy and Surrender.* New York: Paulist Press, 1986.

Conn, Walter. *Conscience: Development and Self-Transcendence.* Birmingham: Religious Education Press, 1981.

Conn, Walter, ed. *Conversion. Perspectives on Personal and Social Transformation.* New York: Alba House, 1978.

Doran, Robert. *Psychic Conversion and Theological Foundations.* Chico: Scholars Press, 1981.

Duggan, Robert, ed. *Conversion and the Catechumenate.* New York: Paulist Press, 1984.

Gaventa, Beverly Roberts. *From Darkness To Light. Aspects of Conversion in the New Testament.* Philadelphia: Fortress, 1986.

Griffin, Emilie. *Turning. Reflections on the Experience of Conversion.* Garden City: Doubleday, 1982.

Happel, Stephen and James J. Walter. *Conversion and Discipleship: A Christian Foundation for Ethics and Doctrine.* Philadelphia: Fortress, 1986.

Haughton, Rosemary. *The Transformation of Man. A Study of Conversion and Community.* Springfield: Templegate Publishing, 1967.

Loder, James E. *The Transforming Moment: Understanding Convictional Experience.* San Francisco: Harper & Row, 1981.

Lonergan, Bernard J. *Method in Theology.* New York: Herder and Herder, 1972.

O'Rourke, David K. *A Process Called Conversion.* Garden City: Doubleday, 1985.

Robb, Paul V. "Conversion as a Human Experience." *Studies in the Spirituality of Jesuits* 14 (1982) 1–50.

Wallis, Jim. *The Call to Conversion.* San Francisco: Harper & Row, 1982.

LITURGY AND SACRAMENTS

Bausch, William J. *A New Look at the Sacraments.* Mystic: Twenty-Third Publications, 1983.

Berger, Rupert and Hans Hollesweger, eds. *Celebrating the Easter Vigil.* Trans. Matthew J. O'Connell. New York: Pueblo, 1983.

DeGidio, Sandra. *RCIA: The Rites Revisited.* Minneapolis: Winston, 1984.

Deiss, Lucien. *Persons in Liturgical Celebrations.* Chicago: World Library Publications, Inc. 1978.

Deiss, Lucien. *Springtime of the Liturgy. Liturgical Texts of the First Four Centuries.* Collegeville: Liturgical Press, 1979.

Duggan, Robert. "Conversion in the Ordo Initiationis Christianae Adultorum." *Ephemerides Liturgicae* 96 (1982) 57–83, 209–252; 97 (1983) 141–223.

Fisher. J.D.C. *Christian Initiation: Baptism in the Medieval West.* London: SPCK, 1965.

Fisher, J.D.C. *Confirmation Then and Now.* London: SPCK/Alcuin, 1978.

Fleming, Austin. *Preparing for Liturgy. A Theology and Spirituality.* Washington, D.C.: The Pastoral Press, 1985.

Fourez, Gerard. *Sacraments and Passages: Celebrating the Tensions of Modern Life.* Notre Dame: Ave Maria Press, 1983.

Gelpi, Donald L. *Charism and Sacrament: A Theology of Christian Conversion.* New York: Paulist Press, 1976.

Guzie, Tad. *The Book of Sacramental Basics.* New York: Paulist Press, 1981.

Hamman, A. ed. *The Paschal Mystery. Ancient Liturgies and Patristic Texts.* Montreal: Palm, 1969.

Hellwig, Monika. *The Meaning of the Sacraments.* Dayton: Pflaum Press, 1972.

Hovda, Robert W. *Strong, Loving and Wise. Presiding in Liturgy.* Washington, D.C.: The Liturgical Conference, 1976.

Huck, Gabe. *Liturgy with Style and Grace.* Chicago: Liturgy Training Publications, 1984.

Huck, Gabe. *The Three Days. Parish Prayer in the Paschal Triduum.* Chicago: Liturgical Training Publications, 1981.

Irwin, Kevin. *Liturgy, Prayer and Spirituality.* New York: Paulist Press, 1984.

Jagger, P.J. *Christian Initiation 1552–1969. Rite of Baptism and Confirmation since the Reformation Period.* London: SPCK, 1970.

Jones, Cheslyn, Geoffrey Wainwright and Edward Yarnold, eds. *The Study of Liturgy.* New York: Oxford University Press, 1978.

Kelly, H.A. *The Devil at Baptism. Ritual, Theology, and Drama.* Ithaca: Cornell University Press, 1986.

Martimort, Aime Georges. *The Church at Prayer: An Introduction to the Liturgy.* Vol. 3 The Sacraments. Trans. Matthew J. O'Connell. Collegeville: Liturgical Press, 1988.

Martos, Joseph. *The Catholic Sacraments.* Wilmington: Michael Glazier, 1983.

Martos, Joseph. *Doors to the Sacred.* New York: Doubleday, 1981.

McMahon, Michael. *The Rite of Christian Initiation of Adults: Liturgical Commentary.* Washington, D.C.: Federation of Diocesan Liturgical Commissions, 1986.

Mitchell, Leonel L. *Baptismal Anointing.* London: SPCK, 1966.

Ostdiek, Gilbert. *Catechesis for Liturgy.* Washington, D.C.: The Pastoral Press, 1986.

Pachence, Ronald A. *Speaking of Sacraments.* Phoenix: WinterSun Publications, 1988.

Power, David N. *Unsearchable Riches: The Symbolic Nature of Liturgy.* New York: Pueblo Publishing Co., 1984.

Riley, H.M. *Christian Initiation. A Comparative Study of the Interpretation of the Baptismal Liturgy in the Mystagogical Writings of Cyril of Jerusalem, John Chrysostom, Theodore of Mopsuestia and Ambrose of Milan.* Washington, D.C.: The Catholic University of America Press, 1974.

Searle, Mark. *Christening. The Making of Christians.* Collegeville: Liturgical Press, 1980.

Searle, Mark. *Liturgy Made Simple.* Collegeville: The Liturgical Press, 1981.

Thurian, M. and G. Wainwright, eds. *Baptism and Eucharist: Ecumenical Convergence in Celebration.* Geneva: World Council of Churches, 1983.

Whitaker, E.C. *The Baptismal Liturgy,* revised edition. London: SPCK, 1981.

Whitaker, E.C. *Documents of the Baptismal Liturgy,* revised edition. London: SPCK, 1970.

Yarnold, Edward. *The Awe Inspiring Rites of Initiation: Baptismal Homilies of the Fourth Century.* Slough, England: St. Paul Publications, 1971.

LITURGICAL MUSIC FOR THE RCIA

Haas, David. *Who Calls You By Name: Music for Christian Initiation.* (two cassette tapes) Chicago: G.I.A. Publications, Inc., 1988.

Haas, David. *Who Calls You By Name: Music for Christian Initiation.* (texts and music) Chicago: G.I.A. Publications, Inc., 1988.

CATECHESIS

Bausch, William J. *Storytelling: Imagination and Faith.* Mystic: Twenty-Third Publications, 1984.

Darring, Gerald. *A Catechism of Catholic Social Teaching.* Kansas City: Sheed & Ward, 1987.

DeBoy, James. *Getting Started in Adult Religious Education.* New York: Paulist Press, 1979.

Elias, John L. *The Foundations and Practice of Adult Religious Education.* Malabar: Robert E. Krieger Publishing Company, 1982.

Fitzmyer, Joseph A. *A Christological Catechism. New Testament Answers.* New York: Paulist Press, 1982.

Foley, Leonard. *Believing in Jesus: A Popular Overview of Catholic Faith.* Cincinnati: St. Anthony Messenger Press, 1981.

Girzaitis, Loretta. *More Radiant than Noonday. Growing in Christian Maturity.* Mystic: Twenty-Third Publications, 1981.

Greeley, Andrew M. *The Great Mysteries: An Essential Catechism.* New York: Seabury Press, 1976.

Groome, Thomas H. *Christian Religious Education.* San Francisco: Harper & Row, 1980.

Hellwig, Monika. *Understanding Catholicism.* New York: Paulist Press, 1981.

Ivory, Thomas. *Looking at Our Faith. A Catechetical Approach for Adults.* New York: Sadlier, 1983.

Knowles, Malcolm. *The Modern Practice of Adult Education: Andragogy Versus Pedagogy.* New York: Association Press, 1975.

Kohmescher, Matthew F. *Catholicism Today. A Survey of Catholic Belief and Practice.* New York: Paulist Press, 1980.

Marthaler, Berard L. *The Creed.* Mystic: Twenty-Third Publications, 1987.

Marthaler, Berard L. *Catechetics in Context.* Huntington: Our Sunday Visitor, Inc., 1973.

McBride, Alfred. *Invitation.* Washington, D.C.: Paulist National Catholic Evangelization Association, 1984.

McBrien, Richard P. *Catholicism.* Minneapolis: Winston, 1980.

McKenzie, Leon. *The Religious Education of Adults.* Birmingham: Religious Education Press, 1982.

O'Hare, Padraic, ed. *Foundations of Religious Education.* New York: Paulist Press, 1978.

Perkins, Pheme. *What We Believe. A Biblical Catechism of the Apostles' Creed.* New York: Paulist Press, 1986.

Warren, Michael, ed. *Sourcebook for Modern Catechetics.* Winona: St. Mary's Press, 1983.

Westerhoff, John W. *Will Our Children Have Faith?* New York: Seabury, 1976.

THEOLOGICAL RESOURCES

Austin, Gerard. *Anointing with the Spirit.* New York: Pueblo Publishing Co., 1985.

Cully, Kendig Brubaker, ed. *Confirmation Re-examined.* Wilton: Morehouse-Barlow, Co., 1982.

Duffy, Regis. *Real Presence. Worship, Sacrament, and Commitment.* San Francisco: Harper & Row, 1982.

Edwards, Denis. *Human Experience of God.* New York: Paulist Press, 1983.

Friday, Robert. *Adults Making Moral Decisions,* revised edition. Washington, D.C.: National Conference of Diocesan Directors of Religious Education, 1986.

Ganoczy, Alexander. *Becoming a Christian: A Theology of Baptism as the Sacrament of Human History.* New York: Paulist Press, 1976.

Haight, Roger. *The Experience and Language of Grace.* New York: Paulist Press, 1979.

Haughton, Rosemary. *The Catholic Thing.* Springfield: Templegate Publishers, 1979.

Kavanagh, Aidan. *Confirmation: Origins and Reform.* New York: Pueblo, 1988.

Kung, Hans. *On Being a Christian.* Garden City: Doubleday, 1976.

Lane, Dermot A. *The Experience of God. An Invitation To Do Theology.* New York: Paulist Press, 1981.

Lane, Dermot. *The Reality of Jesus. An Essay in Christology.* New York: Paulist Press, 1975.

Macquarrie, John. *Principles of Christian Theology,* second edition. New York: Charles Scribner's Sons, 1977.

Marsh, Thomas A. *Gift of Community: Baptism and Confirmation.* Wilmington: Michael Glazier, 1984.

O'Connell, Timothy E. *Principles for a Catholic Morality.* New York: Seabury Press, 1976.

Osborne, Kenan B. *The Christian Sacraments of Initiation: Baptism, Confirmation and Eucharist.* New York: Paulist Press, 1987.

Rahner, Karl. *Foundations of Christian Faith: An Introduction to the Idea of Christianity.* New York: Seabury, 1978.

Richardson, Alan and John Bowden, ed. *The Westminster Dictionary of Christian Theology.* Philadelphia: The Westminster Press, 1983.

Schmeiser, James, ed. *Initiation Theology.* Toronto: The Anglican Book Centre, 1978.

Searle, Mark, ed. *Baptism and Confirmation* (Alternative Futures for Worship, vol. 2). Collegeville: Liturgical Press, 1987.

Shea, John. *Stories of Faith.* Chicago: Thomas More Press, 1980.

Shea, John. *Stories of God. An Unauthorized Biography.* Chicago: Thomas More Press, 1978.

Thompson, William M. *The Jesus Debate. A Survey & Synthesis.* New York: Paulist Press, 1985.

Wagner, J. ed. *Adult Baptism and the Catechumenate.* New York: Paulist Press, 1967.

SCRIPTURE AND SCRIPTURE BASED CATECHESIS

At Home with the Word. Chicago: Liturgy Training Publications, published annually.

Boadt, Lawrence. *Reading the Old Testament. An Introduction.* New York: Paulist Press, 1984.

Brown, Raymond et al. *The Jerome Biblical Commentary.* Englewood Cliffs: Prentice-Hall, Inc., 1968.

Fuller, Reginald H. *A Critical Introduction to the New Testament.* London: Gerald Duckworth & Co., Ltd., 1966.

Fuller, Reginald H. *Preaching the New Lectionary: The Word of God for the Church Today.* Collegeville: Liturgical Press, 1974.

Harrington, Daniel. *Interpreting the New Testament. A Practical Guide.* Wilmington: Michael Glazier, Inc., 1979.

Hinman, Karen and Joseph Sinwell, eds. *Breaking Open the Word of God, Cycle A.* New York: Paulist Press, 1986.

Keegan, Terence J. *Interpreting the Bible. A Popular Introduction to Biblical Hermeneutics.* New York: Paulist Press, 1985.

Maertens, Thierry. *Bible Themes.* Notre Dame: Fides, 1964.

McCauley, George. *The Unfinished Image. Reflections on the Sunday Readings.* New York: Sadlier, 1983.

Miller, John W. *Step by Step Through the Parables.* New York: Paulist Press, 1981.

Powell, Karen Hinman and Joseph Sinwell, eds. *Breaking Open the Word of God, Cycle B.* New York: Paulist Press, 1987.

Powell, Karen Hinman and Joseph Sinwell, eds. *Breaking Open the Word of God, Cycle C.* New York: Paulist Press, 1988.

Scagnelli, Peter. *Sourcebook for Sundays and Seasons.* Chicago: Liturgy Training Publications, published annually.

Share the Word. Washington, D.C.: Paulist National Catholic Evangelization Association, published bi-monthly.

Sloyan, Gerard. *Commentary on the New Lectionary.* New York: Paulist Press, 1975.

EVANGELIZATION

Bohr, David. *Evangelization in America.* New York: Paulist Press, 1977.

Boyack, Kenneth, ed. *Catholic Evangelization Today. A New Pentecost for the United States.* New York: Paulist Press, 1987.

Brennan, Patrick. *The Evangelizing Parish.* Valencia: Tabor Publications, 1987.

Hofinger, J. *Evangelization and Catechesis.* New York: Paulist Press, 1976.

Hoge, Dean R. *Converts, Dropouts, Returnees: A Study of Religious Change among Catholics.* New York: The Pilgrim Press, 1981.

Holash, Lise M. *Evangelization, The Catechumenate and Its Ministries.* Dubuque: Wm. C. Brown Company, 1983.

RELIGIOUS DEVELOPMENT

Duska, Ronald and Whelan, Mariellen. *Moral Development. A Guide to Piaget and Kohlberg.* New York: Paulist Press, 1975.

Dykstra, Craig. *Vision and Character: A Christian Educator's Alternative to Kohlberg.* New York: Paulist Press, 1981.

Fowler, James W. *Becoming Adult, Becoming Christian. Adult Development and Christian Faith.* San Francisco: Harper & Row, 1984.

Fowler, James W. *Stages of Faith: The Psychology of Human Development and the Quest for Meaning.* San Francisco: Harper & Row, 1981.

Gilligan, Carol. *In a Different Voice.* Cambridge: Harvard University Press, 1982.

Joy, Donald, ed. *Moral Development Foundations: Judeo-Christian Alternatives to Piaget/Kohlberg.* Nashville: Abingdon, 1983.

Kegan, Robert. *The Evolving Self: Problem and Process in Human Development.* Cambridge: Harvard University Press, 1982.

Moseley, Romney M. *Religious Conversion: A Structural-Developmental Analysis.* Ph.D. Dissertation. Harvard University, 1978.

Munsey, Brenda, ed. *Moral Development, Moral Education and Kohlberg.* Birmingham: Religious Education Press, 1980.

Rizzuto, Ana-Maria. *The Birth of the Living God.* Chicago: University of Chicago Press, 1979.

Stokes, Kenneth, ed. *Faith Development in the Adult Life Cycle.* New York: Sadlier, 1982.

Toward Moral and Religious Maturity. The First International Conference on Moral and Religious Development. Morristown: Silver Burdett Company, 1980.

Whitehead, Evelyn Eaton and Whitehead, James D. *Christian Life Patterns. The Psychological Challenges and Religious Invitations of Adult Life.* Garden City: Doubleday, 1979.

CHURCH DOCUMENTS

The Code of Canon Law. Latin-English edition. Washington, D.C.: Canon Law Society of America, 1983.

The Documents of Vatican Council II, Austin Fleming, ed. New York: The America Press, 1966.

Environment and Art in Catholic Worship. Washington, D.C.: USCC, 1978.

Liturgical Music Today. Washington, D.C.: USCC, 1982.

Music in Catholic Worship. Washington, D.C.: USCC, 1972.

On Evangelization in the Modern World (Evangelii Nuntiandi), Paul VI. Washington, D.C.: USCC, 1976.

Rite of Christian Initiation of Adults (1986 approved ritual edition for use in the dioceses of the United States). Washington, D.C.: USCC, 1988.

Sharing the Light of Faith: National Catechetical Directory for Catholics of the United States. Washington, D.C.: USCC, 1979.

Sharing the Light of Faith: An Official Commentary. Washington, D.C.: USCC. 1981.

PASTORAL ISSUES

Bishops' Committee on Liturgy and The Catholic University of America Center for Pastoral Liturgy. *The Environment for Worship: A Reader.* Washington, D.C.: USCC, 1980.

Boyack, Kenneth, Robert D. Duggan, and Paul Huesing. *Catholic Faith Inventory.* New York: Paulist Press, 1985.

Coriden, James A., Thomas J. Green, and Donald E. Heintschel, eds. *The Code of Canon Law. A Text and Commentary.* New York: Paulist Press, 1985.

Funk, Virgil C., ed. *Music in Catholic Worship: The NPM Commentary.* Washington, D.C.: National Association of Pastoral Musicians, 1982.

Funk, Virgil C. and Gabe Huck, ed. *Pastoral Music in Practice.* Washington, D.C.: The Pastoral Press, 1981.

Hart, Kevin. *The Juridical Status of Catechumens.* Doctoral Dissertation. Rome: University of St. Thomas in Urbe, 1985.

Lopresti, James. *Penance: A Reform Proposal for the Rite.* Washington, D.C.: The Pastoral Press, 1987.

O'Dea, Barbara. *Of Fast & Festival. Celebrating Lent and Easter.* New York: Paulist Press, 1982.

The Pastorals on Sundays: A Week-by-Week Resource. Chicago: Liturgy Training Publications, published annually.

Simmons, Thomas G. *The Ministry of Liturgical Environment.* Collegeville: Liturgical Press, 1984.

Upton, Julia. *Journey into Mystery: A Companion to the R.C.I.A.* New York: Paulist Press, 1986.

Young, James J. ed. *Ministering to the Divorced Catholic.* New York: Paulist Press, 1979.

Zwack, Joseph P. *Annulment. Your Chance To Remarry within the Catholic Church.* New York: Harper & Row, 1983.

MINISTRIES

Dunning, James B. *Ministries: Sharing God's Gifts.* Winona: St. Mary's Press, 1980.

Holmes, Urban T. *Ministry and Imagination.* New York: Seabury Press, 1976.

Power, David N. *Gifts That Differ: Lay Ministries Established and Unestablished.* New York: Pueblo Publishing Co., 1980.

Sofield, Loughan and Carroll Juliano. *Collaborative Ministry. Skills and Guidelines.* Notre Dame: Ave Maria Press, 1987.

PRAYER, SPIRITUALITY, DISCERNMENT, AND SPIRITUAL DIRECTION

Barry, William A. and William J. Connolly. *The Practice of Spiritual Direction.* Minneapolis: Seabury Press, 1982.

Bloom, Anthony. *Beginning To Pray.* New York: Paulist Press, 1982.

Bloom, Anthony. *Courage To Pray.* New York: Paulist Press, 1973.

Cameli, Louis J., Robert L. Miller, Gerard P. Weber. *A Sense of Direction: The Basic Elements of the Spiritual Journey.* Valencia: Tabor, 1987.

deMello, Anthony. *Sadhana: A Way to God.* St. Louis: Institute of Jesuit Sources, 1978.

Dunne, Tad. *Lonergan and Spirituality: Towards a Spiritual Integration.* Chicago: Loyola University Press, 1985.

Dyckman, Katherine Marie and Patrick L. Carroll. *Inviting the Mystic, Supporting the Prophet. An Introduction to Spiritual Direction.* New York: Paulist Press, 1981.

Edwards, Tilden H. *Spiritual Friend. Reclaiming the Gift of Spiritual Direction.* New York: Paulist Press, 1980.

Green, Thomas H. *Weeds Among the Wheat.* Notre Dame: Ave Maria Press, 1984.

Gutierrez, Gustavo. *We Drink from Our Own Wells. The Spiritual Journey of a People.* Maryknoll: Orbis Books, 1984.

Halpin, Marlene. *Imagine That! Using Phantasy in Spiritual Direction.* Dubuque: Wm. C. Brown, Co., 1982.

Helminiak, Daniel A. *Spiritual Development: An Interdisciplinary Study.* Chicago: Loyola University Press, 1987.

Huck, Gabe. *Teach Me To Pray.* New York: Sadlier, 1982.

Jones, Alan. *Exploring Spiritual Direction. An Essay on Christian Friendship.* New York: Seabury Press, 1982.

Kelsey, Morton T. *The Other Side of Silence. A Guide to Christian Meditation.* New York: Paulist Press, 1976.

Leech, Kenneth. *Soul Friends: The Practice of Christian Spirituality.* San Francisco: Harper & Row, 1977.

Rahner, Karl. *The Practice of Faith. A Handbook of Contemporary Spirituality.* New York: Crossroad, 1986.

Santa-Maria, Maria L. *Growth Through Meditation and Journal Writing. A Jungian Perspective on Christian Spirituality.* New York: Paulist Press, 1983.

Studzinski, Raymond. *Spiritual Direction and Midlife Development.* Chicago: Loyola University Press, 1985.

Wicks, Robert J. *Availability. The Problem & the Gift.* New York: Paulist Press, 1986.

JOURNALS

Catechumenate. A Journal of Christian Initiation. Published bimonthly by Liturgy Training Publications, 1800 North Hermitage Avenue, Chicago, Illinois 60622.

Catholic Evangelization in the United States of America. Published bimonthly by the Paulist National Catholic Evangelization Association, 3031 Fourth Street, N.E., Washington, D.C. 20017.

Forum. Monthly newsletter published by the North American Forum on the Catechumenate, 5510 Columbia Pike, Suite 310, Arlington, Virginia 22204.

The Living Light. An Interdisciplinary Review of Catholic Religious Education, Catechesis and Pastoral Ministry. Published bimonthly by the Department of Education of the United States Catholic Conference in collaboration with members of the Department of Religion and Religious Education at The Catholic University of America. Editorial offices: The Living Light, Department of Religion and Religious Education, The Catholic University of America, Washington, D.C. 20064.

National Bulletin on Liturgy. Published five times a year by the Canadian Conference of Catholic Bishops. Publication Service, 90 Parent Avenue, Ottawa, Ontario K1N 7B1.

PACE (Professional Approaches for Christian Educators). Series of articles published monthly October through May by St. Mary's Press, Terrace Heights, Winona, Minnesota 55987.

Worship. Published bimonthly by the monks of St. John's Abbey, Collegeville, Minnesota 56321.